Comprehensive Nursing Care in Multiple Sclerosis

Comprehensive Nursing Care in Multiple Sclerosis

*Edited by June Halper and
Nancy J. Holland*

demos vermande

Demos Vermande, 386 Park Avenue South, New York, New York 10016

Library of Congress Cataloging-in-Publication Data

Comprehensive nursing care in multiple sclerosis / edited by June
    Halper and Nancy J. Holland.
        p.   cm.
    Includes bibliographical references and index.
    ISBN 1-888799-05-6
    1. Multiple sclerosis—Nursing.   I. Halper, June
    II. Holland, Nancy J.
        [DNLM: 1. Multiple Sclerosis—nursing.   2. Multiple Sclerosis-
    -psychology.   WL 360 C737 1996]
    RC377.C56   1996
    610.73′69—dc21
    DNLM/DLC
    for Library of Congress   96-46912
                                                                      CIP

Made in the United States of America

Dedication

Gail B. Price, RN, BS
11/6/39–12/11/94

It is with great pride and affection that we dedicate this text on nursing care for people with multiple sclerosis to the memory of Gail Price. Gail spent most of her nursing career in efforts to improve the quality of life for those with spinal cord dysfunction, primarily targeting multiple sclerosis. She was particularly known and respected in the rehabilitation community and political arena in Washington, D.C. for her leadership in long-term care.

We wish all nurses who engage in care and advocacy for people with MS some spark of Gail's spirit—expertise, enthusiasm, integrity, and professionalism. Gail's call to action for all of us would be "L'chaim"—To life.

Acknowledgments

A special note of appreciation to Monica Pignotti, MSW, for her significant input in shaping several chapters, and to our publisher, Dr. Diana M. Schneider, and our editor, Joan Wolk, for tireless support during reorganizations, elusive deadlines, and other minor crises!

We acknowledge the National Multiple Sclerosis Society and the Consortium of Multiple Sclerosis Centers for their determination to end the devastating effects of multiple sclerosis, and Labe Scheinberg, M.D., who has always supported the nursing role as vital in delivery of MS care.

We thank our families for their love and support.

Contents

Foreword   **xi**
Amy Perrin Ross

Preface   **xiii**
Jack S. Burks, MD

Contributors   **xv**

1. An Overview of Multiple Sclerosis:
Implications for Nursing Practice   **1**
June Halper and Nancy J. Holland

2. Theoretical Concepts, Current Research,
and Clinical Trials in Multiple Sclerosis   **11**
Stephen C. Reingold

3. Symptom Management in Multiple Sclerosis   **25**
Randall T. Schapiro and Diana M. Schneider

4. Management of Elimination Dysfunction   **45**
Marie A. Namey

5. Prevention of Complications in the Severely
    Disabled   69
    Phyllis Wiesel-Levison and June Halper

6. Psychosocial Issues in Multiple Sclerosis   83
    Nicholas G. LaRocca and Rosalind C. Kalb

7. Sexuality and Family Planning   109
    Rosalind C. Kalb and Nicholas G. LaRocca

8. Women's Issues in Multiple Sclerosis   127
    June Halper

9. Interfacing with Rehabilitation Services   133
    Frances Francabandera and Patricia M. Kennedy

10. Disease Modifying Agents and Nursing
    Implications   159
    June Halper

11. Alternative Therapies   167
    June Halper

12. Patient and Family Education   171
    Nancy J. Holland

13. Advocacy   181
    Gail B. Price

14. Hope as a Unifying Concept   189
    Linda A. Morgante

Appendix A. Resources   203
Appendix B. Medications Commonly Used
                in Multiple Sclerosis   217
Index   281

Foreword

Multiple sclerosis (MS) is a chronic, often disabling disorder that presents significant challenges to the client, family, and the nurses assisting in their care, and people with the disease present many challenges to the nurses who care for them. In recent years there have been many advances in the understanding, diagnosis, and treatment of MS. The nurse caring for people with MS is challenged to keep abreast of these advances so that a complete plan for client education and care can be developed. Nurses involved in the care of people with MS will find this comprehensive text an extremely valuable reference.

The authors and contributors have many years of experience in working with MS clients and their families. They have collaborated to provide a current, comprehensive update on many issues challenging the MS client, family, and nurses involved in their care. As the role of the nurse expands in the care of MS clients, there is a need for experts to collaborate and provide this information to reflect the changes in health care today. This text has been developed with the recognition that care of the MS client requires specialized knowledge.

The book begins with an overview of MS, providing current information about its epidemiology, etiology, and pathophysiology. A discussion of the recently revised categories of MS is provided to assist the nurse in understanding the different courses of the disease. Implications for nursing care are described in terms of a wellness model to guide client care.

Advances in computer technology have led to increased access to information on the World Wide Web. Many clients with MS explore the

Internet regularly to gain information about current research in MS. The second chapter of this text clearly describes current research and clinical trials in MS to better prepare the nurse to discuss these issues with clients and answer questions generated on the World Wide Web.

Issues of concern to clients in everyday life, including symptom management, psychosocial issues, and sexuality, are all comprehensively discussed, with a focus on how the nurse can assist in the care of MS clients facing these issues. Disease modifying agents and alternative therapies are well described to provide the nurse with the indications, rationale, and client care priorities for the person receiving these therapies. The appendixes provide a comprehensive list of various treatments along with the associated nursing care priorities.

This text differs from other books on MS because it presents issues that face the client and nurse today in the era of health care reform and managed care. Prevention of complications in the severely disabled, interfacing with rehabilitation services, as well as women's issues are explored with current nursing implications highlighted.

The text concludes with two very important chapters. Gail Price, one of the strongest advocates for clients with MS, compiled information about the nurse and client advocacy prior to her death. Issues such as disability rights and living wills are vital for the nurse to understand in order to be able to provide truly comprehensive care for the MS client.

The text concludes on a very positive note, addressing the concept of hope in MS. This reflects the current approach to the care of the MS client and family. No longer are we diagnosing and abandoning these clients. There are many opportunities for hope in MS. It is the role of the nurse to integrate this concept into daily care of the MS client and help them utilize it in their daily life.

Comprehensive Nursing Care in Multiple Sclerosis is the collaborative effort of many health care professionals edited by June Halper and Nancy Holland. It represents the most current information on the care of the MS client and family. I am sure this will be an unparalleled resource for all nurses caring for the MS client. Thank you, June and Nancy, for this much needed, wonderful contribution to the MS literature.

Amy Perrin Ross, RN, MSN, CNRN

Preface

Multiple sclerosis has traditionally been viewed as a chronic, frequently debilitating neurologic disease that affects young adults in the prime of their lives. Treatment has remained focused primarily on its symptomatic management, but with the recent advent of potentially disease modifying agents the philosophy of MS management has increased the perspective of patient empowerment and self-care.

This superb volume is the first definitive text on the comprehensive nursing care of people with multiple sclerosis. As the most direct link to our patients and their families, nurses are in a unique position to provide a conduit for physicians and other health care professionals to work with patients, their families, and the community. This book is not simply a nursing text—the lessons that it imparts will be useful in many fields of chronic disease management.

I am honored to recommend this definitive book for nurses developed under the guidance of June Halper, RN, and Nancy Holland, RN, EdD, who have led the nursing field in comprehensive care management strategies in multiple sclerosis for many years. In their respective roles of past President and Executive Director of the Consortium of Multiple Sclerosis Centers and Vice President for Client & Community Services of the National Multiple Sclerosis Society, these outstanding editors have a unique perspective on the critical issues faced both by health care professionals and people affected by multiple sclerosis. This volume is truly a welcome addition to the literature in the nursing field and the general field of multiple sclerosis management. The nurse has a vital role to play in the ongoing care of and interaction with people who have multiple sclerosis and their families and is a key member of the comprehensive team model.

The book opens with an overview of multiple sclerosis and its implications for nursing practice; a discussion of theoretical concepts, research, and clinical trials; and an overview of symptom management. This is followed by chapters dealing with specific areas relating to nursing management of the person with MS, including the management of elimination dysfunction, the prevention of complications in severely disabled individuals, psychosocial issues, sexuality and family planning, issues of special relevance to female patients, and interactions with rehabilitation services. Of particular interest are chapters dealing with the nursing implications of disease modifying agents, the role of complementary therapies, patient and family education, client advocacy, and hope as a unifying concept in managing this unpredictable disease. Appendixes that include an extensive list of resources and medication sheets for the most commonly used agents in the management of multiple sclerosis will be of continuing value.

Jack S. Burks, MD
Rocky Mountain MS Center
Englewood, Colorado

Contributors

Frances Francabandera, EdD, RN, Associate Professor, Department of Nursing, Kean College of New Jersey, 1000 Morris Avenue, Union, NJ 07083

June Halper, MSN, RN.CS, ANP, Executive Director, Bernard W. Gimbel Multiple Sclerosis Comprehensive Care Center, Holy Name Hospital, 718 Teaneck Road, Teaneck, NJ 07666

Nancy Holland, EdD, RN, Vice President, Client and Community Services, National Multiple Sclerosis Society, 733 Third Avenue, New York, NY 10017

Rosalind C. Kalb, PhD, Clinical Psychologist, Medical Rehabilitation Research and Training Center, for Multiple Sclerosis, St. Agnes Hospital and New York Medical College, 303 North Street, White Plains, NY 10605

Patricia M. Kennedy, RN, NP-C, Nurse Consultant, The Jimmie Heuga Center, 100 West Beaver Creek Boulevard, Avon, CO 81620

Nicholas G. LaRocca, PhD, Director of Research, Medical Rehabilitation Research and Training Center for Multiple Sclerosis, St. Agnes Hospital and New York Medical College, 303 North Street, White Plains, NY 10605

Linda A. Morgante, MSN, RN, CRRN, Clinical Nurse Specialist, Division of Neurology, Maimonides Medical Center, 4802 Tenth Avenue, Brooklyn, NY 11219

Marie A. Namey, RN, MSN, Mellen Center for Multiple Sclerosis Treatment and Research, The Cleveland Clinic Foundation, 9500 Euclid Avenue, Cleveland, OH 44195

Gail B. Price, RN, BS (deceased), Former Medical Services Director, National Multiple Sclerosis Society, New York, NY 10017

Stephen C. Reingold, PhD, Vice President, Research and Medical Programs, National Multiple Sclerosis Society, 733 Third Avenue, New York, NY 10017

Randall T. Schapiro, MD, The Fairview Multiple Sclerosis Center, 701 25th Avenue South, Suite 200, Minneapolis, MN 55454

Diana M. Schneider, PhD, President and Publisher, Demos Vermande, 386 Park Avenue South, New York, NY 10016

Phyllis Wiesel-Levison, BSN, RN, C, Clinical Coordinator, MS Care Center, St. Agnes Hospital, 303 North Street, White Plains, NY 10605

CHAPTER 1

An Overview of Multiple Sclerosis: Implications for Nursing Practice

June Halper and Nancy J. Holland

Multiple sclerosis traditionally has been viewed as a chronic, frequently debilitating neurologic disease that affects young adults in the prime of their lives. During the past decade, technological advances such as diagnostic imaging (MRI) and neurophysiologic testing (evoked potentials) have facilitated its diagnosis. However, the treatment of multiple sclerosis has remained focused primarily on symptomatic management rather than disease alteration. The recent advent of potentially disease modifying agents has facilitated the shift in philosophy of MS care from a "diagnose and adios" perspective to one of patient and family empowerment and self-care.

With its emphasis on acute care needs and primary care interventions, basic and advanced nursing education has usually not stressed care of the chronically ill or disabled, including multiple sclerosis. Nurses who enter this field are often confronted with information gaps about the disease, its course, and current treatment.

EPIDEMIOLOGY, INCIDENCE, AND PREVALENCE

It is estimated that 250,000–350,000 people in the United States are afflicted with multiple sclerosis (Anderson, Ellenberg, Leventhal, Reingold, Rodriguez, & Silverberg, 1992). The disease is more common in women than in men by a ratio of 2:1, the difference being most marked at younger ages (Kurtzke, 1993).

Multiple sclerosis appears to have a higher prevalence in Caucasians than any other racial group. A study done in Hawaii (Alter et al., 1971) showed a higher prevalence in Caucasians than in Asians, native Hawaiians, or Blacks living in the same geographic area. Japanese prevalence rates are the lowest of all industrialized countries (Kuroiwa et al., 1983), and the disease is very rare among African blacks (Poser, 1994). The prevalence of MS in those of Scandinavian descent is high, and Bulman and Ebers (1992) showed that the high prevalence of MS in the northern tier of the United States was closely related to the high proportion of people of Scandinavian descent who live there.

It is now believed that MS is the result of an interaction of both genetic and environmental factors (Sadovnick, 1994). It has been theorized that MS susceptibility is under the control of several genes. By inheriting these genes, a person is susceptible to an immunologic stimulus (possibly a virus) that in turn leads to myelin damage and clinical multiple sclerosis (Sadovnick, 1994). The specific genes and how they interact have yet to be identified. For this reason, the interpretation of the data on geographic distribution of MS is difficult (Sadovnick, 1994) and remains a topic of controversy.

There appears to be a markedly uneven geographic distribution of the disease. Kurtzke (1985) identified areas of high, medium, and low risk, according to latitude. In the United States, states south of the 37th parallel of north latitude showed lower death rates than those north of that line, which were well above the national mean. Prevalence studies in groups of Northern Europeans and North Americans who migrated from high risk areas to low risk areas (Moffie, 1996; Dean, 1967; Alter et al., 1971) showed that they remained high risk if they emigrated after the age of fifteen. Those who emigrated prior to age fifteen acquired the low risk of the countries to which they emigrated. Such differences have given rise to a hypothesis that there is a critical age of exposure to unknown causal or triggering factors (possibly a virus) and suggest that there is a long period of latency between exposure and onset of the disease (Granieri et al., 1993).

This geographic model of distribution has been criticized on the basis that the comparison of prevalence rates was "reported from very different areas, countries and communities at different times" (Granieri et al., 1993, p. S17). Granieri also pointed out that more recent European prevalence studies have contradicted earlier studies. A study in Italy showed that prevalence was actually higher in the southern islands of Sicily and Sardinia (Savettieri, 1983; Rosati, 1990), with similar results from studies done in Yugoslavia (Sepcic et al., 1989) and Spain (Martin et al., 1988). According to Granieri (1993), the "lower MS prevalence ascribed to a lower latitude may in part reflect differences in level, quality, and organization of health services as well as accessibility and case ascertainment, variables that affect the accuracy of the reports and produce bias in prevalence estimates" (p. S17). Studies done in Australia, however, support the correlation with latitude, showing higher prevalence rates in the southern regions, where it is cooler, with no significant differences in ethnic composition that might account for this difference (Hammond et al., 1988).

It has also been shown that the prevalence and pattern of MS can vary over time within a given geographic area. One notable study was done in the Faroe Islands, which experienced a dramatic increase in cases of MS after the arrival of British troops during World War II (Kurtzke & Hyllested, 1979). Kurtzke's interpretation of this increase was that the British introduced MS to the Faroe Islands, stating that "the only possible explanations are that the British brought either a persistent toxin or a transmissible infection. A toxin cannot explain successive epidemics. Therefore, the cause of MS in the Faroes is a transmissible infection" and that "MS exists in a widespread, transmissible, but neurologically asymptomatic form" (Kurtzke, 1993, p. 412). Kurtzke goes on to say that this asymptomatic form, which he calls "primary MS affection (PMSA)" is common with a population in which there is MS, but that it only rarely produces clinical MS symptoms.

It should be pointed out that no evidence exists that MS is a directly transmissible disease since it has not been demonstrated that people who live with or have frequent contact with MS patients are at greater risk for the disease. There is no reason to believe that MS patients are infectious (Granieri, 1993).

THE PATHOLOGY AND ETIOLOGY OF MULTIPLE SCLEROSIS

Multiple sclerosis is a disease of the central nervous system in which the myelin sheath surrounding certain nerve fibers becomes damaged, interrupting the conduction of nerve impulses. The pathologic process begins with the destruction of the myelin, which may slow or interrupt conduction (Allen, 1991). Irregularly shaped macroscopic lesions, which appear to be the result of destruction of the myelin sheath, are scattered throughout the central nervous system. These lesions, or *plaques,* are found in the white matter and have a predilection for the optic nerves and the white matter of the spinal cord, brainstem, cerebellum, and cerebrum, especially the area surrounding the ventricles (Pallett & O'Brien, 1985). Recently formed lesions show partial or complete degeneration of myelin and perivascular infiltration with lymphocytes and other mononuclear cells, suggestive of an inflammatory process (Pallett & O'Brien, 1985).

The etiology of multiple sclerosis is not known although there is believed to be a genetic predisposition in susceptible individuals combined with an unknown environmental trigger (Compson, 1991). The environmental factor is not known but has been thought to be viral in origin (Compson, 1991). Multiple sclerosis has been shown to occur frequently in specific families, and current theory is that it is multigenic, i.e., results from more than one gene (Compson, 1991).

THE COURSE OF THE DISEASE

One of the hallmarks of multiple sclerosis is its unpredictability from person to person and within a given individual over time. Its prognosis is usually uncertain although there are general prognostic indicators that can suggest whether or not a patient's disease will follow a specific pattern. In general, women have a better prognosis than men (Coyle, 1996). Onset at an early age, a monoregional versus a polyregional attack, and complete recovery from an exacerbation portend a favorable prognosis (Coyle, 1996). Brainstem symptoms such as nystagmus, tremor, ataxia, and dysarthria, poor recovery from exacerbations, and frequent attack rate are indicators of a poor prognosis (Coyle, 1996). The extent of the patient's level of disability five years after diagnosis usually signifies the long-term picture of the disease.

The diagnosis of MS is usually made by a neurologist after two or more episodes of unexplained neurologic symptoms have occurred. There is no specific laboratory test for MS, and the diagnosis usually depends on a history that indicates the probability of the disease; a neurologic examination with findings consistent with multiple sclerosis; and positive paraclinical evidence (Sibley, 1990). Most patients fall into the age group of 15–60 years although recent data suggest that as many as 10 percent of MS patients have their first symptoms in their sixties (Sibley, 1990). While the average age of onset is between 20 and 30 years, the disease may start in children. Initial symptoms of MS range from numbness, tingling, or weakness of the extremities, visual changes, vertigo, dysarthria, ataxia, and urinary frequency and urgency. L'Hermitte's phenomenon, a transient paresthesia resembling an electrical shock that occurs with forward flexion of the neck, is also common (Sibley, 1990).

Multiple sclerosis is mainly diagnosed on a clinical basis due to the difficulty of obtaining appropriate tissue (Fang & Lublin, 1995). The Poser criteria for clinically definite MS requires two clinical deficits referable to white matter lesions or a physician's observation of one deficit with paraclinical evidence of another, either through magnetic resonance imaging

(MRI) or evoked potentials. Deficits must be separated in onset by at least one month and each must last at least 24 hours (Poser et al., 1983). Additionally, no more appropriate diagnosis should exist to account for clinical findings.

Patients can be categorized as having either relapsing-remitting, primary progressive, secondary progressive, progressive-relapsing, benign, or malignant disease (Lublin & Reingold, 1996; see Figure 1-1).

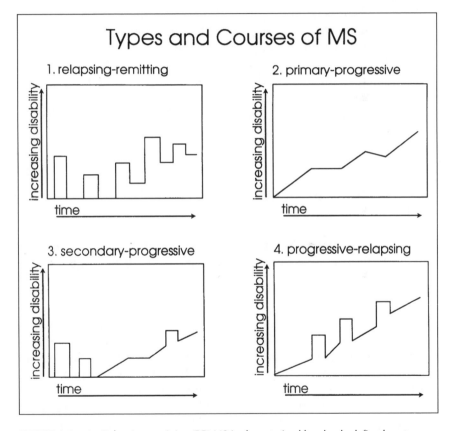

FIGURE 1-1.   1. Relapsing-remitting (RR) MS is characterized by clearly defined acute attacks with full recovery (a) or with sequelae and residual deficit upon recovery (b). Periods between disease relapses are characterized by lack of disease progression. 2. Primary progressive (PP) MS is characterized by disease showing progression of disability from onset, without plateaus or remissions (a) or with occasional plateaus and temporary minor improvements (b). 3. Secondary progressive (SP) MS begins with an initial RR course, followed by progression of variable rate (a), which may also include occasional relapses and minor remissions (b). 4. Progressive-relapsing (PR) MS shows progression from onset but with clear acute relapses, with (a) or without (b) recovery.

⊃ Relapsing-remitting disease is characterized by clearly defined disease relapses with full recovery and periods between relapses characterized by a lack of disease progression.

⊃ Patients with primary progressive MS demonstrate disease progression from the onset with occasional and temporary minor episodes of improvement.

⊃ Secondary progressive multiple sclerosis begins with a relapsing-remitting course followed by progression with or without occasional relapses, minor remissions, and plateaus.

⊃ Progressive-relapsing multiple sclerosis is progressive disease from the onset, but there are clear acute relapses with or without recovery. The periods between relapses are marked by continued progression.

⊃ Benign multiple sclerosis allows patients to remain fully functional in all neurologic systems 15 years after disease onset.

⊃ Malignant MS has a rapid progressive course leading to significant disability or death within a relatively short time after onset (Lublin & Reingold, 1996).

THE WELLNESS MODEL IN MULTIPLE SCLEROSIS NURSING

The variable pattern of MS along with the uncertainty and loss of control in this type of disease impels the nurse to respond with dynamic, individualized interventions that reflect each patient's needs. Clark's wellness model has implications for the nursing process in MS (Clark, 1986; see Table 1-1). In a disease with no cure, the patient and family must assume ongoing responsibility for health care and self-monitoring. In the traditional nursing model, the nurse performs and the patient receives care. The wellness model is a collaboration between the patient and the nurse, a partnership whose goal is self-awareness and self-responsibility. Clark defines wellness as this process, a positive striving that is unique to the individual, in which a person can be ill and still have wellness with a deep appreciation for the joy of living and with a life purpose (Clark, 1986).

CARE MODELS IN MULTIPLE SCLEROSIS

The nurse has a vital role to play in the ongoing care of and interaction with patients who have multiple sclerosis and their families, and is a key member of the comprehensive team model. Comprehensive care in MS is

TABLE 1-1. Comparison of the Traditional Nursing and Wellness Nursing Processes
(Clark, 1986)

Traditional nursing process	Wellness nursing process
Assess client	Model integrates whole person wellness for the client
	Teach client self-assessment procedures
Diagnose	Assess unique learning needs based on client belief systems
Set goals	Teach client to set wellness goals meaningful to him or her
Develop nursing care plan	Client develops plan of action with nurse facilitator and takes responsibility for carrying it out
Carry out nursing interventions	Teach client self-care and self-healing measures consistent with client beliefs
Evaluate results	Teach client to self-evaluate results

an organized system of health care designed to address the medical, social, vocational, emotional, and educational needs of patients and their families (Halper & Burks, 1994). Comprehensive care embraces a philosophy of empowerment, a wellness approach in which the patient takes an active role in planning and implementing health care and self-care activities and acts as a consultant to the team, which may consist of physicians, nurses, rehabilitation specialists, counselors (social workers, psychologists, neuropsychologists), educators, and clergy. Patients must learn to adapt and change in response to alterations in their physical functioning. This implies a total commitment by the health care team and the patient to a clearly defined program of "wellness" that looks beyond impairments to each person's potential (Cobble & Burks, 1985).

Within the past decade, case management has been introduced as a cost-effective and efficient model for restricting patient care delivery. Until the 1980s, health care in multiple sclerosis and other chronic diseases was fragmented, resulting in high costs and duplication of services. With the advent of comprehensive care centers, which have proliferated throughout the United States and Canada, the case management model has taken on new meaning as an addition to the team approach to MS care (Halper & Burks, 1994). Patient care services provided by the interdisciplinary team are coordinated by a case manager or case coordinator (Ignatavicius & Hausman, 1995).

Clinical pathways in multiple sclerosis are the next logical step to providing dynamic care in this perplexing and ever-changing illness. Clinical pathways—also called clinical paths, critical paths or pathways, collaborative plans of care, multidisciplinary action plans (MAPS), care paths, and anticipated recovery paths—are interdisciplinary plans of care that outline the optimal sequencing and timing of interventions for patients with a particular diagnosis, procedure, or symptom (Ignatavicius & Hausman, 1995). They must be designed to minimize delays and utilize resources while maximizing the quality of patient care. They include patient outcomes, timelines, collaboration, and comprehensive aspects of care (Ignatavicius & Hausman, 1995). In multiple sclerosis, clinical pathways should reflect the dynamic nature of the illness, both in the prognosis of each patient, his or her current state of health and function, and the resources available in the health care and other communities.

Thus, the nurse working in the field of multiple sclerosis is faced with numerous questions:

⊃ What is the patient's disease course?

⊃ Are the symptoms ongoing or intermittent?

⊃ How are these symptoms interfering with the patient's functional status?

⊃ How has multiple sclerosis impacted the patient and the family?

⊃ What are the available resources?

⊃ How can I help?

We hope that this book will assist nurses in a variety of nursing settings to develop creative and innovative ways of helping their patients and their families living with a challenging and frightening disease.

REFERENCES

Allen, I. (1991). Pathology of multiple sclerosis. In W.B. Matthews (ed.). *McAlpine's multiple sclerosis.* New York: Churchill Livingstone, 298–378.

Alter, M., Okihiro, M., Rowley, W., Morris, T. (1971). Multiple sclerosis among Orientals and Caucasians in Hawaii. *Neurology, 21,* 122–130.

Anderson, D.W., Ellenberg, J.H., Leventhal, C.M., Reingold, S.C., Rodriguez, M., Silberberg, D.H. (1992). Revised estimate of the prevalence of multiple sclerosis in the United States. *Annals of Neurology, 31,* 333–336.

Bulman, D.E., Ebers, G.E. (1992). The geography of multiple sclerosis reflects genetic susceptibility. *J Trop Geographic Neuro, 2,* 66–72.

Clark, C.C. (1986). *Wellness nursing.* New York: Springer.

Cobble, N.D., Burks, J.S. (1985). The team approach to the management of multiple sclerosis. In F. Maloney, J.S. Burks, S.R. Ringel (eds.). *Interdisciplinary rehabilitation of multiple sclerosis and neuromuscular disorders.* Philadelphia: J.B. Lippincott, 13.

Compson, D.A.S. (1991). Genetics and immunology. In W.B. Matthews (ed.). *McAlpine's multiple sclerosis.* New York: Churchill Livingstone, 298–335.

Coyle, P. Diagnosis, classification, and prognosis in multiple sclerosis. Presentation, February 2, 1996, St. Petersburg, FL.

Dean, G. (1967). Annual incidence: prevalence and mortality of multiple sclerosis in white South-African born and in white immigrants to South Africa. *Br Med J 2,* 724–730.

Fang, J.Y., Lublin, F.D. (1995). Altering the course of multiple sclerosis. *Internal Medicine, 16 (1),* 15–31.

Garnieri, E., Casetta, I., Tola, M., et al. (1993). Multiple sclerosis: does epidemiology contribute to providing etiological clues? *Journal of the Neurological Sciences, 115 (Suppl),* S16–S23.

Halper, J., Burks, J.S. (1994). Care patterns in multiple sclerosis. *NeuroRehabilitation, 4 (4),* 67–75.

Hammond, S.R., McLeod, J.G., Millingen, K.S., Stewart-Wynne, E.G., English, D., Holland, J.T., and McCall, M.G. (1988). The epidemiology of multiple sclerosis in three Australian cities: Perth, Newcastle and Hobart. *Brain, 111,* 1–25.

Ignatavicius, D.D., Hausman, K.A. (1995). *Clinical pathways for collaborative practice.* Philadelphia: W.B. Saunders.

Kuroiwa, Y., Shibasaki, H., Ikeda, M. (1983). Prevalence of multiple sclerosis and its north-south gradient in Japan. *Neuroepidemiology, 2,* 62–69.

Kurtzke, J.F. (1993). Epidemiologic evidence for multiple sclerosis as an infection. *Clinical Microbiology Reviews,* 382–427.

Kurtzke, J.F. (1985). Epidemiology of multiple sclerosis. In P.J. Vinken, G.W. Bruyn, H.L. Klawans (eds.). *Handbook of clinical neurology,* Revised series, Vol. 3. Demyelinating Diseases. Amsterdam: Elsevier, 259–287.

Kurtzke, J.F., Hyllested, K. (1979). Multiple sclerosis in the Faroe Islands. I. Clinical and epidemiological features. *Annals of Neurology, 5,* 6–21.

Lublin, F., Reingold, S. (1996). Defining the course of multiple sclerosis: results of an international survey. *Neurology.*

Martin, R., Matlas-Guiu, L., Calatayud, E., J.M. Molto, J. Aranaz. (1988). Epidemiology of multiple sclerosis in Eastern Spain (Abstr.). *An update on multiple sclerosis,* International MS Conference, Rome, IV/34, September 1988.

Moffie, D. (1996). De geografische, verbreiding van multipele sclerose. *Ned Tijdschr Geneeskd, 110,* 1454–1457.

Pallett, P.J., O'Brien, M.T. (1985). *Multiple sclerosis. Textbook of neurological nursing.* Boston: Little, Brown, 616–619.

Poser, C.M. (1994). The epidemiology of multiple sclerosis: a general overview. *Annals of Neurology, 36(S2),* S180–S193.

Poser, C.M., Paty, D.W., Scheinberg, L.C., et al. (1983). New diagnostic criteria for multiple sclerosis: guidelines for research protocols. *Annals of Neurology, 13,* 227.

Rosati, G. (1990). Epidemiologia della sclerosi multipla. In G. Rosati, E. Garnieri (eds.). *Manual di neuroepidemiologia clinica,* NIS, Rome, 143–182.

Sadovnick, A.D. (1994). Genetic epidemiology of multiple sclerosis: a survey. *Annals of Neurology, 36 (Suppl),* S194–S203.

Savettieri, G. (1983). Epidemiologia della sclerosi multipla in Italia. *Riv Neurol, 52,* 227–237.

Sepcic, J., Antonelli, E., Materljian, D., Rukavina, D. (1989). Multiple sclerosis cluster in Gorski otar, Croatia, Yugoslavia. In Battaglia (ed.). *Multiple sclerosis research.* Amsterdam: Excerpta Medica, 165–169.

Sibley, W.A. (1990). The diagnosis and course of multiple sclerosis. *Neurobehavioral aspects of multiple sclerosis.* New York: Oxford University Press, 5–14.

CHAPTER 2

Theoretical Concepts, Current Research, and Clinical Trials in Multiple Sclerosis

Stephen C. Reingold

Since its most descriptive beginnings, multiple sclerosis research has evolved into a subspecialty that incorporates virtually every discipline of modern biotechnology, ranging from the most esoteric molecular biological laboratory techniques to demographic, socioeconomic, and psychological studies. In spite of the fact that MS has been known and studied as a separate disease since the mid-1800s, its etiology remains a mystery. While many theories abound, none has been directly proven so far. However, current research is leading us closer to a true sense of what causes the disease.

THEORIES OF THE CAUSE OF MULTIPLE SCLEROSIS

Because MS presents clinically as a neurologic disease, research on its basic cause has concentrated on how nervous system pathology in MS might develop (e.g., central nervous system [CNS] inflammation, eventual loss of myelin, astrocytic scarring, and resulting problems with conduction of nerve signals).

Although many theories of the underlying cause of MS have been explored over decades, a relationship to MS has not been unequivocally demonstrated. Among some of the more prominent theories that seem *not* to be related to the cause of MS are:

Congenital defects in nervous system structure or function. Considerable research has claimed that CNS myelin in people with MS is compositionally normal. Thus, it was generally believed that there is nothing intrinsically "wrong" with myelin in MS that results in its loss. However, the advent of magnetic resonance spectroscopy (MRS) has shown that "normal appearing white matter" in brains of individuals with MS is in fact *not* normal. It is not known whether this is a contributor to the development of MS (i.e., a developmental abnormality that makes the person's white matter disease-prone) or a consequence of disease that is not (yet) grossly apparent. Studies on the genetic makeup of myelin have provided conflicting results. Some studies show genetic differences in key myelin proteins in those with MS compared to healthy control subjects; other studies have failed to confirm this.

Direct damage by a virus or other infectious agent of central nervous system white matter. Although viral infections can damage the nervous system and cause other diseases in both humans and animal demyelinating disease models, such direct viral effects have not been shown to be relevant to MS despite detailed research in this area. Over the years, intensive search using increasingly sophisticated techniques has led to proposals of the involvement of a variety of common and uncommon viruses, ranging from canine distemper virus to retroviruses to herpes viruses, with none yet proven to be related to the disease. Problems of sampling, artifact, and an apparent increased immune reactivity to most or all viruses in MS patients have confounded results over the years.

Environmental toxic substance or dietary imbalance. No research has supported such theories, although toxic substances and diet are known to cause other nervous system problems that may have some clinical similarities to MS.

While significant research has not uncovered data that support such theories of the cause of MS, these hypotheses are still being explored by some scientists. One often hears of "findings" suggesting that one or the other chemical or virus or heavy metal causes MS. In spite of the attention and excitement drawn to such reports, further exploration has usually found the claims to have little scientific merit.

Current theories about multiple sclerosis focus on four hypotheses that, together with psychosocial, health care delivery, and experimental therapy studies, drive most of today's research efforts:

⊃ MS is believed to be an autoimmune disorder.
⊃ There is a genetic susceptibility that may predispose certain individuals to the disease.
⊃ There is probably an infectious trigger for the disease.
⊃ The ultimate neurologic damage that produces the signs and symptoms of the disease results from inflammation, T-lymphocyte infil-

tration, myelin breakdown, and astrocytic scarring that slow or block the conduction of nerve signals in fibers of the brain, spinal cord, and optic nerves.

IMMUNOLOGY AND MULTIPLE SCLEROSIS

Significant research on the cause of MS in the past 20 years has focused on the possibility that MS is a disease of immune system function that is clinically apparent in signs and symptoms of the CNS. More specifically, many scientists concentrate their research efforts on the hypothesis that MS is an "autoimmune" disease, in which cellular elements of immune function are misdirected and, instead of doing the normal job of defending our bodies against viral, bacterial, and parasitic infections, also mistakenly turn against a part of our body—the white matter or myelin insulation around nerve fibers in the CNS.

The evidence for immune system *involvement* in MS is fairly clear, while evidence that it is an *autoimmune disease* is more indirect. First, people with MS seem to have clear-cut abnormalities in immune function. These include, among many other factors, unusually high reactivity of immune system T-cells to proteins of myelin in the CNS (which are termed "antigens" because they can trigger immune responses); an over-representation of cells that enhance immune responses (so-called "helper T-cells") and a relative under-representation of cells that suppress immune responses (so-called "suppressor T-cells"); and the presence of immune system cells in MS lesions in the brain, spinal cord, and optic nerves.

Direct evidence that the immune problem in MS is "autoimmune" is difficult to obtain in humans but is quite clear in a laboratory model disease of rats, mice, guinea pigs, and primates, called experimental allergic encephalomyelitis (EAE), in which T-lymphocytes sensitized to myelin antigens can transfer disease to healthy, syngeneic animals—the true test of autoimmunity.

While this key experiment to "transfer" MS from a sick individual to a healthy one using activated T-cells alone cannot be done in humans for obvious practical and ethical reasons, the similarities of CNS lesion pattern between EAE and MS and, in some regards, of clinical signs, have led most scientists to conclude that MS must surely be autoimmune as well.

In mid-1990, for the first time, several studies on people with MS detected reactivity of specific immune cells in the blood and central nervous system against a protein component of normal myelin, called myelin basic protein, which makes up some 30 percent of all myelin proteins. Other myelin proteins, such as proteolipid protein, can also trigger specific immune system responses in MS. Even though healthy individuals may also show immune reactivity in the blood against myelin antigens, this sort of evidence enhances our belief that MS is an autoimmune disorder, primarily involving T-lymphocytes directed against apparently normal myelin proteins in the CNS. As a result of these studies, major focus has been brought on the nature of immune system reactivity to myelin in MS, including specificity of antigens, immune responses of cytokines (soluble mediators of immune function), control of pro-inflammatory vs. anti-inflammatory responses, and the movement of activated immune cells from the blood to the CNS, all with the aim of better understanding MS immune responses and harnessing this information to develop more specific therapies.

It is clear that immune function is under strict genetic control. The genes that control immune function in people with MS may differ in one or more key ways from those of healthy individuals. In the early 1990s, molecular genetic research identified two types of immune system genes that were thought to be involved in MS. The first type consists of genes that help the immune system differentiate between body tissues that are "self" and substances that are foreign—such as a bacteria or virus, or even a transplanted liver or kidney from a genetically different donor. This "self-recognition" mechanism helps to signal the immune system to mount an effective response against foreign antigens but not against "self" antigens. Genes involved in "self-recognition" are variously called histocompatibility genes, human leukocyte antigens (HLA), or major histocompatibility complex (MHC) genes, and there is evidence from population and family studies of characteristics of HLA genes in people with MS that differ from healthy individuals.

The second important gene type that has been hypothesized to be involved in immune function in MS is that responsible for the structure and function of receptors on T-cells of the immune system. Such receptors are essential in recognizing targets of immune attack—foreign or perhaps "auto" antigens—and consequently are essential in determining immune responses. Suspicion of a T-cell receptor genetic relationship in MS came from animal model studies and from small early MS studies, but a clear immunogenetic role related to T-cell receptors in MS has not yet been confirmed or proven.

GENETICS AND MULTIPLE SCLEROSIS

The identification of genetic factors that may underlie immune function in MS is only one step in our effort to clarify the long-known fact that there is a genetic susceptibility to the disease. A genetic relationship is borne out by a number of findings:

⊃ It has long been known that there are ethnic groups in the world that are genetically "isolated" (i.e., they rarely or never marry or bear children outside of their own group, and thus have developed a relatively restricted and unique gene pool) and rarely or never get MS. These include such religious sects as the Hutterites in Canada and such groups as Eastern European gypsies.

⊃ There are racial differences in MS prevalence that are also most likely genetically based. The disease occurs less frequently in African-Americans than among Caucasians in North America, is rarely seen in Eskimos or in pure African Bantus, and is also rarely seen—and in a form quite different from Caucasians—among Asians.

⊃ Evidence from family studies has demonstrated an increased susceptibility to MS (and possibly to other known autoimmune diseases as well) in families in which MS already occurs. In fact, some 20 percent or more of individuals with MS may have another family member with the disease.

Even though there is a clear increased family susceptibility, the risk of disease is still quite low in families in which the disease already exists. In the United States, a little more than 1/1,000 people have MS. When a family member (parent, sibling, aunt/uncle, etc.) has the disease, the risk increases to about 1–5/100 for other family members, depending on the degree of relationship. This represents an increased susceptibility but still a relatively low risk. For twins, an important finding is that among dizygotic (nonidentical) twins, the risk resembles that for any other sibling. However, among monozygotic (identical) twins, who are genetically identical, the risk of both having MS rises dramatically to as high as 30 percent if one twin has been diagnosed, a clear indication of the importance of genetic factors in disease susceptibility.

Recent population studies from a large clinic-based sample in Canada demonstrated clearly that the occurrence of multiple cases of MS in families is certainly genetically, not environmentally, caused. Adopted siblings with their different genetic backgrounds do not share a family's overall risk for MS, even though the environment in which they are reared may be identical to that of nonadopted siblings who are genetically related to each other.

By the mid-1900s, genetic molecular technology had advanced to the point at which genome screening in MS was possible. At least three independent studies in the United States, Canada, and Great Britain have focused on understanding the specific genetic associations and links in MS, using families in which MS occurs more often than once. Early data from these studies make it clear that MS is a complex, multigenic disease with areas of genetic "interest" on several chromosomes.

ENVIRONMENTAL TRIGGERING FACTORS

Although genetic factors are key in MS, the fact that only 30 percent of monozygotic twins are concordant for MS means that nongenetic factors must play a major role in the development of the disease. Over decades, population studies have suggested that some triggering factor from the environment must initiate the autoimmune disease process. Epidemiologic data from migration studies suggested that some factor—most likely viral—must be encountered before the age of 15 years in order for the disease to be triggered.

While somewhat controversial, these data have resulted in a search over the last half century for a specific virus that triggers the disease. Although many common and uncommon viruses have been proposed as causative agents for MS, in each case further scientific analysis has failed to support the initial claim. This has not stopped the search for a specific MS virus, but in recent years it has made such a search somewhat unpopular and subject to skepticism. Retroviruses have been among the most recent candidates for a specific viral trigger for MS, with initial findings based on serologic studies for antibodies against HTLV-1 in MS patients, followed by polymerase chain reaction (PCR) analysis looking for viral "footprints." However, studies from multiple laboratories around the world have been unable to confirm the initial findings, using the same technologies. In 1995–1996, serologic, PCR, and immunohistochemical studies pointed to a possible role of an ubiquitous human herpesvirus, HHV6, a virus more easily recognized as the cause of the childhood disease roseola. As of this writing, attempts are being made to confirm, and if possible expand upon, these findings.

In the absence of evidence for a specific viral trigger for MS, increased attention has been paid to the possibility that many viruses (and perhaps bacteria and other pathogens as well) could serve as a trigger for the disease process. If so, it may well be the *manner* in which a genetically susceptible immune system reacts to such infectious challenges that results in MS. This possibility has decreased the likelihood that a vaccine against a specific triggering agent could be found to prevent disease. However, it has increased research efforts to understand more about how immune responses to infectious agents might result in autoimmunity.

A common theory of how the autoimmune process might be triggered by infectious agents involves "molecular mimicry," in which the immune system normally reacts to a foreign antigen but also reacts against a component of "self"—such as myelin—if the foreign antigen and myelin share some components of molecular structure. Molecular mimicry has been demonstrated to contribute to autoimmune reactions in animals with EAE and may contribute to the human disease as well. Work in 1995 showed that molecular mimicry may occur between certain viral and bacterial antigens and human myelin. Importantly, human T-cells were found to react against the mimicking antigens as well as myelin. This lends credence to the "molecular mimicry" hypothesis of how autoimmunity may develop in MS.

DEMYELINATION: THE CAUSE OF SYMPTOMS

The damage done by an immune reaction against myelin in brain and spinal cord might truly be considered the "cause" of MS since it is this process that results in symptoms. Immune system T-cells normally in the blood stream become activated to a myelin antigen and cross the blood-brain barrier, which separates the blood stream from the CNS and normally keeps such immune system cells out of the nervous system. Local inflammation in scattered places—most often around blood vessels and ventricles of the brain—results in damage to the myelin insulation around nerve fibers. Myelin is broken down and scavenged by macrophages but nerve fibers themselves remain relatively intact, at least in the early stages of disease. Lost myelin is ultimately replaced by gliotic scars produced by astrocytes.

Inflammation, loss of myelin, and scarring result in reduced conduction of nerve signals within the CNS. Conduction deficits result from changes in membrane properties and relocation of ion channels in nerve fibers from which myelin is lost. These conduction problems produce the symptoms that characterize the disease.

Historically, oligodendrocytes that make myelin in the CNS were believed to be incapable of regenerating the insulating material in an adult once it had been lost. This may be one key difference between MS and Guillian-Barré disease, in which recovery of function after an acute episode is often seen, and in which the Schwann cells that make myelin in the peripheral nervous system are more easily capable of regeneration. However, in recent years, the dogma concerning the lack of CNS remyelination after an MS attack has been challenged, even in the most advanced disease and the most serious lesions. Neuropathologic evidence from autopsy specimens shows clear but "weak" remyelination in massively demyelinated CNS lesions. An absence of necessary growth factors, an inability to "penetrate" astrocytic scars, and even immune responses that may inhibit the remyelination process are among the theories as to why remyelination after MS damage is difficult and incomplete. As of the 1990s, a variety of treatments—for instance, galactocerebroside and even common immunosuppressive drugs—have been shown to enhance CNS remyelination in animal models of MS, and myelin development is being actively studied for the lessons it might teach about myelin regeneration. Oligodendrocyte "precursor" cells in the CNS have been identified that may be primed for proliferation and differentiation, and may thus be capable of forming new myelin after initial myelin damage. Finally, animal studies have demonstrated the capability of transplanted oligodendrocytes to form functional myelin insulation around nerve fibers in genetically myelin-deficient mouse strains and in experimentally induced myelin lesions. Each of these findings raises the possibility of regeneration of myelin after disease. Since proper nervous system conduction depends on functioning myelin insulation, such studies raise the hope for recovery of function in people with MS.

RESEARCH INTO NEW TREATMENTS FOR MULTIPLE SCLEROSIS

In the long run, all research—the most basic or the most applied—is directed to developing and testing new drugs or devices that can alter the disease course, prevent the disease from occurring, or improve function in people who already have MS. The ultimate research experiment, then, is the clinical trial.

A clinical trial is the scientific study of the efficacy and safety of a drug or device for a given disease on people who have that disease. As scientific studies, clinical trials are complex and must be done as carefully as any other experiment.

Clinical trials in MS are aimed at one or more of a number of desired outcomes: inducing a disease remission; maintaining that remission; altering the disease course; improving or eliminating symptoms; and prevention and cure. No one therapy is likely to satisfy all of these goals, and it is likely that management of MS will include use of multiple treatments.

MS clinical trials are particularly difficult to undertake. First, people with MS are generally highly motivated to seek a "cure" for their disease, and thus a patient's motivation can actually interfere with the objective assessment of any drug or device. This often results in a placebo effect— the tendency to improve simply because of participation in a clinical trial even if no active drug is administered. Well-documented clinical studies in MS have shown that sham therapies can result in improvement in as many as 50–60 percent or more of patients. A largely psychological phenomenon, the placebo effect has a basis in the physiologic responses a person can have as a consequence of experiencing increased hope or excitement in the prospect of helping to find a useful therapy. While the true physiologic basis for placebo effects is unknown, hormonal factors surely play a role—pain research, for instance, has shown that sham therapies can cause a release of endorphins and actually result in amelioration of pain if the patient is in the right psychological state. While important and potentially useful, such placebo effects are generally short-term and must be carefully separated from a true therapeutic drug effect. In fact, any useful drug for MS must have an effect that is greater than the placebo effect.

The high degree of individual and unpredictable variability in MS also makes the design of clinical studies problematic. A useful drug effect must be separable from the natural variability in disease course.

Additionally, since different drugs may have different effects on various disease types, trials must be designed to answer questions of effect of one type of disease, such as relapsing-remitting or secondary progressive disease.

Finally, some drugs may seem to cause improvement but actually only have indirect effects. Understanding the true effect of any drug on the MS disease process requires a detailed knowledge of the drug's action as well as careful clinical assessment for effects on the disease. These and other problems associated with MS clinical trials can best be overcome by extremely rigorous experimental design for the studies. The generally accepted methods of study are time-consuming and expensive but hold the best chance of obtaining a clear-cut answer to efficacy and safety for any agent in MS.

The first step, and perhaps the most essential, is that any new agent should have a strong scientific rationale for being tested in MS. Based on current knowledge, immunoregulatory agents, antiviral agents, and those that may promote remyelination or improve conduction of nerve fibers or otherwise target specific disease symptoms all have a sound rationale for possible use in MS.

Based on knowledge of the MS process, on the biological action of any proposed treatment, and on basic experimental studies of the drug (including preliminary toxicity studies), a physician-scientist may conclude that the drug could have a potential role in the treatment or management of MS. A drug or any other substance without a scientific rationale related to MS should not be given strong consideration for disease testing.

Given a strong scientific rationale, human studies almost always begin with toxicity studies in a very small number of people who have the disease (called a "preliminary" or "phase I" clinical trial). In such early experiments, usually only a few very seriously ill people will be asked to participate, since they may find the potential risk of any new agent to be worthwhile given the grave nature of their disease. If such studies demonstrate acceptable safety and risk, a physician may choose to pursue further studies to get a sense of possible efficacy.

"Pilot" or "phase II" studies usually involve larger, statistically relevant numbers of patients (often 20 to 100 or more) with a disease type and severity that seem appropriate to the hypothesized drug effect. Key objectives in such a study are: (1) determining effectiveness of the drug in halting progression, reducing relapse rate, or improving function; (2) obtaining additional information about toxicity and safety; and (3) refining knowledge about the best dose and route of delivery (i.e., oral, by injection, etc.). Such studies aim to be objective in obtaining the required answers. Thus, patient performance on drug may be compared to pre-drug status, but, even better, should be compared to an identical, matched group of patients in a control group, using either a sham treatment— a treatment that looks identical to the actual drug but which is known to be therapeutically inactive—or using a currently accepted treatment against which the new agent is being tested. True objectivity and elimination of placebo effects are enhanced if both the patients and the physicians who periodically check for efficacy are "blinded" as to each individual's treatment status in the study.

Results from such studies, which can often take several years to obtain, may or may not show statistical benefit for people on drug compared with people on control treatment, as well as acceptable levels of side effects of the drug. If there is no benefit or if there are uncontrollable or dangerous side effects, the agent is usually abandoned as a possible therapy. On the other hand, if there is benefit and side effects are minimal and acceptable, a larger clinical trial will be undertaken to confirm and expand the studies.

Such "pivotal" or "phase III" trials are the final experimental step toward making a decision about the value of any proposed therapy. As previously, the key questions concern efficacy and safety. Statistically relevant numbers of participants are essential, and the study is usually conducted at a number of different sites (a "multicenter" study) to ensure that the drug can be used in an equivalent fashion by many physicians. Rigorous adherence to blinding of patients and examining physicians, as well as careful random assignment of patients into treatment and control groups, is essential to ensure objectivity. There should be sufficient information to determine if the tested agent is truly useful and safe at the conclusion of the study period, when the blinding code is broken and performance of drug-treated patients can be compared with the control group.

While there are variations in this outlined scheme, often depending on the amount of information available from use of the agent in other diseases, the elements and data described are required to determine true benefit and safety. Importantly, these are also the elements and data required by the U.S. Food and Drug Administration, which monitors such studies closely at every step. It is ultimately the FDA's assessment of the data and the care with which a study is done that determines whether any agent may be sold in the United States as a treatment for MS.

Once FDA approval has been granted and the drug can be sold and advertised as a treatment for MS, there are often series of further studies done, which are called "post-market analyses" or "phase IV" studies. These are designed to test further for possible adverse reactions to the drug, to explore its use for different forms of disease (for instance, an approved drug for progressive MS might be tested in relapsing-remitting disease in a phase IV analysis), or to test the effects of the drug on related disorders (e.g., testing efficacy and safety of an MS-approved drug on rheumatoid arthritis).

FINANCING AND PARTICIPATING IN CLINICAL TRIALS

Drug studies are time-consuming and expensive. Such studies are most often supported financially by drug companies that invest significant research and development resources in these ultimate experiments. Grants from the federal government or health agencies like the National Multiple Sclerosis Society sometimes also fund part or all of the clinical trials. It is extremely rare (and often considered unethical) to require that a patient who volunteers to participate as an experimental subject pay for that privilege.

The decision for anyone with MS to participate in an experimental clinical trial is intensely personal and highly subjective. Since there is always the potential for risk of any untested agent, a potential subject must be fully informed by the physician and must consider the risk factor in any decision-making process. Since good studies require a control treatment group that may be given a sham or placebo agent with no benefit, individuals may balk at volunteering to be in a study in which there is a chance of being in the untreated, sham group. A true sense of altruism—since participation in either treatment or control group may ultimately help tens of thousands of people with MS—is often needed to agree to volunteer. Finally, a sense of frustration and even adventure may help sway a potential study volunteer.

One of the most unfortunate dilemmas occurs when a patient decides that he or she wants to be in a clinical trial and finds that it is impossible. A frequently asked question is, "Doctor, why can't I be in your clinical trial?" Clinical trials are limited in practice to a relatively small number of individuals who must be located geographically close to the clinical center(s) where the study is undertaken. The design of trials is such that generally only one type of MS—such as relapsing-remitting disease—is involved in a study. This excludes people with any other form of disease.

Further restrictions also may be enforced: disease limited to a certain duration, a certain level of disability, age of participants, exclusions based on prior or current medications, or participation in previous trials of agents where there might be dangerous or confusing effects with the experimental treatment medication. For any particular test drug, other restrictions may apply. These practical factors can often result in an eager patient being refused a place in a new clinical trial. If this is the case, a potential participant should take solace from the realization that positive findings from a clinical trial will be of eventual benefit to many more people than could ever hope to participate in the initial studies.

Finding out about clinical trials in MS should be a joint project of the patient and his or her physician. There is an ever-growing network of physicians who organize and run studies in MS. An interested patient and physician team can usually learn of pending studies nearby, often with the assistance of the National Multiple Sclerosis Society.

In summary, the ultimate research in MS is the development and testing of new therapies for use in the disease. Clinical trials designed to objectively test efficacy and safety are difficult and expensive to undertake. While people with MS are always needed to participate in such research, the decision to volunteer is often a difficult and personal one, and the practical restrictions involved in conducting clinical trials in MS often exclude many patients who would gladly participate.

HEALTH SERVICES AND REHABILITATION RESEARCH

When one thinks of research concerning particular diseases, the first assumption is that all research is aimed at understanding the basic disease process and then developing therapeutic agents that alter disease course. However, in recent years, the obvious fact that diseases affect the entire person, his or her family, and even society has entered into the consideration of research topics for serious clinical investigators.

Increasing focus is being placed on research aimed at improving rehabilitative care for people with chronic diseases like MS. Long ignored as a research enterprise, rehabilitation medicine has focused instead on acute and ongoing care for disabled individuals. However, research has a critical role in bringing new methodology to the field and improving care and management. Studies of exercise programs, cognitive rehabilitation, strategies for occupational and physical therapy, and others, have become common in comprehensive MS care groups.

The impact of chronic disease on society and the impact of society entitlements and attitudes on those with disabilities is also an area for much needed research. From questions of accessibility to delivery of services to preconceptions about disabilities that affect employment, insurance, and family and community structure, health care delivery research can provide hard data that can effect societal change.

CONCLUSION

Research related to multiple sclerosis is broad in scope and touches all aspects of the disease, from its basic pathology to understanding how individuals with MS cope with their disease in society today. While most focus is, and should be, aimed at understanding the disease process, improving the quality of life for those with MS, and developing safe and effective treatments, the "whole person" is the subject of modern research in MS.

CHAPTER **3**

Symptom Management in Multiple Sclerosis*

Randall T. Schapiro and Diana M. Schneider

All too often people with multiple sclerosis (MS) are told that there is little that can be done for their disease. In fact, the appropriate management of MS includes a variety of medical, rehabilitative, and psychological approaches. This chapter focuses on the management of specific symptoms that may develop as the result of the disease process in multiple sclerosis. For each type of problem encountered, appropriate medications and rehabilitative therapies are considered.**

SYMPTOMS OF MULTIPLE SCLEROSIS

Because different areas of the brain and spinal cord are responsible for different movements and sensations, the neurologic symptoms and signs (deficits) are dependent on the location of the lesion (scar). For example, coordination is affected when demyelination occurs in the cerebellum. Because of the variability of scarring, no two cases of MS are exactly alike.

Uncertainty can be one of the major problems in dealing with MS. Studies indicate that if a person is doing reasonably well five to six years after diagnosis, he or she will likely continue to do reasonably well. The

---

* This chapter is based on Randall T. Schapiro, *Symptom Management in Multiple Sclerosis*, 2nd edition. New York: Demos, 1994.

** Appendix B, "Medications Commonly Used in Multiple Sclerosis," contains detailed information on specific medications.

prognosis is better if the predominant early symptoms are sensory. If the early symptoms and findings include tremor and weakness, the prognosis is not as good and a more aggressive management program is in order. Although MS is often thought of as seriously disabling, studies indicate that the majority of patients have a relatively benign disease pattern, with over two-thirds remaining ambulatory 20 years after diagnosis. The majority of patients may be expected to live fairly normal lives, and some may have only one or two attacks of neurologic deficit.

A specific characteristic of the disease is the presence of clinical symptoms that affect several sensory or motor functions in the central nervous system (CNS), reflecting the existence of multiple sites of damage. Symptoms may fluctuate or steadily progress in severity. Many patients have periods of stability for years, and even those who ultimately progress to severe disability often have long periods of more moderate symptoms.

THE MANAGEMENT OF MULTIPLE SCLEROSIS

Management strategies utilized to treat MS fall into two general categories: those used to treat the underlying disease by shortening exacerbations and slowing the progress of the disease, and those used to minimize and control specific symptoms, such as spasticity, bowel and bladder problems, or fatigue.

Some general principles have been developed for managing the disease, including minimizing fatigue, emotional stress, and increases in body temperature, all of which can magnify symptoms.

Acute attacks are generally treated with corticosteroids (prednisone, methylprednisolone, dexamethasone), which appear to shorten exacerbations, in part by reducing the amount of swelling in areas of demyelination. Studies have shown that a short course of high-dose cortisone works best to shorten the attack. High doses of methylprednisolone (intravenously) or dexamethasone (intramuscularly) are most often used. The course of therapy, which lasts from a few days to a week, is initiated at the onset of a sudden attack, followed by tapering the oral dose over about a month. Administration in this manner minimizes many of the side effects produced by corticosteroids, including degeneration of bones, cataracts, ulcers, obesity, decreased ability of the body to combat infections, and problems of salt and water balance. The goal is to decrease swelling within the CNS, thus allowing unaffected nerves to function normally.

Multiple sclerosis may involve a defect in the way the immune system "sees" myelin so that it reacts to myelin as if it were a foreign tissue. Thus, much of the focus of general management of the disease involves decreasing the activity of the immune system. Corticosteroids work in part through an effect on this system. Other drugs that depress the activity of the immune system without the serious side effects of the corticosteroids are now being used in the long-term management of MS. These include a series of drugs first used to treat cancer, which also involves a defect in the immune system. Imuran® (azathioprine) or Cytoxan® (cyclophosphamide) are examples of such drugs. Their use in certain selected patients may allow for a slowing of the progression of some kinds of MS.

Immunosuppression remains somewhat controversial. Azathioprine, cyclophosphamide, plasmapheresis (plasma exchange), and total lymphoid irradiation all remain as possible treatments for progressive MS. What *can* be said is that the trend of research for progressive MS involves modulating and redirecting the immune system. To date, the methods used have all been nonspecific. The future will involve more specific methods of immunosuppression.

Interferons are proteins made by the body in response to a foreign stimulus, e.g., a virus, and which appear to regulate or modulate the immune system. There are three broad categories of interferons: alpha, beta, and gamma. Gamma interferon appears to stimulate the immune system, worsening symptoms of MS. Beta interferon appears to "calm" the system. Two drugs have now been approved for use by the Food and Drug Administration for the treatment of MS, Betaseron® and Avonex®, slightly modified beta interferons. In recent studies in relapsing-remitting MS patients, these substances decreased the fluctuations commonly seen and also decreased the number of lesions seen on MRI when compared to placebo. They are the first drugs to be used for the actual demyelinating process, as opposed to symptomatic or inflammatory management.

In addition to these general treatments, a variety of therapies are available to treat the specific symptoms that can occur during the course of the disease. The remainder of this chapter is organized around these specific problem areas; bladder and bowel symptoms and their management are among the most common seen in MS, and are discussed separately in Chapter 6. By no means do all or even many of these difficulties occur in every individual. Virtually all of them, however, do have management strategies that can be utilized to minimize discomfort and inconvenience.

SPASTICITY

Increased tone and resistance to movement produce spasticity in MS. In the extreme, spasms become prominent and are often quite uncomfortable. Spasticity tends to occur most frequently in the muscles responsible for maintaining upright posture, the antigravity or postural muscles.

The increased stiffness in the muscles may mean that a great amount of energy is required to perform everyday activities. Reducing spasticity can produce greater freedom of movement and strength, frequently accompanied by less fatigue and increased coordination. The major ways in which spasticity is reduced include stretching range of motion exercise, aerobic exercise, and the use of medications. When spasticity does not respond to these measures and is clearly uncomfortable, a surgical procedure may be necessary.

The simplest and often most effective way to reduce spasticity is *passive stretching*, in which each affected joint is slowly moved into a position that stretches the spastic muscles. Once the muscles reach their stretched position, they are held there for about a minute to allow slow relaxation and release undesired tension. This stretching program begins at the ankle, to stretch the calf muscle, then proceeds upward to the muscles in the back of the thigh, the buttocks, the groin, and, after turning from back to stomach, the muscles on the front of the thigh.

Range of motion exercises differ from stretching exercises in that the movement about the joint is not held for any specific length of time. Although range of motion is important, holding the stretch is significant, and patience in doing the stretches is essential. An independent stretching program based on some of the same principles used in physical therapy can be used at home.

Exercising in a pool may also be beneficial because the buoyancy of water allows movements to be performed with less energy expenditure and more efficient use of many muscles. We recommend using the pool for both stretching and range of movement exercises, which consist of easy, slow, rhythmic, and flowing calisthenics that allow most of the joints of the body to move through their full stretching range. The pool temperature should be cool to lukewarm, about 85°; this may feel cold to some, but warmer temperatures should be avoided because they produce fatigue, while cooler temperatures may result in shivering.

Many people with MS have limited range of movement in at least some joints and muscles, and *the key to managing spasticity is to expand the number and kind of movements that can be performed.* The exercises should be done utilizing a minimum of effort.

Spasticity may also be reduced by the use of relaxation techniques that involve a combination of progressive tensing and relaxing of individual muscles, accompanied by deep breathing techniques and imagery.

Mechanical Aids

Specific devices can be made for individual patients to counteract spasticity and prevent contractures. For example, a "toe spreader" or "finger spreader" can be used to relax tightness in the feet and hands and to aid mobility.

Braces (orthoses) for the wrist, foot, and hand can be made to maintain a natural position and to prevent limitations on movement and deformities. For example, an ankle-foot orthosis (AFO) can be made to place the foot at many different angles to the ankle. A good orthotist can make the brace to take stress off the knee. Hinges in the material can add to its flexibility. All orthoses should be customized to allow for maximal benefit.

Medications

Lioresal® (baclofen) is the most common antispasticity drug used in MS, and most patients respond well to it. The dose must be carefully determined for each individual; too little will be ineffective, whereas too much produces fatigue and a feeling of weakness because it interferes with the proper degree of stiffness needed for balance and erect posture. The correct dose is usually determined by starting at a low level and slowly increasing the amount until a maximum beneficial effect is achieved. The most common error when taking baclofen is to give up on it before it has reached the dose necessary to obtain proper relaxation. That dose may be as low as 5 mg per day, but as much as 40 mg four times a day may be necessary in some patients.

Zanaflex® (tizanidine) has effects on spasticity that are similar to those of baclofen. It produces greater sedation than baclofen but less weakness, and may therefore be a useful medication for those in whom sedation is less of a concern than weakness.

Another drug that is sometimes helpful in relieving spasticity is Dantrium® (dantrolene sodium), which acts directly at the level of the muscle. It can be helpful, but hepatotoxicity limits its use. Spasticity may also be reduced by Valium® (diazepam), which is most often used for the relief of spasms that occur at night since its calming effect also helps to induce sleep. Its strong sedative effect limits its use during the daytime. Klonopin® (clonazepam) is closely related to Valium®. Its main use has been to treat certain types of epilepsy. It produces significant relaxation and thus may be used as an antispasticity medication. Like Valium®, it sedates and is therefore best used at night. When using Valium® and Klonopin®, both the physician and the person with MS must keep in mind the potential for chemical dependency.

Another drug commonly used for spasms in the muscles of the back is Flexoril® (cyclobenzaprine HCl). This medication acts quite specifically on such spasms, but may settle limb spasms as well. It usually works best when used in combination with another spasticity medication. Any of these drugs may become less effective when taken for a prolonged period as tolerance may develop; it may be necessary to stop taking them for a period of time, after which they may again become effective.

People with MS occasionally develop "paroxysmal" or "tonic" spasms, in which an entire arm or leg may draw up (flexor) or out in a stiff, clenched, or extended (extensor) position. Tegretol® (carbamazepine) is generally used to control such spasms, although Lioresal® may also be effective. Cortisone may decrease spasticity in general and is effective for paroxysmal spasms when used on a short-term basis; its long-term use is not advocated because of numerous risks.

Surgical Management

Occasionally spasms become so severe that no medication is effective. When this occurs, nerves controlling specific muscles of the leg may be deactivated by using a phenol motor point block. This produces decreased tone in the muscles, which may be more comfortable but usually does not increase functional mobility. Botulinum toxin (Botox®) has been approved by the FDA for managing facial spasms. Botulinum toxin causes a temporary blockage within the muscle; it is somewhat easier to control than phenol but may need more repetitive injections. This treatment is practical for small muscle spasms, especially around the eye or face. Severe spasms may be managed by surgical procedures that involve cutting nerves or tendons to decrease the contraction of specific muscles that are producing serious stiffness.

A new approach to the management of severe spasticity involves the use of a pump to deliver baclofen directly into the spinal canal. A tube is placed in the canal, then connected (underneath the skin) to the pump placed in the abdominal region, through which the drug is delivered into the spinal canal at prescribed levels. The newest pumps can be programmed by computer via radio waves so that the dose can be changed as needed. For some patients, this technique may provide relief of intractable spasticity. Because the doses of baclofen needed with this approach are so low (micrograms), side effects are also low and there is almost always a significant decrease in fatigue and malaise. This treatment is aggressive and expensive. It should be reserved for only those with severe spasticity that can not adequately managed by oral medications.

The faithful use of an exercise program and the appropriate use of drugs when needed significantly increase the level of function and avoid the development of more severe problems.

TREMOR

Tremor is one of the most frustrating symptoms to treat in MS. There are many different kinds of tremors; some have gross oscillations, others are fine; some occur at rest, others occur only with purposeful movement;

some are fast, others are slow; some affect the limbs, others may involve the head, trunk, or speech; some are disabling, others are merely a nuisance; and some are treatable, others are not. As with all symptoms, because of this wide variation, proper diagnosis is essential before correct management decisions can be made.

The Pharmacologic Management of Tremor

The most common tremor seen in MS—and also the most difficult to treat—occurs as the result of demyelination in the cerebellum, which often results in a gross tremor that is relatively slow and occurs with purposeful movement of the arm or leg.

This type of tremor is almost always exaggerated during times of stress and anxiety, so one mode of managing the problem is treatment with drugs that have a calming or sedative effect. Atarax® and Vistaril® (hydroxyzine) are antihistamines that may settle a minor tremor that has been magnified by stress. Klonopin® (clonazapam) may also decrease a tremor via its sedative effect. The anti-tremor effect must be balanced against the generally unwanted effects of sedation by carefully monitoring the dosage until the desired effect is achieved.

Inderal® (propranolol), a beta-blocker, is helpful in controlling some tremors seen in MS. The effect may not be great but even a small decrease in tremor may allow greater function.

Some studies have shown that the anticonvulsant Mysoline® (primidone) may alleviate this difficult symptom, although it is heavily sedating. Low doses may be worthwhile. Diamox® (acetazolamide) is a diuretic that has some anti-tremor properties and may be of value in selected patients.

Because a component of spasm is often involved in gross tremors, baclofen may provide some relief. The potential but reversible side effect of weakness must be balanced against the tremor-reducing effect of the drug, again by careful adjustment of the dosage.

High doses of INH (isoniazide), a drug used primarily for the treatment of tuberculosis, can alleviate gross tremors that are influenced by posture. It is sometimes worth a trial if tremor is especially incapacitating, but toxicity to the liver must be monitored.

Recent studies indicate a reasonable response to the anti-anxiety drug Buspar® (buspirone), which is nonsedating and nonaddictive.

Other Treatments for the Management of Tremor

Drugs are not the complete solution to the management of tremor. Physical techniques provide another approach. Physical treatments fall into three general categories:

Patterning is a technique used by physical and occupational therapists to trace and repeat basic movement patterns. It is based on the theory that certain muscles can be trained to move in a coordinated fashion by repeatedly using the nervous circuit involved in a movement. These normal movements are guided and assisted by the therapist until they become automatic. Minor resistance is then added and removed while the patient repeats the patterns independently. The muscles gradually appear to develop increased endurance for these learned movements and manage to retain control when the patterns are applied to functional tasks.

Immobilization is the placement of a rigid brace across a joint, fixing it in one position and dampening the severity of a tremor by reducing random movement in the joint. Bracing is most helpful in the ankle and foot, providing a stable base for standing and walking. It may also be used for the arm and hand. The desired position of function is defined by the tasks that are to be facilitated, such as writing, eating, or knitting; the brace is used to immobilize the arm or hand for these tasks and then removed.

Weighting involves the addition of weight to a part of the body to provide increased control over its movements. The underlying theory behind this approach is that more muscles will be used to stabilize a distant point in the body (hands, wrists, feet, ankles) when a heavier object is involved. This stabilizing action tends to reduce tremor and provide greater sensory feedback to the brain. In practical terms, either the limb itself may be weighted or the object being used may be made heavier, including utensils, pens and pencils, canes, or walkers.

These techniques are used primarily for tremors that affect the limbs. Their goal is to teach the person with MS to compensate for tremor by providing as much stability for the limbs as possible. It may be important to develop postural adjustments, such as using one's arms close to the body. Adaptive equipment and/or assistive devices that are nonskid, easy to grasp, and stable are helpful and can be used for many activities.

Tremors of the head, neck, and upper torso are more difficult to manage than those of the limbs. Stabilizing the neck with a brace may be helpful.

Tremors of the lips, tongue, or jaw may affect speech by interfering either with breath control for phrasing and loudness or with the ability to form and pronounce sounds. Speech therapy may involve changing the rate of speaking or the phrasing of sentences. Suggestions may be made as to the placement of the lips, tongue, or jaw for the best possible sound production. A simple pace board—a pattern of rectangles set next to each other—may slow the person down and allow for improved understanding. The person points to each square while uttering a single syllable. If he or she can slow down to keep pace with the pointing, a dramatic increase in clarity of speech often results. Pace boards may be simple and effective at virtually no cost. In some instances, tremor may make it impossible to speak, in which case alternative communication devices must be used.

None of these techniques completely eliminates the problem of tremor. The goal is continued function, which can often be managed by combining some of these therapies.

BALANCE

Vestibular stimulation involves increasing the amount of stimulation received by the "balance centers" in the brainstem, thus allowing the brain to function more normally. The techniques used challenge the patient's sense of balance by rocking, swinging, or spinning, using such activities as sitting on a beach ball or swinging in a hammock.

Along the same lines are exercises performed with a "Swiss ball." This large ball may become part of a balance program designed to stimulate the different balance centers within the body.

If a person can stand, computerized balance stimulation via a machine called the "Balance Master" may be helpful. The person stands on a platform that is in contact with a video screen via a computer. Movements of the feet influence the screen much like a video game, teaching people how to achieve better control of balance.

WEAKNESS

Weakness results from difficulties in transmitting electrical impulses from within the central nervous system to the muscles as a result of demyelination, usually in the spinal cord but occasionally in the brain.

It is vital that the source of weakness be understood in order to properly manage it. If weakness is caused by lazy, weak muscles, they may be strengthened by lifting weights (progressive resistive exercise). When weakness is the result of poor transmission of electrical impulses, lifting weights may only fatigue the nerve and further increase muscle weakness. For people with MS, it is important to realize that *exercises that involve lifting weights or repetitive movements of muscles to the point of fatigue do not increase strength; they increase weakness.*

A weak muscle that is not stimulated at all will result in atrophy. It is important to determine what exercises are appropriate, which will likely require the assistance of a trained physical therapist who has knowledge of both the neuromuscular system and the specific problems involved in MS. The problems experienced by the person with MS should not be treated as if they were the result of broken bones.

It is impossible to separate the management of weakness from that of spasticity and fatigue. If muscles are less stiff, less energy needs to be expended in movement. Drugs or other treatments that lessen spasticity also frequently increase strength. Similarly, lessening fatigue may also increase strength.

Efficiency is the key to increasing strength in patients with MS. Energy should be conserved and wisely used. This means using one's muscles for practical, enjoyable activities and planning the use of time accordingly; difficult activities should frequently be done before those that are easier to perform. The wise use of assistive devices may also be helpful in increasing overall efficiency.

Strength may also be increased with an aerobic exercise machine such as an exercycle or a rowing machine. The principle of not becoming fatigued and exercising those muscles that can be strengthened to compensate for the weaker muscles must be applied. Exercise in general is good, but the wrong exercise may be harmful.

FATIGUE

Fatigue is one of the most common and annoying problems for people with MS. It is difficult for others to understand since it is not manifested by a highly visible symptom. "MS fatigue" is a lassitude or overwhelming fatigue that can come at any time of day and without warning. Symmetrel® (amantadine) and Prozac® (fluoxetine) effectively manage this type of fatigue, although the manner in which they work is not yet understood. Stimulants such as Cylert® (pemoline) and Ritalin® (methylphenidate) may provide relief but they have the unwanted side effect of disrupting sleep. Some people cannot tolerate such medications and adjustment or discontinuance may be necessary.

Occupational therapists are in many ways "efficiency experts," and their advice on planning, work simplification, and performing activities in the most efficient manner can help relieve fatigue. Allowing for frequent rest periods is also helpful for rejuvenating the mind and body to enhance overall performance.

AMBULATION

Movement impairment is frequently associated with multiple sclerosis, and difficulties in walking represent one major type of such impairment. It is fitting that this section follows those dealing with weakness, spasticity, and tremor because walking becomes difficult as the result of losses in strength, muscle tone, and balance.

If walking becomes impaired, a more practical means to accomplish the same goal should be substituted, hopefully without too much emotional trauma. This is easy to say, but people value being ambulatory far beyond its true value.

When foot muscles are weak, "foot drop" results, in which the toes of the weak foot touch the ground before the heel, thereby disrupting balance. As discussed in the section dealing with weakness, there is no way to strengthen a weakened foot, and compensation techniques become essential.

It is particularly important to wear proper shoes. A leather-soled oxford is recommended. The tie gives maximum stability to the foot, and the smooth leather sole prevents the sticking that can occur with crepe soles to throw the walker off balance. A plastic (polypropylene) insert is often added to the shoe to keep the foot from dropping. This lightweight brace—an ankle-foot orthosis or AFO—picks up the foot and allows it to follow through in the normal heel-foot manner.

Ankle-foot orthoses can also be designed to decrease spasticity by tilting the foot to a specified angle and keeping it from turning in or out (inverting or everting). The proper use of AFOs decreases fatigue while increasing stability.

A metal brace that fits outside the shoe may be needed if there is a significant increase in tone (stiffness) at the ankle. This is a "springloaded" device that keeps the toe from dropping.

If the hip muscles are also weak, the leg will swing out in front to allow the foot to clear the ground. In order to maintain stability, the knee is often forced back into hyperextension, which puts significant stress on the knee. After a period of time, the knee begins to hurt and may become swollen as the result of arthritis. To prevent this condition, a metal device called a Swedish hyperextension cage can prevent the knee from snapping back. Alternatively, a custom-made knee brace may be necessary.

Walking with less fatigue may again become realistic with the aid of such devices. If balance is also a problem, another assistive device such as a cane may be needed. Two canes may be needed if weakness is pronounced in both legs.

If balance and weakness are more severe, it may be necessary to use forearm (Lofstrand) crutches. Forearm crutches provide greater stability than a standard cane, and their use does not require as much strength in the upper extremities.

If walking is still difficult or impossible, a wheelchair may be the correct choice. A three-wheeled motorized chair can be a boon for people with MS because it does not carry the stigma associated with a regular wheelchair. Although extremely useful, a motorized chair is best utilized by those who have retained some means of walking, as the seating system of a motorized chair is not designed for all-day sitting.

Those who do not possess the ambulatory skills necessary to use a three-wheeler appropriately may achieve independence using a lightweight motorized wheelchair. A standard manual wheelchair often does not offer the person with MS sufficient independence because of the fatigue generated by operating the chair and the coordination necessary to control it. The key in choosing a chair or scooter is *independence.* The proper device should be selected to regain control and independence in the environment. Help from a physical therapist or a physician who understands the use of the chair is necessary to select the most appropriate one.

PREVENTING IMMOBILITY

People with MS are too often told to rest and not overdo, and the fear of fatigue becomes almost unbearable. There is no real basis for this fear. *People with MS are not fragile!* Proper exercise leads to increased fitness and less fatigue. The process is slow, and it begins with a carefully developed exercise prescription. Like medicine, it should be prescribed by a professional—usually a physical therapist or a physician—who knows how to tailor the exercises to the individual.

The exercise prescription should have four elements:

1. The type of exercise (aerobic, strengthening, balance, stretching);
2. The duration of exercise (how long to exercise);
3. The frequency of exercise (how often to exercise);
4. The intensity of exercise (how hard to exercise).

The role of exercise in MS has become somewhat controversial, partly because the meaning of exercise is misunderstood. To many, exercise is defined as stressing one's body to the point of pain, an approach whose watchwords are "no pain, no gain." But in MS it has become quite clear that if one exercises to the point of pain, fatigue sets in and weakness increases.

Rigorous exercise also increases core body temperature. Because the protective shielding of the nerves has been destroyed, this rise in temperature increases short-circuiting in the central nervous system and further increases weakness. Thus, it is fairly obvious why exercise originally fell into bad repute with those knowledgeable about MS.

Our understanding of what is "good" exercise for people with MS and how they should train has increased considerably in the past few years as the concept of fitness has developed. Fitness implies general overall health. It is a holistic concept that strives for improvement in function of the heart, lungs, muscles, and other organs, and is attained by adhering to a proper diet, not smoking, and exercising appropriately.

Two major concepts underlie the term *appropriate*. First, because of the wide variability of the disease, what is "good" exercise for one person may not be good for another. *It is important to tailor an exercise program for each individual rather than to have a set program for everyone who has MS.* The second factor is that there are many kinds of exercise—not just those that involve running, jumping, or similar activities.

Exercises that increase mobility through stretching and maintaining range of motion play an important part in combating weakness by reducing the stiffness so commonly present in MS. As discussed previously, balance exercises are helpful in managing tremor. Relaxation exercises are particularly helpful in reducing stress, which can increase weakness; techniques for learning how to relax must be considered as part of any overall program designed to reduce weakness and fatigue.

Moderate aerobic exercises, which may involve a bicycle, rowing machine, treadmill, brisk walking, running, or a self-wheel in a wheelchair, will all result in a slow but definite increase in endurance.

The proper exercise prescription takes into account that each exercise should not bring on pain. *"No pain, no gain" is absolutely the wrong approach to exercise for the person with MS.* The proper exercise prescription is a balanced one that includes many different types of exercises with the goal of improving overall condition.

PAIN

Although MS is generally considered to be a painless disease, over 20 percent of all individuals with MS find pain to be a significant problem.

There is a difference between headaches and head pains. Headaches occur commonly in people with or without MS. They are one of the most common symptoms seen by neurologists in people who do not have MS. Head pains with sharp, stabbing qualities can be associated with the neuralgias of MS and can occur in the distribution of many of the cranial nerves. The most common is trigeminal neuralgia or tic douloureux.

Trigeminal neuralgia is a sharp pain in the facial area, often brought on by touch or movement of the face. It can be treated with Tegretol® (carbamazepine). To avoid its primary side effect of sleepiness, the drug is initially given at low doses and slowly increased to the point at which it adequately controls pain. Other drugs that may be used to control trigeminal neuralgia include Dilantin® (phenytoin), whose action is similar to but milder than Tegretol®, and Lioresal® (baclofen), used most commonly for spasticity. If drugs fail, a surgical procedure can usually be performed to eliminate pain, leaving a less disturbing numbness in its place. This procedure, percutaneous rhizotomy, can now be performed under local anesthesia with laser technology. Although not the first line of therapy, it is a viable backup. Other neuralgias may affect the glossopharyngeal and splenopalatine nerves.

Occasionally an unusual electrical sensation is felt down the spine and into the legs when the head is nodded. This is a momentary sensation, called L'Hermitte's sign, that is usually surprising and disturbing. It is a signal of loss of myelin within the spinal cord in the cervical region but has no significance in predicting the course of the MS.

The predominant type of pain seen in MS is a burning, tooth-achy type of pain that occurs most commonly in the extremities, although it may also occur in the trunk. The same medications used for trigeminal neuralgia are used for these burning dysesthesias, but they appear to be less effective than they are for facial pain. Capsaic acid (Axsain®, Zostrix HP®) was recently made available, is safe, and can be of value for this type of pain. The cream is applied sparingly three times per day and has few side effects. It feels like a different type of burning as it soothes the irritant feeling.

Electrical stimulation (TNS, transcutaneous nerve stimulation) applied over the painful area occasionally provides relief. However, it frequently has produced the opposite effect and is therefore not often recommended.

Mood-altering drugs such as tranquilizers and antidepressants may be effective in some cases because they alter the interpretation of the message of pain. A number of such drugs are available, and some relief may be provided with careful manipulation of the type and dosage. Biofeedback, meditation, acupuncture, and similar techniques may help in specific circumstances. Since pain is a symptom that clearly increases in severity when dwelt upon, a concerted effort to treat the reaction to pain is an important part of the overall treatment plan.

What is clear is that standard pain medications, including aspirin, codeine, and narcotic analgesics, are not effective because the source of pain is not the typical one that occurs with injury. *Pain medications are therefore to be avoided; they are ineffective and can be addictive.*

Although "MS pain" may be severe and bothersome, it usually does not lead to decreased ambulation and is not a predictor of a poor prognosis. Studies have shown that people who have these sensations as the major feature of MS do better than average in movement activities.

Low back pain is one of the most common symptoms treated by the neurologist, so it is therefore not unexpected that it is also relatively common in people with MS. Multiple sclerosis itself rarely causes low back pain; it is more commonly caused by a pinched nerve or other problem. This situation occurs fairly frequently because abnormal posture or an unusual walking pattern resulting from MS places stress on the discs of the spinal cord (padlike structures that cushion the areas between the vertebrae). This stress may cause slippage of the discs, compressing one or more of the nerves as they leave the spinal cord and resulting in pain in the part of the body innervated by these nerves. Obviously, heavy lifting and inappropriate turning and bending compound the problem. Such movements irritate the spinal nerves, causing the muscles on the side of the spinal column (the paraspinal muscles) to go into spasm; it is this spasm that causes low back pain. If a spinal nerve is significantly irritated, the pain may extend down a leg to the muscles in the leg that are served (innervated) by that nerve.

If the problem is one of poor walking posture, the pattern needs to be corrected; if spasticity contributes to the problem, it must be lessened. Local back care with heat, massage, and ultrasound waves are frequently helpful, and exercises designed to relieve back muscle spasm may be recommended. Drugs designed to relieve back spasms may also be used, including Parafon Forte®, Flexoril®, and Robaxin®, and some arthritis medications are frequently useful. If the problem is the result of a faulty disc, surgery may be needed to relieve the spinal irritation.

Spinal manipulation (rapid twisting or pushing of the spinal column) is not recommended for the person with MS because it can irritate the spinal cord and increase neurologic problems.

It is critical that a correct diagnosis of the cause of any type of pain be made to ensure proper treatment. Diagnostic X-rays, including CT scanning, may be needed to pinpoint the cause of pain, after which the appropriate mode(s) of treatment can be prescribed.

Other types of musculoskeletal problems of an orthopedic nature may be commonly seen in MS. Ligament damage may result if there is significant hyperextension of the knee while walking. The knee may swell and become painful. Many orthopedic specialists are unfamiliar with MS and do not understand why this occurs. As a result, they may recommend exercises to increase the strength of the weak leg. Unfortunately, if strength could be restored to the leg, the problem would not have occurred in the first place. Exercising the leg with orthopedic exercises produces fatigue and increased weakness. A more appropriate approach is to take weight off the leg with an assistive device (cane or crutch). A knee brace may be necessary and helpful to prevent hyperextension.

SPEECH DIFFICULTIES

Speech patterns are controlled by many areas of the brain, especially the brainstem. Depending on the location of demyelinated areas, many different alterations of normal speech patterns are possible. Most affect speech production, resulting in dysarthria, ranging from mild difficulties to severe problems that make comprehension impossible.

If the cerebellum is primarily involved in speech difficulties, speech generally becomes slow and fluency is diminished. Words may be slurred, but they are usually understandable. If the tongue, lips, teeth, cheeks, palate, or respiratory muscles become involved, the speech pattern becomes even more slurred (dysarthric). In either case, speech therapy can increase both fluency and rhythm. Although exercises are sometimes advocated, they are not usually successful for this type of speech problem. Nevertheless, they may be worth trying. For example, oral motor exercises may be utilized to maintain muscle coordination.

Tremors of the lips, tongue, or jaw may affect speech by interfering either with breath control for phrasing and loudness or with the ability to voice and pronounce sounds. Speech therapy focuses on changes that increase the ability to communicate efficiently. It may involve making changes in the rate of speaking or in the phrasing of sentences.

Pacing and pausing techniques may be helpful if speech is slurred and rapid. Pausing is used between one or two words. As discussed previously, a paceboard may be used to initially assist with this technique.

VISION

The two major components of effective vision are the ability to correctly image what one sees and the proper coordination and strength of the muscles that surround the eye and control its movements. Both may be affected by MS.

Inflammation and demyelination in the optic nerve produce optic or retrobulbar neuritis, resulting in an acute overall loss of vision with accompanying pain in the eye. This is often managed simply by waiting for the inflammation to abate, after which function returns. If the problem is sufficiently disabling, cortisone may be given to reduce inflammation. Recent studies indicate that if cortisone is used, it should be administered in relatively high doses. The end results are no better than without treatment but the time needed for a return to usual clarity may be reduced. Nonsteroidal anti-inflammatory drugs may alleviate the pain. It is becoming increasingly clear that not all optic or retrobulbar neuritis requires treatment.

In some cases, vision remains imperfect even after inflammation has been reduced. This is especially noticeable at night when light is dim, although colors may appear "washed out" in normal lighting. Leaving a lamp on at night may be helpful. Additionally, there may sometimes be "holes" in the vision, with part of the area one is looking at obscured. This cannot be treated with eyeglasses, which only tend to magnify these areas. The problem can be adjusted to with time.

A weakening of coordination and strength of the eye muscles sometimes produces double vision, which can be treated acutely with steroids. Over time, the brain usually learns to compensate for double vision so that images are perceived as normal despite the weakened muscles. This compensation does not occur if the eye is patched. Patching should be reserved for reading, situations in which there is fatigue, or while driving or performing other essential tasks. Prisms placed into eyeglasses may bring the images together and provide another relatively simple way to manage this difficult problem.

Multiple sclerosis can be accompanied by various varieties of nystagmus, which is usually more of a nuisance than anything else. Klonopin® (clonazepam) and related drugs occasionally decrease nystagmus.

Cataracts often develop at a younger age in the MS population because cortisone promotes their development. The surgical removal of the abnormal lens sometimes brings about a substantial improvement in vision.

As with all symptoms of MS, significant fluctuations can occur in visual symptoms. Visual acuity often falls, and double vision increases, with fatigue, increases in temperature, stress, and infection.

DIZZINESS AND VERTIGO

In MS, vertigo usually results from an irritation of brain stem structures that are involved in maintaining balance. The inner ears also play a major role in balance. Disturbance in the conduction of inputs to the brain from the inner ear may be distressing. Dizziness and the sensation of lightheadedness are less severe than vertigo, but nonetheless are uncomfortable. Other diseases that involve these structures produce similar symptoms, so it should not be assumed that they are necessarily caused by MS.

Antihistamines, including Benadryl®, Antivert®, and Dramamine®, frequently provide relief when vertigo or sensations of dizziness are relatively mild. Vitamin B (niacin) is occasionally used to dilate blood vessels in the hopes that this will reduce the problem. The class of medications that include Valium® (diazepam), Klonopin® (clonazepam), and Serax® (oxazepam) are direct suppressants of the structures of the inner ear that stimulate dizziness. They are potent treatments that should be used judiciously. These medications—individually or occasionally in combination—provide sufficient relief to allow the patient to continue functioning reasonably well.

A physical therapist can teach exercises that are effective if dizziness is worsened by positional changes. The therapist determines which positions of the head make the dizziness worse. Therapy consists of holding the head in these positions as long as can be tolerated. If done successfully, tolerance develops and comfort results.

Dizziness frequently accompanies an attack of influenza. When flu and its accompanying fever and muscle aches occur, the symptoms are managed with aspirin or other medication; dizziness often disappears as the flu symptoms abate.

If vertigo is severe and vomiting prevents the use of oral medications, intravenous fluids are administered in combination with high doses of cortisone to decrease inflammation in the region that produces the symptoms—the brainstem area at the base of the brain.

SEIZURES

Seizures occur twice as often in people with MS as in the general population. No studies have attempted to predict which person with MS is more likely to have a seizure, but cerebral involvement may be an indicator. Since MS is a disease that involves the subcortical transmission systems of the brain, patients with significant cognitive disturbances quite possibly are at increased risk for seizures.

While seizure management in MS is similar to the management of seizures that result from other causes, it often is more difficult to control seizures in the setting of MS. Treatment may necessitate the use of higher doses or various combinations of anticonvulsant medication.

WEIGHT GAIN

Weight gain can be a problem in MS if a person's activity level drops but caloric intake remains constant. There are no data indicating that weight gain causes weakness, but it is not good for one's overall health and is unattractive. It can make general movement and especially aided transfers more difficult than necessary. People who are overweight universally know they are overweight. It does little good to point that out on a continuous basis.

Those confined to a wheelchair show weight gain first in the abdominal area. Although stomach firming exercises may be of some benefit, it is not usually possible to perform enough repetitions to cause an effective redistribution of weight, and the problem is practically unavoidable.

The same basic dietary guidelines that apply to others apply to people with MS. A balance between exercise, calories, and fatigue must be achieved. This starts with eating smaller meals. Many people find that eating small but frequent meals results in both lower overall caloric intake and greater satisfaction.

NUMBNESS

Numbness is one of the most common complaints in MS, usually as an annoyance rather than as a disabling symptom. Numbness occurs when the nerves that transmit sensation do not conduct information properly, so that one is unable to feel sensations from that area.

Little can be done to treat numbness, and there is no real need to do so since it is usually a harmless symptom. Steroids may improve sensation by decreasing inflammation, but their use is reserved for instances of real need.

Focusing on numbness can magnify the problem and make it especially bothersome. The best approach is the realization that it does not indicate a worsening of the disease. A more aggressive approach with cortisone treatments may be considered if numbness involves the hands, impairing fine movements, or the genitalia, making sexual relations difficult. No medications are available that specifically treat numbness.

COLD FEET

The complaint of cold feet is common in MS, even in the milder forms of the disease. The maintenance of skin temperature is an involuntary process, under the control of the autonomic nervous system. Short-circuiting in the interconnections that control the diameter of blood vessels and those nerves that sense temperature is responsible for the perception of cold feet.

This symptom can be annoying, but it is innocuous; there is nothing wrong with the circulatory system itself in the legs or feet, and there is nothing dangerous in the slight drop in temperature that produces this sensation. Warm socks, electric blankets, and similar devices are the best way to manage the problem. Niacin or medications that dilate blood vessels may be used to alleviate the symptom when it is particularly annoying.

ANKLE EDEMA

Swollen ankles result from an accumulation of lymphatic fluid, which most often results from reduced activity of the leg muscles. Unless the swelling is extreme, it is usually painless.

Diuretics usually fail to reduce this type of swelling because they cannot stimulate upward movement of fluid. Treatment is relatively simple and consists of keeping the feet sufficiently elevated so that gravity can begin to move the fluid toward the trunk. Support hosiery may help by keeping the lymphatic fluid within normal channels; elastic stockings must be properly fitted to avoid pinching the muscles of the leg. Special stockings are now available that literally pump the muscles, allowing the fluid to be mobilized and carried away; they are expensive and should be reserved for special situations.

Despite continued leakage of fluid, swollen ankles are essentially only a nuisance, requiring looser shoes, not a symptom of a major problem. Swelling may be more noticeable in summer because blood vessels and lymph channels dilate (swell) more when the temperature is higher.

If a cardiac problem exists, swelling may be accompanied by shortness of breath, coughing, and a general feeling of unwellness. If swelling occurs rapidly, especially in one leg, and is accompanied by redness and pain, it is important to rule out the possibility of thrombophlebitis.

CHAPTER 4

Management of Elimination Dysfunction

Marie A. Namey

Approximately 80 percent of patients with multiple sclerosis experience significant bladder dysfunction at some point in their illness. Reports of bowel problems range from 50 percent to 68 percent of the MS population. Bladder and bowel symptoms can be distressing and may interfere with personal, social, and vocational activities; sleep may also be disrupted. Alteration in elimination patterns can create feelings of loss of control, embarrassment, dependency, and isolation.

Nursing plays a major role in the assessment and treatment of bladder and bowel conditions. Nursing interventions focus on helping the individual to achieve a predictable and effective elimination plan and to minimize complications. Most bladder and bowel symptoms are manageable for most patients after proper assessment and intervention. Although nursing research is limited in the areas of bladder and bowel for the individual with MS, a significant amount of information is available from practice.

Normal bladder function and changes due to multiple sclerosis will be detailed in this chapter. The three common types of bladder dysfunction will be discussed: failure to store, failure to empty, or a combination of these. A step-by-step assessment leading to appropriate intervention will be reviewed. Treatment goals include:

1. Maintain renal function.
2. Keep patient dry.
3. Establish normal voiding patterns.

4. Reduce symptoms and improve quality of life.
5. Motivate patient to comply with treatment.

Bowel management issues are also of concern for the individual with MS. Although constipation is common, involuntary bowel is particularly distressing. Techniques for assessment and intervention will be reviewed.

BLADDER MANAGEMENT

Normal Bladder Anatomy and Function

The main function of the urinary bladder is to store and expel urine. Urine is continuously produced by the kidneys and carried to the bladder through the ureters. The bladder is a hollow muscular organ and is supported anteriorly and anterolaterally by loose connective tissue attachments to the pubic symphysis and pelvic diaphragm. The trigone and lower portion of the base of the bladder rest upon the anterior vaginal wall. The wall of the bladder consists of an inner mucous membrane, with transitional cell lining and underlying lamina propria; a layer of smooth muscle, the detrusor; and an outer adventitial layer of connective tissue.

The urethra has an internal and external sphincter mechanism. The internal sphincter has three components (urethral mucosa, periurethral connective tissue and periurethral vascular plexus), and each is responsible for one third of the urethral closure pressure. The internal sphincter is composed of small muscle bundles and is not under voluntary control. The external sphincter has those components of the internal sphincter and is augmented by striated muscle fibers that are under voluntary control (Figure 4-1).

The bladder is innervated by sympathetic fibers from the hypogastric nerve at T-10 through L-2 and parasympathetic fibers from the pelvic nerve at S-2 through S-4 (Figure 4-2). As the bladder distends with urine, its fundus rises into the lower abdominal cavity. To initiate voiding, the urethra relaxes first, then the bladder contracts and expels the urine through the relaxed sphincter. These functions occur automatically.

Average bladder capacity for an adult is 300–500 ml. Initial (first) urge occurs when approximately 200 ml has accumulated in the bladder. Contractions of the bladder are inhibited by the nervous system until at least 300 ml has collected. An individual can sense bladder fullness and can initiate or postpone emptying as it is convenient. Normally, a person urinates

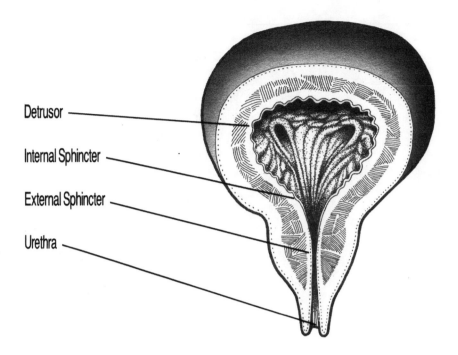

FIGURE 4-1. The bladder.

four to six times during a twenty-four hour period (depending on fluid intake, amount, and type). Generally, our bodies produce approximately 1 ml/minute of urine. Although urinary tract infections are more common in women than men, more than one urinary tract infection per year is considered abnormal.

For voiding to occur, the valve-like muscle (sphincter) and the urethra relax so urine can pass easily; then the bladder detrusor muscles contract to expel urine through the urethra. As bladder fullness is sensed by the individual, emptying can be postponed by voluntarily contracting the external sphincter until a convenient time for voiding.

Problems Occurring with Multiple Sclerosis

Bladder dysfunction in multiple sclerosis is primarily associated with demyelination in the spinal cord, the pontine cerebellar micturition control areas, or other CNS points in between. Interruption of the spinal cord pathways may result in excessive detrusor contractions, involuntary sphincter relaxation or contraction, or detrusor areflexia with urinary retention.

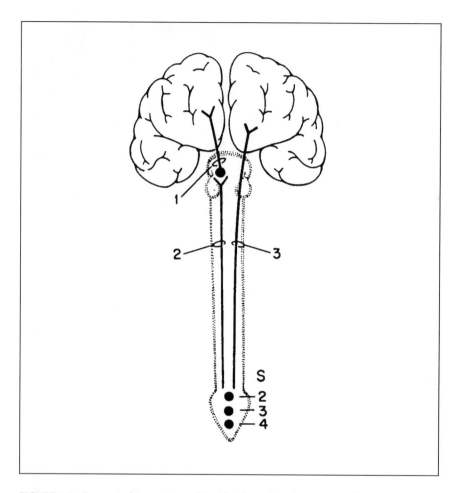

FIGURE 4-2. Supraspinal innervation of the bladder and urethra. 1. Frontal cortex to pontine-mesencephalic reticular formation. 2. Pontine-mesencephalic recticular formation to parasympathetic nucleus (reticulospinal tract). 3. Frontal cortex to pudendal nucleus (corticospinal tract).

Bladder dysfunction is referred to as neurogenic bladder and may produce a variety of symptoms:

⌛ Urinary urgency: A strong sensation to urinate that cannot be controlled. Urination cannot be postponed until convenient.

⌛ Urinary frequency: Having the need to urinate more often than every two to three hours.

⊃ Urinary hesitancy: Difficulty initiating the flow of urine. Although a person may experience an urge to void, urination may not be easily initiated.

⊃ Nocturia: Waking up more than once at night to urinate.

⊃ Incontinence: Losing control of urine. This may be "leaking," "dribbling," or loss of a larger amount of urine prior to reaching the toilet.

⊃ Incomplete emptying: Feeling that some urine is left in the bladder after urinating.

⊃ Urinary tract infections (or cystitis): Resulting in "classic" symptoms of burning or pain upon urination, itching, change in odor or color of urine, pain in the lower back or abdomen, chills and fever. Urinary tract infections in individuals with MS can result in temporary worsening of MS symptoms, or as a first sign a person may experience a change in the usual bladder pattern. Increased lower extremity stiffness or spasticity is often associated with a urinary tract infection.

The presence of one or more of the symptoms is suggestive of a neurogenic bladder. The specific abnormality, however, cannot be identified by report of symptoms alone.

The three common types of bladder dysfunction in MS are the result of:

⊃ hypercontractility of the detrusor muscle of the bladder;

⊃ inability of the sphincter to relax and open or detrusor areflexia; and

⊃ incoordination of the detrusor and sphincter activity (detrusor/ sphincter dyssynergia).

Simply stated, bladder dysfunction in MS can result in:

⊃ failure to store;

⊃ failure to empty; or

⊃ combined failure to store/failure to empty.

Similar symptoms may be present in all three types of bladder dysfunction. A patient may report symptoms of urgency, frequency, and incontinence as a result of inability to store or inability to completely empty. In fact, combined bladder dysfunction commonly presents with a mix of symptoms that can be confusing to the practitioner.

Diagnosis of Bladder Dysfunction

A key to accurate diagnosis of bladder dysfunction is obtaining a complete history of bladder symptoms from the patient. Often it is helpful for the patient to keep a diary of bladder function for a few days for an accurate report (see Appendixes C and D).

Critical questions to ask include:

1. What is your chief concern about bladder function? What bothers you the most about how your bladder is currently working?
2. How often do you void during the waking hours (including voluntary versus involuntary voiding)?
3. How often do you awake at night to void (nocturia)?
4. Do you leak urine when you cough, sneeze, or laugh?
5. Do you experience a strong urge to void that sometimes results in an accident? How often does this occur?
6. Do you feel you completely empty your bladder when you void?
7. Do you find it hard to begin urinating?
8. Do you wear pads or protection? How often?
9. Have you had bladder, urine, or kidney infections? If so, how often and when was the most recent infection?
10. Do you experience pain or discomfort when you urinate?
11. Have you had blood in your urine?
12. What medications are you currently taking?
13. Have you had your bladder function evaluated before? If so, what tests were done?
14. For women: How many pregnancies have you experienced? How many births?
15. Have you had abdominal surgery? If so, what type of surgery, and when?

After a complete history is obtained, it is important to have the patient spontaneously void and measure the amount of urine voided. A urine specimen for urinalysis and culture & sensitivity should be obtained, either from the spontaneous void or the post-void residual urine. (It is important to note that a urinary tract infection can cause bladder symptoms and change in bladder habits.) If the urinalysis and urine culture are suggestive of a urinary tract infection (+ nitrites, bacteria, >100,000 colonies of organism), appropriate antibiotic therapy should be prescribed.

Following the patient's spontaneous void, the patient should be catheterized for measurement of post-void residual urine (PVR). Based on the results of the initial history and bladder assessment, assumptions can be made regarding bladder function and probable diagnosis and possible interventions can be entertained. Reports of bladder symptoms and a post-void residual volume of < 60 ml suggest failure to store syndrome. Often a trial of anticholinergic medications is effective treatment. Reports of bladder symptoms and a post-void residual volume of > 100 ml suggest failure to empty. Intermittent catheterization (IC) is a first step in treatment. If symptoms persist with performance of IC, addition of anticholinergic medication may be considered. Table 4-1 may be of assistance.

Additional Bladder Studies

An ultrasound of the bladder and kidneys can yield useful findings to rule out any structural abnormalities causing bladder symptoms. An intravenous pyelogram (IVP) is a method of outlining the urinary passages and also a test of kidney function. The position of the ureters and kidneys is studied following injection of a radiopaque solution. The ultrasound and

TABLE 4-1.

DIAGNOSIS	SYMPTOMS	PVR	INTERVENTIONS
Urinary tract infection (UTI)	Urgency Dysuria Frequency Hesitancy Incontinence Nocturia Change in usual pattern of voiding	Varying amounts	Treat with appropriate antibiotics
Failure to store	Urgency Frequency Incontinence Nocturia	< 60 ml	Anticholinergic medication Bladder training Protective pads
Failure to empty	Urgency Frequency Hesitancy Nocturia Incontinence Incomplete emptying UTI	> 100 ml	IC

(Continued)

TABLE 4-1. *(Continued)*

DIAGNOSIS	SYMPTOMS	PVR	INTERVENTIONS
Combined dysfunction*	Urgency Frequency Hesitancy Nocturia Incontinence Incomplete emptying UTI	Inconsistent PVR amounts	Anticholinergic medication and IC

* Can only truly be diagnosed by urodynamic testing

IVP are common tests of upper urinary tract function to determine diagnosis or rule out other abnormalities.

Urodynamic studies clarify the functional process of the lower urinary tract, specifically focusing on bladder function. Urodynamic testing helps to qualify and quantify bladder function. Complete urodynamic testing includes uroflowmetry, the quantitative and qualitative analysis of urinary stream. Uroflowmetry is a measurement of the rate of urination and force of the bladder's expulsive ability. It is the first test of the detailed urodynamic studies. This test is not invasive and is easily performed in an outpatient setting.

The patient should be instructed to drink approximately one liter of fluid two hours prior to the evaluation. The patient is then instructed to void into a commode-like device that funnels the urine to a container on a sensor pad. The urine flow rate is measured in milliliters per second and a flow pattern is obtained. Uroflowmetry serves as a "baseline" of the patients voiding patterns.

A normal flow pattern is represented as a bell curve (Figure 4-3). The maximum or peak flow is greater than 12 ml per second and the average flow is greater than 8 ml per second. Poor flow pattern, intermittent flow pattern, or explosive pattern are represented.

Generally, poor flow pattern indicates bladder outlet obstruction or deficient detrusor function. Intermittent flow rate indicates deficient detrusor function or bladder outlet obstruction caused by anatomic or functional factors. Stress urinary incontinence is a common cause of explosive flow pattern.

The urodynamic pressure flow parameters in the study include bladder pressure, rectal pressure, differential pressure, urethral pressure, flow rate, volume, as well as electromyogram (EMG) sphincter activity. The goals of urodynamic studies are to define the pathophysiology of the bladder and urethra in patients, suggest therapy, and provide a prognosis. Ideally, urodynamic evaluation can be carried out in a setting that reproduces

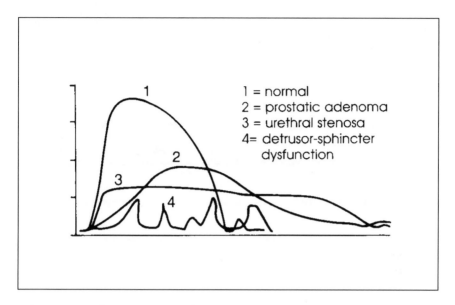

1 = normal
2 = prostatic adenoma
3 = urethral stenosa
4= detrusor-sphincter
     dysfunction

FIGURE 4-3. Uroflowmetry. 1. Normal curve. 2. Significantly decreased max. flow-rate, prolonged flow-increase time, beginning plateau formation in cases of prostatic adenoma. 3. Severely reduced max. flow rate and plateau formation. 4. Splash-like voiding in cases of reflex bladder detrusor-sphincter dyssynergia.

that of the patient's naturally occurring symptoms. Urodynamic studies are likely to include a filling cystometrogram (CMG), voiding cystometrogram, electromyography (EMG) of the striated sphincter, and pressure flow analysis.

Commonly, sterile water or saline solution is used to fill the bladder through a catheter. Either a single multi-lumen catheter or two catheters are placed in the bladder. One tube measures intravesicle or total bladder pressure (VES). Additionally, a rectal tube is inserted to provide simultaneous measurement of abdominal pressure (Pabd) evacuation. During filling the patient is asked to report sensation of filling, initial urge to void, and strong urgency.

A computer recording of cystometric results provides the measurements from the CMG, VES, (the sum of pressure placed against the bladder from the detrusor muscle and abdominal muscle), and PDET. The detrusor pressure (PDET) represents the intravesicle pressure produced by detrusor contractions during bladder filling and evacuation.

The filling CMG is accompanied by an EMG of the sphincter muscles. As the bladder fills, muscles are recruited and the EMG sweeps more vigorously as the bladder approaches capacity. Both needle or surface EMG in conjunction with the CMG are helpful in diagnosing detrusor-sphincter dyssynergia.

Urodynamic testing can yield the following type of printout:

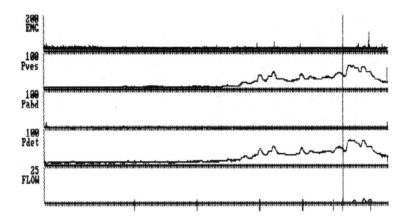

Depending on patients' symptoms and initial nursing diagnosis, a variety of interventions can be recommended to the patient for improved bladder function. Common interventions can include:

Bladder Management Interventions

⊃ Bladder training, timed voiding, and prompted voiding are behavioral techniques that are often suggested to improve bladder functioning. Bladder training generally consists of education, scheduled voiding, and positive reinforcement. A bladder retraining program requires that the participant resist or inhibit the sensation of urgency to postpone voiding, and to urinate according to a timetable, rather than according to the urge to void. Bladder training may also involve tactics that allow the bladder to hold more volume. Initially, the interval goal is set at 1–1/2 to 2 hours (this voiding schedule is not generally enforced during sleep). Drinking an adequate amount of fluid at one sitting will generally result in an urge to void within the retraining time frame. Patients need to know that certain fluids, especially caffeine, NutraSweet®, and alcohol are bladder irritants and cause additional urgency with frequency. Eliminating these products or limiting intake can relieve bladder symptoms. For an individual who has multiple sclerosis, the functional difficulty of getting to the bathroom and removing clothes can also cause problems. A voiding schedule can help deter the effects of these functional problems.

⊃ Absorbent products have proliferated for individuals with incontinence. Protective pads, either disposable or reusable, are worn to absorb involuntary urine flow. These absorbent products include minipads, maxipads, diaper-like garments, shields, undergarment pads, and absorbent chair or bed pads. Absorbent products provide "protection" and can be a useful and rational way to manage bladder problems. Male external catheters (condom catheters) are available in a variety of sizes and styles. Most external catheters are disposable and indicated for one-time use. Individuals may have a preference for brand types.

⊃ Medications have been beneficial in treating bladder problems, including urgency, frequency, and incontinence. Specifically, anticholinergic medications are helpful to block contraction of the detrusor muscle of the bladder. Common anticholinergic medications used specifically for multiple sclerosis include oxybutynin (Ditropan®), lyoscyamine sulfate (Levsinex®) and propantheline bromide (Probanthine®). Tricyclic antidepressant agents (i.e., Tofranil®) can be beneficial in decreasing urgency, frequency, and incontinence.

⊃ Using a Credé method is contraindicated with sphincter hyperreflexia or detrusor–sphincter dyssynergia. Instead, intermittent self-catheterization allows an individual to empty the bladder at regular intervals and thereby reduce the risk of urinary tract infection and structural damage and other distressing bladder symptoms. The use of intermittent self-catheterization was first reported in 1972 by Lapides as an effective therapy for individuals who experience overflow incontinence, sphincter dyssynergia, and urinary retention. This technique of catheterization is preferable to an indwelling catheter due to a lower incidence of symptomatic urinary tract infections, bladder stone formation, and social consequences. The technique of intermittent catheterization has been widely supported in the literature for bladder management in individuals with multiple sclerosis. Basically, an individual is taught to catheterize using a clean technique. Teaching guides are included in Appendixes A and B.

⊃ An indwelling catheter may be needed for either short-term treatment or long-term use. An indwelling catheter allows for continual bladder drainage by gravity. Indwelling catheter use should be restricted to individuals whose incontinence cannot be managed effectively by combining the use of anticholinergic medications and intermittent catheterization. The use of an indwelling catheter would also be suggested for an individual with chronic urinary retention that results in frequent urinary tract infections when he/she cannot perform intermittent catheterization. Individuals who have developed pressure sores of the sacral area may utilize indwelling catheters to eliminate urinary incontinence that may complicate healing of decubitus.

⊃ Long-term use of indwelling catheters is a significant source of bac-teriuria and urinary tract infections. Management of indwelling catheters varies, but the usual practice is to change the catheter a minimum of every thirty days or prn. If the patient has a sympto-matic urinary tract infection, the entire system (catheter and bag) must be changed and a urine culture obtained when the new catheter is inserted.

⊃ A person with MS may still experience urinary incontinence with an indwelling catheter. In this instance, the indication is not to increase the size of the catheter or balloon, but to suggest the use of an anticholinergic medication to decrease spasms of the detru-sor muscle of the bladder.

⊃ *Surgical Procedures*

1. Suprapubic catheters are sometimes an alternative to long-term urethral catheter use for male patients. They are also used in women who have developed severe urethral irritation secondary to an indwelling Foley catheter. The use of suprapubic catheters can create potential problems, and consultation with a urologist is strongly recommended before this procedure is undertaken.
2. Sphincterectomy may be recommended for very disabled male patients who experience intractable hesitancy and retention. The use of anticholinergic medications and an external condom catheter can be combined to manage bladder activity.
3. Diversion procedures including cystostomy (performed for obstruction of bladder outlet or males needing long-term indwelling catheter) or transurethral resection (removal of excess tissue of the area where the bladder connects with the urethra) to provide a clear passageway for the urine to flow freely. This proce-dure is rare in occurrence and generally a treatment for male patients.

BOWEL MANAGEMENT

Normal Bowel Function

Normally, communication from the brain through the parasympathetic nerve center located at S2–S4 to the rectum and anal sphincter results in defecation. When sensory nerves are stimulated because of a bowel filled with stool, the message sent to the brain is interpreted as an urge to defecate. If it is convenient to do so, the internal anal sphincter is voluntarily relaxed and stool is allowed to pass. However, if it is not an appropriate time to defecate, the external anal sphincter is kept tonically contracted until the defecation reflex is suppressed and disappears for several hours. Then, at an appropriate time, the person can stimulate the defecation reflex by abdominal straining. However, abdominal straining is not usually as effective as a natural reflex.

Elimination of stool is actually accomplished by the aid of the Valsalva maneuver. This action may be described as "bearing down" as a person takes a deep breath and attempts to exhale against a closed glottis, while at the same time tightening the abdominal muscles. In order to accomplish this maneuver, intact enervation to the lower thoracic cord (T6–T12) is required.

Most people with MS gave little thought to bowel function before the onset of their illness, and many continue without bowel dysfunction throughout the course of the disease. However, approximately 60 percent of individuals who have MS develop and report bowel dysfunction.

The most common bowel complaint of a person with MS is constipation, but the most distressing bowel complaint is probably that of involuntary bowel.

Diagnoses of Altered Elimination

Constipation

Factors related to constipation in the individual with multiple sclerosis include correlating pathophysiology as described below, inadequate fluid intake, inadequate bulk in the diet, decreased physical activity or immobility, and/or medications such as anticholinergics used for bladder control. Constipation may result directly from multiple sclerosis involvement of that portion of the nervous system that controls the bowel function, the sacral area. This produces a slow bowel, in which waste moves slowly through the digestive system. Another indirect MS influence on bowel movements is weakened abdominal muscles, making it difficult to "bear down" strongly enough to create sufficient abdominal pressure for easy evacuation of stool.

Additionally, decreased physical activity because of impaired walking or easy fatigability is a common secondary cause of slow bowel syndrome. Constipation also results when the amount of fluid a person drinks is voluntarily limited due to bladder problems. Often, individuals decrease fluid to "manage" bladder problems, and then develop additional bowel problems. For better bowel habits, it is therefore important to improve bladder function so that individuals can tolerate adequate fluid intake.

Usually an individual reports decreased frequency of defecation, less than the usual pattern. It is important to remember that "normal" frequency of bowel movements is dependent upon the individual and not necessarily a daily activity. Individuals usually complain of straining on defecation, difficulty evacuating stool, and hardened fecal matter.

Commonly, the nurse would observe distended abdomen, decreased bowel sounds, or oozing of stool around fecal impaction.

Specific nursing interventions for constipation include:

1. Determine premorbid pattern of elimination, including frequency and time of day, and factors that facilitate elimination.
2. Assess current pattern of elimination.
3. Palpate abdomen for distention or abdominal mass, and auscultate abdomen for bowel sounds.
4. Identify related factors contributing to the problem, including issues of privacy, ability to get to a bathroom facility, or inadequate fluid or fiber in diet.
5. Implement interventions to promote normalization of bowel function based on assessment.

Initial interventions to relieve constipation include: (1) fluid intake of 1.5–2 liters of fluid per day; (2) high fiber diet (minimum 15 grams of fiber per day; (3) routinize bowel schedule and encourage patient to evacuate at the same time each day (the best time to attempt defecation is about one half hour after mealtime, when the gastrocolic reflex is the strongest).

The next line of defense includes bulk formers, which add substance to the stool by increasing bulk and water content. In order to be effective, bulk formers should be taken with one to two glasses of liquid. Action usually occurs within 12 to 24 hours, but results may be delayed in some individuals. Daily use is recommended for maximum effectiveness. (Bulk formers are not habit-forming.) Common bulk formers include Metamucil®, Perdiem®, FiberCon®, and Citrucel®.

Stool softeners can also be helpful to draw increased amounts of water from body tissues into the bowel, thereby decreasing the hardness of stool and facilitating elimination. Stool softeners usually act within 24 to 48 hours. Consistent use is recommended to achieve the most benefit. As bulk formers, stool softeners are not habit-forming. Common stool softeners include Colace®, Surfak®, and Correctol® syrup.

Oral stimulants are utilized to provide a chemical irritant to the bowel, which increases bowel activity and aids in the passage of stool. A number of oral stimulants are available over-the-counter. Bowel movements are induced gently, usually overnight or within 8 to 12 hours. Common oral stimulants include Pericolace®, Modane®, Perdiem Granules®, Dialase®, and Milk of Magnesia®.

Harsher laxatives such as Ex-Lax®, Feen-A-Mint®, Dulcolax® tablets, and castor oil have a high potential of becoming habit-forming.

Rectal stimulants can provide chemical stimulation combined with localized mechanical stimulation and lubrication to promote elimination of stool. These may be used only as needed or on a routine basis (every other day) in conjunction with other bowel regimens included in this chapter. Suppositories usually act within 15 minutes to one hour. Glycerine or Dulcolax suppositories are most commonly used.

Frequent use of enemas should be avoided because the bowel will become dependent on them if used routinely to stimulate the elimination of stool. A Therevac® mini-enema is a stool softener evacuant that can be used for relief of chronic constipation. Other enemas include Fleet®, oil retention, saline, and soapsuds.

Developing a bowel routine may take some time. Consistency and reevaluation of the bowel management program is key to success.

Diarrhea

Diarrhea may occur secondary to fecal impaction, diet or irritating foods, inflammation or irritation of the bowel, stress or anxiety, medications (antacids or antibiotics), and overuse of laxatives or stool softeners. Diarrhea may result from a gastrointestinal virus or influenza. Usually the patient complains of abdominal cramping or pain with urgency of bowel.

Nursing interventions include basic assessment, including characteristics of stool (color, odor, amount, frequency), bowel sounds, signs and symptoms of dehydration, medication, and anxiety or stress factors. If diarrhea has been persistent, monitoring electrolytes, client weight, and intake and output are helpful parameters, as are monitoring dietary habits and discontinuing the intake of irritating foods (high fiber bran, fruits, or vegetables).

An additional complication of diarrhea is alteration in skin integrity. Scrupulous skin care is important when diarrhea occurs. Certain medications can be helpful to decrease gastrointestinal mobility and fluid loss (Lomotil®, Imodium®). Bulk-forming fiber supplements (Metamucil®, Citrucel®, Perdiem®) might improve consistency of stool.

Involuntary Bowel

Uninhibited bowel elimination can result due to loss of or diminished sphincter control or hyperreflexic bowel. The patient reports involuntary stools, urgency, or a lack of awareness of need to defecate.

Nursing interventions include complete assessment of normal bowel patterns or habits, including frequency, time of day, color, consistency, amount of stool, and use of laxatives or enemas. Nutritional patterns or habits may contribute to this problem.

A structured daily plan for bowel management can lead to more predictable bowel habits. Patients should be encouraged to utilize the gastrocolic reflex by establishing a consistent daily time for bowel elimination within 30 minutes of a meal. They should select a time of day that is most convenient for their home schedule. The use of a suppository may be helpful to structure a daily bowel movement. Anticholinergic medication can relieve bowel hyperreflexia when this is a causative or contributing factor.

Managing bowel symptoms with an MS client is often the result of trial and error. Generally, success does not come quickly, but rather over a period of weeks or months (remember, haste does not make waste!). It is important to remember the goal of any bowel management program is for a patient to move his or her bowels comfortably in an appropriate setting.

Appendixes

A. Steps to Clean Intermittent Catheterization—Females

1. Assemble equipment and place in an accessible area. Equipment needed: catheter, water soluble lubricant, moist towelette or soap and water, and dry hand towel.
2. Wash hands thoroughly with soap and water and dry.
3. Position yourself comfortably with thighs spread apart. Many women prefer to sit on the toilet or in a chair across from the toilet.
4. Lubricate the catheter end that will go into the urethra. Use Lubri-Wipe™ or a similar water soluble lubricant and lubricate the tip and approximately 2″ up the catheter. (Lubricant may be optional for women.)

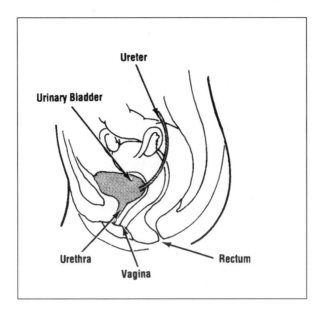

5. Slowly and gently insert the catheter into the urethra until the urine begins to flow (approximately 1–1.5″). Then insert the catheter about 1″ further and hold it there until urine stops flowing.

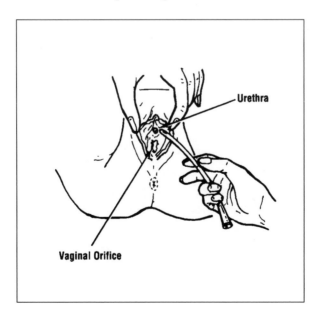

Illustrations courtesy of Mentor Urology, Inc.

6. When urine stops, slowly begin to withdraw the catheter. It is recommended that you slightly rotate the catheter as you withdraw and stop each time more urine drains out.

7. Check the color, odor, and clarity of the urine to be aware of any changes that you may need to report to your doctor or nurse.

8. Never reuse a catheter that appears rough, stiff, worn discolored, or damaged in any way. Consult with your physician or nurse as to how frequently a new catheter should be used.

B. Steps to Clean Intermittent Catheterization—Men

1. Assemble equipment and place in an accessible area. Equipment needed: catheter, water soluble lubricant, moist towelette or soap and water, and dry hand towel.

2. Wash hands thoroughly with soap and water and dry.

3. Position yourself in front of the toilet or in a chair across from the toilet. Men may prefer to stand during the catheterization process.

4. Lubricate the catheter end that will go into the urethra. Use Lubri-Wipe™ or a similar water soluble lubricant and lubricate the tip and the first 6″ of the catheter.

5. Hold the penis straight up from the body at a 60–70° angle from the body. Slowly and gently insert the catheter into the urethra until the urine begins to flow (approximately 6–8″). Then insert the catheter about 1″ further and hold it there until urine stops flowing.

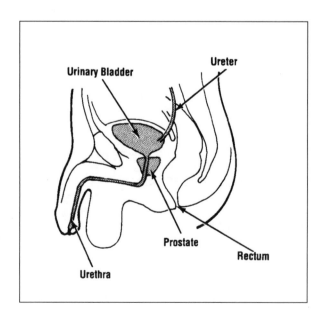

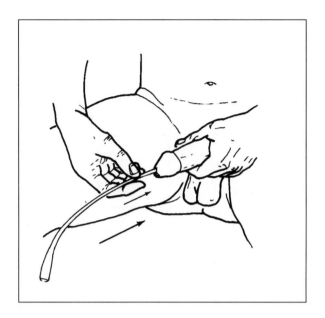

6. When urine stops, slowly begin to withdraw the catheter. It is recommended that you slowly rotate the catheter as you withdraw it and stop each time more urine drains out.

7. Check the color, odor, and clarity of the urine to be aware of any changes that you may need to report to your doctor or nurse.

8. Never reuse a catheter that appears rough, stiff, worn discolored, or damaged in any way. Consult with your physician or nurse as to how frequently a new catheter should be used.

C. Sample Voiding Diary.

Time	Amount Voided	Activity	Leak Volume	Urge Present	Amount/ Type of Intake

D. Sample Bladder Diary.

In the first column, write the time whenever you void in the toilet. In the second and third columns, write the time whenever you have an accident. For every accident, write the reason in the fourth column.

Urinated in Toilet	Small Accident	Large Accident	Reason for Accident

REFERENCES

Blaivas, J. (1980). Management of bladder dysfunction in multiple sclerosis. *Neurology*, *30 (7)*, 12–18.

Caruana, B., Wald, A., Hinds, J., Eidelman, B. (1991). Anorectal sensory and motor function in neurogenic fecal incontinence: comparison between multiple sclerosis and diabetes mellitus. *Gastroenterology*, *100 (2)*, 465–470.

Catanzaro, M., O'Shaughnessy, E., Clowers, O., Brooks, G. (1982). Urinary bladder dysfunction as a remedial disability in multiple sclerosis: a sociologic perspective. *Archives of Physical Medicine & Rehabilitation*, *63*, 472–473.

Doughty, O. (1991). *Urinary and fecal incontinence: nursing management.* St. Louis: Mosby Yearbook.

Edlich, R., Westwater, J., Lombardi, S., Watson, L., Howards, S. (1990). Multiple sclerosis and asymptomatic urinary tract infections. *Journal of Emergency Medicine*, *8*, 25–28.

Guyton, A. (1986). *Textbook of medical physiology.* Philadelphia: W.B. Saunders.

Henderson, J. (1989). Intermittent clean self-catheterization in clients with neurogenic bladder resulting from multiple sclerosis. *Journal of Neuroscience Nursing*, *21*, 160–164.

Hinds, J., Bach, M., Wald, A. (1989). Colonic and anorectal dysfunction associated with multiple sclerosis. *American Journal of Gastroenterology*, *84 (6)*, 587–595.

Hinds, J., Eidelman, B., Wald, A. (1990). Prevalence of bowel dysfunction in multiple sclerosis. *Gastroenterology*, *98*, 1538–1542.

Holland, N. (1982). Intermittent catheterization: application in multiple sclerosis. *AUAA Journal*, *2 (3)*, 5–8.

Holland, N., Wiesel-Levison, P., Madonna, M. (1985). Rehabilitation research: pathophysiology and management of neurogenic bladder in multiple sclerosis. *Rehabilitation Nursing*, *10 (4)*, 31–33.

Kelly, B., Mahon, S. (1988). Nursing care of the patient with multiple sclerosis. *Rehabilitation Nursing*, *13 (5)*, 238–242.

Lapides, J., Diokno, A., Gould, F., Lowe, B. (1975). Further observations on self-catheterization. *American Association of Genitourinary Surgeons*, *67*, 15–17.

Lapides, J., Diokno, A., Silber, S., Lowe, B. (1972). Clean intermittent self catheterization in the treatment of urinary tract disease. *Journal of Urology*, *107*, 458–461.

McCourt, A. (1993). *The specialty practice of rehabilitation nursing: a core curriculum*, Third Edition. Skokie, IL: Rehabilitation Nursing Foundation.

Mohler, J., Cowen, D., Flanigan, R. (1987). Suppression and treatment of urinary tract infections in patients with an intermittently catheterized neurogenic bladder. *Journal of Urology 1*, 336–40.

Moore, K. (1991). Intermittent catheterization: sterile or clean? *Rehabilitation Nursing*, *16 (1)*, 15–18.

Namey, M., Morgante, L., Clesson, I., et al. (1994). Developing proposals for nursing research. *Journal of Neurologic Rehabilitation 8 (3)* 13–18.

Shapiro, R. (1994). *Symptom management in multiple sclerosis*, Second Edition. New York: Demos Publications.

Scheinberg, L., Holland, N. (1987). *Multiple sclerosis: a guide for patients and their families.* New York: Raven Press.

Schoenberg, H. (1983). *Bladder dysfunction in multiple sclerosis, Neurology clinics.* Philadelphia: W.B. Saunders.

Urinary Incontinence Guideline Panel. (1992). *Urinary incontinence in adults: clinical practice guidline.* HCPR publication No. 92-0038. Rockville, Maryland: Agency for Health Care Policy and Research, Public Health Service, U.S. Department of Health and Human Services.

CHAPTER 5

Prevention of Complications in the Severely Disabled

Phyllis Wiesel-Levison and June Halper

As discussed in Chapter 1, a small percentage of patients with multiple sclerosis become severely disabled and dependent on others for most or all activities of daily living. Caregivers are faced with many ongoing tasks as well as the special needs of this segment of the MS population, which include adequate nutrition and hydration, eating problems and swallowing complaints, severe spasticity, and prevention of skin breakdown. In caring for the severely disabled, the nurse is both a caregiver and the educator of the patient, family, and other caregivers.

NUTRITION IN MULTIPLE SCLEROSIS

Adequate nutrition has traditionally been recognized as a key factor in health maintenance both for people in good health and for those with altered health states. Good nutrition is characterized by a well-developed body, ideal weight for body composition (ratio of muscle mass to fat), healthy hair and skin, and mental alertness (Williams, 1995).

Recommended dietary allowances (RDAs) have been developed by the U.S. Department of Agriculture and are shown in Figure 5-1 (Welsh, 1992). Table 5-1 summarizes the USDA's guide to daily food choices. Major changes include increased servings in the bread and cereal group and the vegetable and fruits groups, as well as limiting fat intake.

The role of nutritional factors in the course of multiple sclerosis has been of considerable interest for both patients and health care profession-

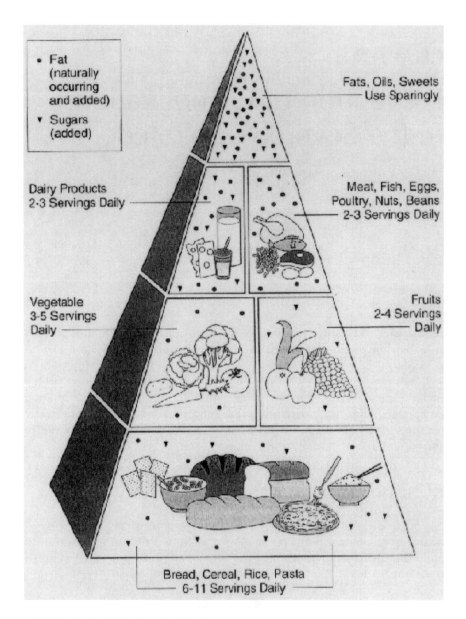

FIGURE 5-1. A guide to daily food choices.

SOURCE: U.S. Department of Agriculture/U.S. Department of Health and Human Services (1992).

als during the past 50 years (Wozniak-Wowk, 1993). A number of diets have received a great deal of attention, including the Swank diet, the gluten-free and other elimination diets, as has the use of supplements such as vitamins,

TABLE 5-1. The Guide to Daily Food Choices—A Summary

Food Group	Servings	Major Contributions	Foods and Serving Sizes[1]
Bread, cereals, rice, pasta	6–11	Starch Thiamine Riboflavin[2] Iron Niacin Folate Magnesium[3] Fiber[3] Zinc	1 slice of bread 1 oz ready-to-eat cereal $1/2$–$3/4$ cup cooked cereal, rice, pasta
Vegetables	3–5	Vitamin A Vitamin C Folate Magnesium Fiber	$1/2$ cup raw or cooked vegetables 1 cup raw leafy vegetables
Fruits	2–4	Vitamin C Fiber	$1/4$ cup dried fruit $1/2$ cup cooked fruit $3/4$ cup juice 1 whole piece of fruit 1 melon wedge
Milk, yogurt, cheese	2 (adults[4]) 3 (children, teens, young adults, pregnant or lactating women)	Calcium Riboflavin Protein Potassium Zinc	1 cup milk $1 1/2$ oz cheese 2 oz processed cheese 1 cup yogurt 2 cups collage cheese 1 cup custard/pudding $1 1/2$ cups ice cream
Meat, poultry, fish, dry beans, eggs, nuts	2–3	Protein Niacin Iron Vitamin B6 Zinc Thiamine Vitamin B12[5]	2–3 oz cooked meat, poultry, fish 1–$1 1/2$ cups cooked dry beans 4 T peanut butter 2 eggs $1/2$–1 cup nuts
Fats, oils, sweets	Foods from this group should not replace any from the other groups. Amounts consumed should be determined by individual energy needs.		

Adapted from the U.S. Department of Agriculture, revised edition of former *Basic Four Food Groups Guide*, 1994.

[1]May be reduced for child servings.
[2]If enriched.
[3]Whole grains especially.
[4]25 years of age.
[5]Only in animal food choices.

food additives, and oil of evening primrose. No dietary regimens have to date been subjected to scientifically controlled trials that have demonstrated them to be of significant therapeutic merit for multiple sclerosis (Wozniak-Wowk, 1993).

It is essential to recognize the educational needs of people with multiple sclerosis and to support them by providing information about the value of good nutrition as well the pitfalls of fad diets or undocumented therapeutic claims. Lack of adherence to accepted regimens places the patient in a vulnerable state for inadequate nutrition and potential development of secondary complications of multiple sclerosis (Phair & Holland, 1993).

The nurse is in an excellent position to assist patients and families to recognize their nutritional needs and teach ways to incorporate them into their lifestyle. These needs do not differ greatly from those of the general population, but they should be individually evaluated based on the patient's disease course, functional status and activity level, and age. The underlying dysfunctions and associated symptoms in MS that impact nutrition are numerous and variable (Phair & Holland, 1993). Tremor, weakness, and paralysis may interfere with the patient's ability to eat or drink. Dysphagia, a problem frequently seen in MS, not only can compromise adequate nutrition but also could result in pneumonia secondary to aspiration of either liquid or solid food. Fatigue may result in inadequate dietary intake due to the energy required to prepare meals, cut food, chew, and swallow large portions.

Excess body weight, whether a patient's premorbid physical characteristic or a result of reduced activity, interferes with mobility and requires dietary intervention (Phair & Holland, 1993).

The patient's weight should be monitored to determine early changes so that modifications in intake and activity can be recommended promptly. A registered dietitian or nutritionist can help determine individual caloric needs based on an in-depth interview that takes individual preferences into consideration. For example, someone with limited mobility (a person using a wheelchair or a walker) might function on 1,200 calories a day while a person with mild disease might continue on his or her usual intake. A patient who is in bed all or most of the day and is dependent on others for activities of daily living (ADLs) will require restricted calories with an adequate intake of nutrients and fluid. A patient with skin breakdown will require additional intake of calories and protein to promote healing and replace loss of nutrients and fluid through wound drainage.

If the person is totally dependent, his or her family will need assistance in learning feeding techniques and may need information about positioning the patient to avoid choking. Referrals to home health programs to relieve the caregiver should be explored, as should information about community programs such as food stamps and meals-on-wheels for those with fixed and limited incomes.

The person with decreased energy should be encouraged to adopt techniques such as precooking and freezing meals, using a microwave to heat food, eating small portions frequently rather than having large meals, and purchasing frozen foods for use when tired. Assistive devices such as weighted utensils and elongated straws can be helpful for patients with tremor or weakness. A consultation with an occupational therapist may promote the use and fitting of these special aids (Phair & Holland, 1993). Another helpful technique is to use liquid nutritional supplements, both for energy conservation and to insure an adequate intake of basic nutrients. These supplements are available in pudding form for patients who have difficulty swallowing liquids or prefer a solid form of supplementation.

HYDRATION

It is extremely important that adequate fluids are taken in order to maintain all bodily functions at the highest level. Food without fluid is akin to a car without oil. Fluid is the lubrication needed to assist in swallowing; the hydration for body tissues; the liquid needed to form waste products and body fluids (blood, lymph, perspiration); and the moisture for skin, hair, and nails. Inadequate fluid intake contributes to constipation, urinary tract infections, and skin breakdown. A minimum of eight glasses of fluids should be ingested daily. People with frequent urinary tract infections can reduce their risk by drinking cranberry or prune juice to acidify their urine. Fluids can also be obtained indirectly through gelatin and other desserts made from liquids.

Nursing outcomes related to nutrition and hydration should include:

⊃ maintenance of optimum body weight within ± 5 pounds;

⊃ maintenance of fluid intake of 1500–2000 ml/24 hours;

⊃ daily intake of basic nutritional requirements;

⊃ utilization of appropriate assistive devices for eating (Phair & Holland, 1993).

DYSPHAGIA

Dysphagia in MS patients with and without swallowing complaints has been found to vary from 10–15 percent (Poser, 1979) to 55 percent (Daly, Code, & Anderson, 1962). In practice, it is believed that dysphagia occurs frequently, yet specific swallowing therapies have not been validated in multiple sclerosis (Sorensen et al., 1993). This problem must be identified by the nurse by asking questions such as: "Do you have difficulty swallowing? Are you having problems with liquids? Solids? Do you ever have choking episodes? Have you ever had pneumonia? Have you maintained your current weight or have you experienced weight loss?" Once the problem is identified, referral to a speech-language pathologist is indicated, usually followed by testing. The most commonly used diagnostic tests for evaluating dysphagia include the bedside swallow examination, a modified barium swallow with videofluoroscopy, or other endoscopic procedures (Glenn, 1995). The purpose of the swallow evaluation is to determine whether the cricopharyngeal sphincter is not opening and the epiglottis is not protecting the airway (Glenn, 1995). The modified barium swallow with videofluoroscopy allows viewing of the oral cavity, laryngopharynx, and esophagus while the patient swallows barium of various consistencies (Glenn, 1995). Videotaping of the study allows clinicians to review the procedure repeatedly and with slow-motion analysis (Glenn, 1995). An abnormal study may indicate alternatives to normal feeding methods such a positioning of the head and chin, changing consistency of food and fluid (chopping or blenderizing foods or adding thickening agents), and planning rest periods prior to mealtime to reduce fatigue (Phair & Holland, 1993). A study that reveals swallowing to be unsafe may require a surgically placed feeding tube. The most commonly used feeding tube in multiple sclerosis is the percutaneous endoscopic gastroscopy (PEG), which can be inserted under local anesthesia and results in fewer complications than surgical procedures (Glenn, 1995). Patient and family education is required for tube feeding at home, and the discharge planner must make arrangements to supply the appropriate equipment.

Although maintenance of adequate nutrition is an inherent principle of nursing care, nutrition in multiple sclerosis is complicated by the variability of the disease course. Dynamic interventions are required in response to the changing needs of patients with multiple sclerosis.

SPASTICITY

Spasticity or muscle hypertonia occurs as a result of abnormal spinal and brainstem reflexes and is a common and treatable symptom of multiple sclerosis. Lesions in several cerebrospinal or propriospinal fiber systems may contribute to this symptom (Stein et al., 1987). Its severity varies depending on the size and location of plaques (Chan et al., 1993). The measurement of spasticity is subjective via patient report or objective using the Ashworth scale (Table 5-2) and the spasticity scale (Table 5-3) (Chan et al., 1993).

TABLE 5-2. Ashworth Scale

Score	Criteria
1	No increase in tone
2	Slight increase in tone, giving a "catch" when the affected part(s) is moved in flexion or extension
3	More marked increase in tone but affected part(s) easily flexed
4	Considerable increase in tone—passive movement difficult
5	Affected part(s) rigid in flexion or extension

TABLE 5-3. Spasticity Scale

Score	Criteria
0	No spasms
1	No spontaneous spasms (except with vigorous motor stimulation)
2	Occasional spontaneous spasms and easily induced spasms
3	More than 1 but less than 10 spontaneous spasms/hour
4	More than 10 spontaneous spasms per hour

The management of spasticity in MS is a challenge because of intercurrent symptoms such as weakness and fatigue. The primary management of spasticity consists of regular stretching programs and pharmacologic agents such as baclofen (Lioresal®), diazepam (Valium®), dantrolene sodium (Dantrium®), and tizanidine (Zanaflex®) (Chan et al., 1993). Baclofen has been the drug of choice for many years although its side

FIGURE 5-2. Pyramid approach to the management of spasticity.

effects of drowsiness and weakness are problematic for many patients (Chan et al., 1993). Diazepam has been successful in the management of spinal cord injury but has been rarely appropriate for MS, other than for nighttime relief of spasticity, due to its sedative and addictive side effects (Chan et al., 1993). Dantrolene is used infrequently due to its side effects of hepatotoxicity, nausea, malaise, dizziness, and weakness (Katz, 1988). Tizanidine, expected to be available in late 1996, inhibits the polysynaptic reflexes whereas baclofen inhibits monosynaptically (Stein et al., 1987).

Phenol blocks and surgical techniques such as neurectomy, rhizotomy, and myelotomy have been greatly reduced with the advent of intrathecal baclofen, which is delivered by an implantable and programmable pump (Penn, 1992) (Figure 5-3). After test dosing via lumbar puncture to evaluate efficacy, the pump is inserted under the skin of the abdomen and connected to a catheter in the spinal canal. Baclofen is delivered continuously throughout the day and may be titrated to deliver variable doses depending on the patient's needs (activity level and the need for some spasticity to transfer, sit, etc. and for rest and sleep at night). Up to 10 doses can be delivered throughout a 24-hour period. Maintenance of the pump is relatively simple and refilling is performed with a computerized programmer either via a home care nursing service or in the physician's office.

A wide variety of treatment options are available for managing spasticity in multiple sclerosis. Management of this symptom can promote improved patient and family function and facilitate improved quality of life.

SKIN CARE

The importance of skin care in the prevention of decubitus ulcers is widely accepted in multiple sclerosis. The economic and emotional costs of prolonged hospital and home management of decubiti are obvious. Prevention of skin breakdown has traditionally been viewed as part of nursing practice and is essential in caring for the MS patient (Phair & Holland, 1993). The goal of risk assessment is to identify patients at risk of breakdown. The Braden and Norton Scales have been tested and validated in many settings (LaMantia, 1995). The Norton Scale consists of five factors: physical condition, mental condition, activity, mobility, and incontinence. Each factor is rated 1 to 4; a score of 14 indicates onset of risk and a score of 12 and below a high risk of pressure ulcer formation (LaMantia, 1995). The Braden Scale (see Table 5-4) consists of six factors: sensory perception, moisture, activity, mobility, nutrition, and friction and shear. The subscales are rated 1 to 4. A score of 4 to 23 is possible, with 16 or below being considered at risk (LaMantia, 1995).

FIGURE 5-3. The SynchroMed® Infusion Pump from Medtronic, Inc., is implanted under the skin in the patient's abdomen or chest. A drug, placed in a reservoir inside the pump, is delivered to its destination in the body through a small-diameter catheter inserted into a blood vessel or the spinal space and connected to the pump.

There is significant potential for impaired skin integrity in MS patients, especially those who have alterations in mobility. Several factors predispose the MS patient to this problem, including the use of assistive devices such as braces or splints, which could increase friction or pressure; decreased sensation or paresthesias, which may interfere with the perception of irritation or pain; urinary or bowel incontinence, which can chemically irritate the skin; nutritional deficiencies; and cognitive impairment,

TABLE 5–4

BRADEN SCALE FOR PREDICTING PRESSURE SORE RISK

PATIENT'S NAME _____   EVALUATOR'S NAME _____

SENSORY PERCEPTION	**1. Completely limited**	**2. Very limited:**
Ability to respond meaningfully to pressure-related discomfort	Unresponsive (does not moan, flinch, or grasp) to painful stimuli, due to diminished level of consciousness or sedation, *or* limited ability to feel pain over most of body surface.	Responds only to painful stimuli. Cannot communicate discomfort except by moaning or restlessness, *or* has a sensory impairment that limits the ability to feel pain or discomfort over half of body.
MOISTURE	**1. Constantly moist:**	**2. Moist:**
Degree to which skin is exposed to moisture	Skin is kept moist almost constantly by perspiration, urine, etc. Dampness is detected every time client is moved or turned.	Skin is often but not always moist. Linen must be changed at least once a shift.
ACTIVITY	**1. Bedfast:**	**2. Chairfast:**
Degree of physical activity	Confined to bed.	Ability to walk severely limited or nonexistent. Cannot bear own weight and/or must be assisted into wheelchair.
MOBILITY	**1. Completely immobile:**	**2. Very limited:**
Ability to change and control body position	Does not make even slight changes in body or extremity position without assistance.	Makes occasional slight changes in body or extremity position but unable to make frequent or significant changes independently
NUTRITION	**1. Very poor:**	**2. Probably inadequate:**
Usual food intake pattern	Never eats a complete meal. Rarely eats more than 1/3 of any food offered. Eats 2 servings or less of protein (meat or dairy products) per day. Takes fluids poorly. Does not take a liquid dietary supplement, *or* is NPO and/or maintained on clear liquids or IV for more than 5 days.	Rarely eats a complete meal and generally eats only about half of any food offered. Protein intake includes only three servings of meat or dairy products per day. Occasionally will take a dietary supplement, *or* receives less than optimum amount of liquid diet or tube feeding.
FRICTION AND SHEAR	**1. Problem:**	**2. Potential problem:**
	Requires moderate to maximum assistance in moving. Complete lifting without sliding against sheets is impossible. Frequently slides down in bed or chair, requiring frequent repositioning with maximum assistance. Spasticity, contractures, or agitation leads to almost constant friction.	Moves feebly or requires minimum assistance. During a move skin probably slides to some extent against sheets, chair, restraints, or other devices. Maintains relatively good position in chair or bed most of the time but occasionally slides down.

NPO, nothing by mouth; IV, intravenously; TPN, total parenteral nutrition.
Source: Barbara Braden and Nancy Bergstrom. Copyright, 1988. Reprinted with permission.

TABLE 5–4 (*Continued*)

	DATE OF ASSESSMENT				

3. Slightly limited:

Responds to verbal commands but cannot always communicate discomfort or need to be turned,
or
has some sensory impairment that limits ability to feel pain or discomfort in 1 or 2 extremities.

4. No impairment:

Responds to verbal commands. Has no sensory deficit that would limit ability to feel or voice pain or discomfort.

3. Occasionally moist:

Skin is occasionally moist, requiring an extra linen change approximately once a day.

4. Rarely moist:

Skin is usually dry; linen requires changing only at routine intervals.

3. Walks occasionally:

Walks occasionally during day but for very short distances, with or without assistance. Spends majority of each shift in bed or chair.

4. Walks frequently:

Walks outside the room at least twice a day and inside room at least once every 2 hours during waking hours.

3. Slightly limited:

Makes frequent though slight changes in body or extremity position independently.

4. No limitations:

Makes major and frequent changes without assistance.

3. Adequate:
Eats over half of most meals. Eats a total of 4 servings of protein (meat,dairy products) each day. Occasionally will refuse a meal but will usually take a supplement if offered,
or
is on a tube feeding or TPN regimen, which probably meets most of nutritional needs.

4. Excellent:
Eats most of every meal. Never refuses a meal. Usually eats a total of 4 or more servings of meat and dairy products. Occasionally eats between meals. Does not require supplementation.

3. No apparent problem:
Moves in bed and in chair independently and has sufficient muscle strength to lift up completely during move. Maintains good position in bed or chair at all times.

	TOTAL SCORE				

which may alter judgment regarding self-care activities (Phair & Holland, 1993).

Prevention is key to the treatment of skin impairment. The nursing assessment will provide areas of concern, and a comprehensive management plan can then be developed to reduce pressure. Pressure reduction encompasses all activities and modalities from bed to wheelchair, transfer activities, clothing fit, and mobility (LaMantia, 1995). Additionally, reduction of spasticity is key to the prevention of skin breakdown of the lower extremities, the sacrum, and other areas with bony prominences. Maintenance of desired weight and promotion of maximum health all contribute to the prevention of skin breakdown.

Long-term outcomes of skin care should include freedom from skin breakdown and its complications (Phair & Holland, 1993). Short-term outcomes should focus on compliance and preventative treatments that involve patient and family education, professional activities, and prompt treatment. These should include:

⊃ the identification of predisposing factors;

⊃ patient and family demonstration of activities to relieve ongoing pressure (wheelchair push-ups, change of position in wheelchair, transfers to other seats);

⊃ the use of appropriate seating cushions or mattress adaptations to relieve pressure;

⊃ the use of assistive devices to facilitate changes in bed lying positions (side-rails, trapeze);

⊃ the inspection of the skin by patient, family, home health aides, or the nurse to identify early signs of skin impairment (redness, excoriation, blanching, etc.);

⊃ the provision of early intervention and treatment.

The nurse, in conjunction with the patient and family, is the primary team member in the prevention and treatment of skin impairment. The appropriate use of modalities and patient and family education provide for decreased emotional and monetary cost to the patient, family, and the healthcare system (LaMantia, 1995).

REFERENCES

Chan, A., Hugos, C., Morrison, S., et al. (1993). Balance and spasticity: what we know and what we believe. *Journal of Neurologic Rehabilitation, 7,* 119–130.

Daly, D., Code, C., Anderson, H. (1962). Disturbances of swallowing and esophageal motility in patients with multiple sclerosis. *Neurology, 12,* 250–256.

Glenn, N.H. (1995). Eating and swallowing. In S.P. Hoeman (ed.). *Rehabilitation nursing, process and application*. St. Louis: Mosby.

Katz, R.T. (1988). Management of spasticity. *American Journal of Physical Medicine and Rehabilitation, 67 (3),* 108–116.

LaMantia, J.G. (1995). Skin integrity. In S.P. Hoeman (ed.). *Rehabilitation nursing, process and application*. St. Louis: Mosby, 273–306.

Penn, R.D. (1992). Intrathecal baclofen for spasticity of spinal origin: seven years of experience. *Journal of Neurosurgery, 77,* 236–240.

Phair, L.S., Holland, N.J. (1993). Nursing outcomes in multiple sclerosis. *J Neuro Rehab, 7,* 131–138.

Poser, C. (1979). Diseases of the myelin sheath. In Marritt, H.H. (ed.). *A textbook of neurology,* Sixth edition. Philadelphia: Lea & Febiger, 767–824.

Sorensen, P., Brown, S., et al. (1993). Communication disorders and dysphagia. *Journal of Neurologic Rehabilitation, 7,* 140.

Stein, R., Nordal, H.J., et al. (1987). The treatment of spasticity in multiple sclerosis: a double-blind clinical trial of a new anti-spastic drug tizanidine compared to baclofen. *Acta Neurologica Scandinavica, 75,* 190–194.

Welsh, S.I., et al. (1992). Development of the Food Guide Pyramid. *Nutrition Today, 27 (8),* 12.

Williams, SR. (1995). *Basic nutrition and diet therapy*. New York: Mosby

Wozniak-Wowk, C.S. (1993). Nutrition intervention in the management of multiple sclerosis. *Nutrition Today,* November-December, 12–22.

CHAPTER 6

Psychosocial Issues in Multiple Sclerosis

Nicholas G. LaRocca and Rosalind C. Kalb

INTRODUCTION

The Impact of Multiple Sclerosis on the Individual and on Family Life

Multiple sclerosis (MS) has wide ranging effects on both individuals with the disease and those around them. These effects can last a lifetime and range from mild interruption in daily routine to complete disruption of everyday life. Some people with MS also report that the illness has some positive impact. Many think it has helped them to discover new inner resources and heightened their sensitivity to others. Thus, although it is possible to see MS as a life challenge, there can be little doubt that it also represents a burdensome and often devastating intrusion in people's lives.

This chapter focuses on the psychosocial impact of MS and describes how it affects the thoughts, feelings, and relationships of the people it touches. The broad sweep of MS derives in part from its vast array of symptoms, including impaired ambulation, fatigue, bladder and bowel dysfunction, tremor, spasticity, sexual dysfunction, and cognitive and emotional changes. Every facet of daily life may be invaded. Difficulty in walking can interfere with important activities of daily living and perhaps lead to unemployment, loss of self-esteem, and a dramatic erosion in the lifestyle of the family. Memory impairment can make basic activities such as reading a book or learning a new skill difficult or impossible. Individuals and families may experience the tension and distress caused by these symptoms before they understand the role that MS has in causing these feelings. Grief, stress, conflict, and confusion can all become part of the person's daily life. The nurse can help the individual and the family to understand the effects of MS, to deal with those effects, and to rebuild damaged lives.

The Role of the Nurse

The nurse is the health care provider with whom many people have the most regular and extensive contact. The nurse can play a pivotal role in facilitating individual and family adjustment to the illness. Early signs of new or worsening symptoms may first come to the attention of the nurse, thus providing opportunities for early intervention and education. In particular, the nurse can recognize the signs of cognitive, emotional, and family problems—those effects of MS that often go untreated. While the nurse may not be able to provide the actual treatment for many of these psychosocial problems, she (or he) can act as a valuable resource for information and education about a variety of MS-related problems. The nurse will often be the one who makes the referral that will get things back on track. The psychologist, psychiatrist, social worker, and vocational counselor often rely on the nurse to act as an "early warning system" for new symptoms.

Goal of This Chapter

This chapter delineates some of the cognitive, emotional, and family problems that result from MS, describing them in terms of their various signs and symptoms. It also discusses the challenges facing nurses who work with people who have MS and how they can be met. Additionally, attention is paid to the effect that MS problems may have on the work of the nurse. For example, memory loss can make the nurse's patient education efforts seem fruitless at times. Readers of this chapter will acquire a basic understanding of the psychosocial problems that arise in MS and how to respond to them. The goal is to assist nurses to (1) incorporate an understanding of MS psychosocial issues into their work; and (2) know what type of help is needed to begin solving these problems.

THE EMOTIONAL CHALLENGES OF MULTIPLE SCLEROSIS

Stress

There has been much speculation, many anecdotes, and some research into the question of the impact of emotional stress on MS. Many believe that stress can precipitate the onset of the disease or trigger exacerbations. Almost everyone can cite some emotionally stressful event that took place just before an MS attack. While some studies have found limited evidence to support the stress-MS link (Warren, Greenhill, & Warren, 1982; Franklin et al., 1989), many others have not (Fischer et al., 1994). Many of the stress studies have used methods that were scientifically weak. As a result, the question of the stress-MS link remains cloudy and controversial. However, there is little doubt that the belief in this link can cause much unnecessary heartache. Family members may express guilt because they think they caused emotional stress that worsened their loved one's MS. Many people with MS have quit their jobs because a misguided physician told them that they needed to avoid "occupational stress" to keep their MS from worsening. Such ideas have no scientific basis whatsoever. People with MS should be discouraged from making major life changes based on "avoiding stress." Most sources of stress are beyond our control in any case. The key is to learn how to deal with stress in one's life, not to try to escape it.

There are more productive ways to look at stress. Recent studies that have begun to investigate the relationship between stress and the immune system (Foley et al., 1988) are finding that the relationship between stress and illness is not a simple one and may vary depending on how long the person has had MS. Other studies have shown what is self-evident, that MS is a tremendous source of stress and can lead to emotional dis-stress (LaRocca, 1984). There is evidence that psychological distress is likely to increase when an exacerbation occurs and to abate as remission ensues (Dalos et al., 1983). We need to be particularly sensitive to a person's emotional state and potentially increased need for help when he or she is dealing with an exacerbation. Because MS can disrupt a person's physical and social life and undermine self-esteem, it may aggravate preexisting personality problems. Here is an example:

Mary has always been a person who needed to be in control. Some would have described her as "bossy" or "picky." She had an opinion about everything and was generally critical about the way people in the family did things. Nothing was ever "good enough" for her. After she developed MS, Mary was no longer able to walk and had to rely more and more on other family members to do things around the house. Gradually she progressed from picky to petulant. Since no one could do anything to her satisfaction, she would loudly berate members of the family concerning their shortcomings. Gradually everyone in the household began to avoid her and Mary became increasingly isolated and lonely within her own family.

The individual described here has become a caricature of her former self. She and her family need the help of a psychotherapist to sort out the feelings that MS has engendered. Mary will probably always be somewhat perfectionistic. However, at present she has become impossible to live with—even for herself—and some intervention is needed.

Many stresses accompany MS; they may be roughly divided into two types: major life events and everyday stress. The major life events are those things such as losing one's job that require change or readjustment on the part of the individual and/or family. Everyday stress, sometimes referred to as "hassles," are the many day-to-day occurrences, such as being stuck in a traffic jam, that do not require major life changes but are emotionally taxing. Let us look at some of the psychosocial issues in MS that are sources of stress and how we can respond to them. Each is illustrated with a vignette. While these vignettes have been prepared so that in their details they do not resemble any real person, each situation is drawn from actual clinical experience and exemplifies the real-life challenges of MS.

Uncertainty and Unpredictability

Uncertainty is probably the first of the stresses that MS places on the individual. Fleeting and ambiguous symptoms such as numbness or blurred vision may be the first signs of MS. It may take months or years to establish a definite diagnosis, during which time these symptoms may be attributed to fatigue, depression, hysteria, or any of a host of other causes. Shock and disbelief may ensue once the concept of having a degenerative illness sinks in. The person with MS wants to know his or her "prognosis" and soon discovers that predicting the course of MS is a little like picking the winner of the Kentucky Derby ten years from now. Building a sense of security and stability in the face of such uncertainty is a significant challenge that carries with it the potential for significant emotional turmoil. Here is an example:

> Tom walks with difficulty, using a cane. He has worked for a number of years at a large telecommunications company that is currently downsizing. He has been able to work out an arrangement in which he telecommutes three days per week and works at his office the other days. He feels fairly secure in his job since he has received excellent evaluations. However, the company has a number of employees with disabilities, and no one is exempt from downsizing. Tom has another job offer from a different company. The new company has a reputation as a good employer and has made him a good offer. However, he would have to travel over an hour to the new job, and because of the nature of his duties he would not be able to telecommute more than one day a week. Tom thinks that he could handle the new job so long as his MS does not get worse. However, if driving became more difficult or fatigue became a problem, he would

probably not be able to do it. When he comes in for a medical visit, he discusses how his uncertainty about his illness is making it hard for him to make a decision.

Tom needs to express some of his feelings of anxiety about the unpredictability and uncertainty of his illness. A psychotherapist could help him to do this. Tom might also find it helpful to talk to an employment specialist and/or an attorney to make sure that he understands his rights and options. He cannot escape the uncertainty of MS. His challenge in the face of uncertainty is to make an informed decision that is neither overly optimistic nor pessimistic.

Denial and Adaptation

When the diagnosis of MS is established, a sense of relief may ensue because at least some of the initial sense of uncertainty has been resolved. However, many soon find themselves in a state of mild shock. Most people's expectations in life do not include an incurable, degenerative disease such as MS. Some sense of disbelief is a normal and healthy reaction. Denial may be helpful in that it gives the psyche time to absorb a shocking reality for which it was totally unprepared. In most instances, this initial sense of shock and disbelief gradually passes as people learn to accept and adapt to MS. Most people with MS will say that they have never really "accepted" the disease any more than one would "accept" a toothache. However, acceptance means that the person with MS is able to recognize the existence of the illness and deal with it. Once someone has accepted the existence of MS, the person can begin the work of making the adaptations that are necessitated by the disease. When health care providers find that such changes are not being made, it is often because denial has persisted long after it has outlived its usefulness. When denial begins to get in the way of adaptation, it is time to consider other strategies. Here is one example:

Jennifer is a favorite customer at the auto body shops. She has had eight automobile accidents in the last three years, two of them total wrecks. She had a spotless driving record prior to being diagnosed with MS at age 34. By age 36 her physical symptoms included numbness and weakness in the legs, episodic double vision, and some memory loss. Her first serious accident occurred shortly after her thirty-sixth birthday when she took out a utility pole on a clear night when she had nothing to drink. Her family has pleaded with her to either stop driving or at least have her driving skills evaluated. She vociferously refuses, attributing her mishaps to "bad luck," "faulty brakes," or "the other guy."

Jennifer appears to be engaging in a particularly dangerous form of denial. Unfortunately, denial is often hard to break through because, by its very nature, it shuts out ideas. Driving is a major bulwark of independence and, for many people, giving it up is worse than not being able to walk. Jennifer needs a carefully measured combination of confrontation and understanding. Her need for independence should be acknowledged even as she is presented with the incontrovertible proof that something is not right. However, understanding and confrontation might not be enough. Family and friends may have to refuse to ride in a car if Jennifer is driving. Jennifer should be tested to determine if she has any specific visual or spatial deficits. In some states, such evidence of impaired ability to drive must be reported to the state motor vehicle agency. Jennifer has not injured anyone yet, but she stands a high likelihood of doing so. Her denial is standing in the way of adaptation and she will need a lot of help to break through it.

Grief and Depression

The shock and denial that can occur at some points in MS are akin to what people feel when they first hear of the sudden and unexpected death of a loved one. Shock and denial normally give way to grief as people mourn the loss of someone who was an important part of their life. In MS, grief plays out in a slightly different way. The losses that are mourned are largely losses of self. The old, able-bodied self is no more and needs to be mourned. Long-held expectations concerning the future may have to be abandoned. Valued physical abilities, such as running or skiing, may be lost and need to be mourned.

Family and friends do not always have an easy time with MS-related grieving. It is sometimes hard for them to understand why the person with MS is down in the dumps when his or her symptoms are "not so bad." However, grief is a normal reaction to the types of changes that occur in MS. Grieving can encompass several reactions and may include (1) sadness and crying, (2) fear and denial, (3) anger and irritability, (4) asking "why me?", (5) reminiscing about the past, and (6) longing for happier times. At times, feelings of anger and resentment borne of the person's feelings of loss may be directed against others, adding to family strain and confusion. Here is an example:

> Before she developed MS at age 37, Saundra had been a successful account representative for a major office technology company. Although her cognitive abilities are intact, she is no longer able to walk. She had been in a competitive field and her inability to get around to her accounts spelled the end of her career. Her company had excellent dis-

ability insurance but was planning to scale it back along with other cost-ly parts of the benefit package. Saundra agonized over whether to go out on disability or try to transfer to a lower paying position in the company. Since she has a family—a husband and two daughters—she opted for the financial security that disability payments based on her old salary would provide. The first few weeks of "retirement" went fine as she caught up on reading, saw friends whom she had not seen for a long time, and worked on long-neglected hobbies. However, after several months went by, Saundra became increasingly moody, alternating between periods of somber withdrawal and extreme irritability. Formerly a mellow and loving wife and mother, she now seems to find fault with everything. Unknown to her husband, she cries every morning when he leaves for work. She spends a lot of time thinking and talking about her old job. Her husband cannot understand what is going on. She has a nice pension and lots of time to do whatever she wants. He wishes he had it so easy. He urges her to stop thinking about the old days and try to enjoy the present. She has always been good with people and once considered going to school to become a social worker. However, she simply cannot face the prospect of starting over again.

Saundra is grieving. She needs space to engage in this process and live through the feelings that go with it. If her husband can develop a better understanding of the process of grieving, he can be helpful in allowing her to give vent to her emotions. In time she will probably be ready to build a new life for herself, perhaps even getting her degree in social work.

When we encounter someone who is grieving, we are likely to say that they are "depressed." What is the difference between grief and depression? Grief is often focused on a specific event or set of events and is generally time-limited. The individual who is grieving may be sad, but is usually able to engage in stimulating activities and enjoy the company of others. In con-trast to grief, clinical depression is generally more severe, pervasive, and persistent. Clinical depression is typically diagnosed in the form of a major depressive episode. Such an episode consists of persistent (daily for two weeks or more) sadness and/or lack of interest or pleasure in previously enjoyable activities, along with at least three of the following: (1) loss of or increase in appetite; (2) sleep disturbance; (3) feelings of hopelessness; (4) persistent thoughts of death or suicide; (5) feelings of worthlessness, self-reproach, or guilt; (6) lassitude; (7) inability to concentrate.

In practice, it is often difficult to distinguish between severe grief and clinical depression. Professional help may be *useful* in both instances; it is *essential* in clinical depression. There is evidence that psychotherapy can relieve some of the symptoms of depression in MS (Foley et al., 1987). Anti-depressants have also been used successfully. The tricyclic antidepressants such as Elavil® and Tofranil® have been used for many years, although in the last few years, the SSRI antidepressants (including Paxil®, Prozac®, and Zoloft®) seem to have become more popular.

The term *depression* is a potential source of confusion in MS because it is used in so many different ways. When used as defined previously, it refers to a specific set of conditions that, taken together, constitute a particular psychiatric diagnosis: major depressive episode. However, the term is often used to refer to a less specific and less severe state of dysphoria (sadness) and generalized psychological distress. Thus, a person who is having a bad day in which everything goes wrong may describe him- or herself as "depressed." Because MS has such wide-ranging effects, people with MS frequently experience some emotional distress, especially when they have an exacerbation.

Both clinical depression and less severe emotional distress are common in MS. It has been estimated that 50 percent of people with MS experience a major depressive episode at some time during the course of their illness, a rate much higher than in the general population or in other conditions with similar disabilities, e.g., spinal cord injury. In fact, the very high frequency of depression in MS has led many to theorize that some of the clinical depression seen in MS may be the direct result of damage to parts of the brain concerned with the regulation of emotions, such as the limbic system. In all probability, there are various causes for the clinical depression seen in MS, including demyelination, altered life circumstances, and inherited susceptibility to affective disorders. Whatever the cause, clinical depression should be taken seriously and treated. The rate of suicide is much higher in people with MS than in the general population and is one of the leading causes of death in MS. If you recognize the signs of clinical depression, you should strongly recommend evaluation by a psychiatrist. Here is an example:

Margaret has had MS for 16 years, having been diagnosed at age 32. She did well for a number of years, walking with a cane and keeping close tabs on the availability of rest rooms. About two years ago, however, she experienced a severe flare-up that required hospitalization for the administration of high-dose intravenous steroids followed by inpatient rehabilitation. Although Margaret improved somewhat, she never regained the ability to walk and now must use a wheelchair. She seemed to be making a good adjustment and had a lot of friends, numerous interests, and a part-time job doing computer work at home. About two months ago she began to become increasingly withdrawn, stopped seeing friends, and lost interest in her hobbies. She had been an avid reader but now rarely picks up a book, saying that she cannot concentrate. Food had always been important to her, but she only eats if reminded to do so and then picks at her food. She has lost 15 pounds in two months. She has one son who is away at college. Her husband tries to engage her in conversation, but she seems listless and uninterested. In occasional moments of intimacy, she confides to him that she feels completely useless and that her life has no purpose. Margaret fantasizes about being dead so that she can escape her pain and cease being a burden to her husband. She has not received treatment for depression but her internist has given her a prescription for sleeping pills since she has been having trouble falling asleep. One day Margaret's husband found a plastic bag containing about 30 of the sleeping pills hidden in her night table.

Margaret has progressed well beyond grief or simple emotional distress. She is clinically depressed and has at least a rough plan to take her own life. This represents an abrupt and recent change for her. She had been enjoying life, work, and friends until recently. She needs professional help quickly, probably a combination of medication and psychotherapy. With such help, she should be able to resume her former activities and will likely see things in a more positive light.

Mood Swings and Personality Change

The bouts of grief and depression described so far are part of a much larger picture of emotional upheaval that occurs in MS. For want of a better term, we often refer to these collectively as "mood swings." In reality, we all fall prey to mood swings from time to time. However, it appears that having MS makes one particularly vulnerable to emotional upheaval of many types. The possible exacerbations and remissions of MS can create their own emotional instability. Mood swings may also occur on an hour-to-hour or minute-to-minute basis. Families often mention that the person with MS may be cheerful and loving one minute and angry and critical the next. Other families describe a different phenomenon in which the person with MS is extremely sensitive, cries easily, and finds it difficult to stop crying once it has begun. A third type of emotional instability involves fits of laughing and crying that seem unrelated in any obvious way to what is happening in the environment. Let's look at each of these in more detail.

Emotional Instability   Most people experience some emotional instability when they are placed under tremendous stress. It may manifest itself as irritability, hypersensitivity, and fragility of mood. A good mood may be toppled easily, like a house of cards, and replaced by darker thoughts and a pessimistic outlook. These mood swings may not be confined to the person with MS. Families members, responding to life pressures and their own issues, may also have them. However, the ups and downs sometimes experienced by people with MS may also be fueled in part by demyelination in those parts of the brain responsible for the regulation of emotion, i.e., the limbic system. While research on this topic is lacking, it could help to explain why many people with MS are so emotionally labile. Whatever the cause, dealing with mood swings can be challenging. Brief family therapy can help everyone understand the phenomenon. Therapy can also help to clarify and resolve some of the psychosocial issues that may contribute to the mood swings. Sometimes several members of the family are experiencing the same pain and concerns but are unable to share them effectively with one another. Through therapy, family members can be helped to air some of their concerns and work toward solutions.

Increased Sensitivity Emotional sensitivity in which crying is easily provoked and difficult to stop is not confined to MS. However, it seems to be much more common in MS than in other populations. While research on this topic is sadly lacking, this sort of mood alteration is likely due in part to demyelination. Once people become aware of this problem, it is possible for them to handle it constructively. Being aware of the situations likely to provoke a strong reaction may help people prepare for the rush of emotions that may result. Taking a few deep breaths or pausing for several moments before saying anything in response to the emotions can help the person control the strong emotions. Finally, trying to see individual events in a larger context may be helpful. Sometimes each event is treated as if it were a life or death situation. Trying to see the larger picture can have a calming effect.

Emotional Release The third and most extreme form of mood alteration was previously called *pseudobulbar affect* but is now referred to as *emotional release*. This is a "classic" symptom of MS in which the individual has "fits" of laughing or crying that seem to be out of their control. Additionally, these episodes of laughing or crying may have little or no precipitant or the precipitant, if any, may have little or nothing to do with the emotion being expressed. The person having a crying jag may report later that he or she did not really feel sad and cannot say why the crying started. There is little doubt that such episodes are a direct result of demyelination in the brain, probably in the limbic system. One small study found some success with the use of Elavil® (amitriptyline) in the treatment of this problem (Schiffer et al., 1985).

MAKING REFERRALS THAT WILL BE ACCEPTED

Referring people for help with psychosocial problems can be compared to diffusing a bomb. When it is done carefully, you may be successful. When it is done carelessly, not only are you not successful but you might not get a second chance. A person who confides private problems is likely to "clam up" in the future if he finds that his confidences are handled clumsily or abruptly. A person may reveal psychosocial problems yet feel ambivalent about discussing family and emotional problems with physicians and nurses who deal primarily with physical problems.

Many people become incensed when you suggest that they see a therapist or a psychiatrist. They have barely gotten accustomed to the idea that their body is not working properly and may misinterpret a referral to a therapist as an indication that they are "crazy" or have "mental" problems as well as physical ones, or that they are too "weak" to handle their problems. Psychosocial interventions need to be presented as another facet of comprehensive medical care. Showing people that psychiatry, psychology, and social work are routine components of the team, just like the nurse, physical therapist, and speech pathologist, can help diffuse some of the anxiety. Multiple sclerosis presents a variety of challenges and there are a variety of tools available to help people in dealing with it. Psychosocial interventions are important additional tools.

COGNITIVE CHANGES

Multiple sclerosis is a disease that produces demyelination of the nerves in the brain and spinal cord. It is thus not surprising that upwards of 50 percent of people with the disease show some cognitive deficits when properly evaluated. The frequency of cognitive changes was grossly underestimated in the past. This underestimate occurred because people relied on the brief mental status exam performed by a physician (Peyser et al., 1980). The so-called "bedside mental status" can readily detect only major and obvious traumas to the brain. More subtle insults to the brain may require a more sophisticated assessment using standardized tests such as those administered by a psychologist or speech pathologist. Research using brief batteries of tests have met with some success (Beatty & Goodkin, 1990). However, approximately five to six hours of standardized testing are required in order to assess the nature and severity of cognitive deficits properly.

During the last few years, numerous studies using magnetic resonance imaging (MRI) have demonstrated that the overall extent of demyelination is related to the presence and severity of cognitive dysfunction. More recent studies have begun to show that lesions clustering in particular areas of the brain are likely to be associated with specific functional deficits. For example, the corpus callosum is the heavily myelinated structure that connects the right and left halves of the brain. Lesions in this area tend to be associated with slowing in the ability to process information as well as any tasks that require the transfer of information between the left and right hemisphere. In contrast, lesions in the frontal lobes are often found in those with memory deficits.

While debate continues concerning the exact cognitive functions affected, consensus has been building over the years. In contrast to conditions such as Alzheimer's disease, in which most intellectual functions are severely affected in the space of just a few years, the deficits seen in MS are more limited. Typically, MS affects some cognitive functions while leaving others intact. This preservation of functions is important because it gives the person valuable assets with which to compensate for more compromised functions. Only about 5–10 percent experience cognitive changes severe enough to interfere seriously with daily activities. Let us examine some of the cognitive functions that can be affected in MS and what can be done about them.

Memory

Memory loss is the most commonly cited cognitive dysfunction in MS. It has generally been thought that people with MS are able to learn new material adequately but then have trouble recalling or retrieving that information (Rao, 1986). More recent research has suggested that many individuals with MS learn new information with greater difficulty than controls (DeLuca & Johnson, 1993). This has important implications since those who are attempting to teach new skills to people with MS may find it a frustrating experience. MS memory problems impinge on everyday life in myriad other ways. Those affected may find that they forget appointments, misplace things, have trouble following the plot of a book or movie, and cannot remember family social events. Families are often unaware that MS may be causing memory problems. A person with MS may forget to do important things, angering other family members. An example serves to illustrate:

> Don is a respected attorney in his early fifties. He has had MS for about 15 years. He walks with a cane and works full-time. He and his wife, a guidance counselor, have two children in college. Don has always handled the family finances, including the taxes, financial aid applications, and refinancing the mortgage. During the past few months, he has made a number of major slip-ups such as forgetting to pay certain bills and losing track of a couple of important documents. Recently he and his wife had a major blow-up because he forgot to submit the annual financial aid form for their younger son. They were able to get an extension but his wife was furious. She accuses him of being "all wrapped up in himself," careless, and lazy. She is also irritated at him because he often forgets

things that she has told him. When he was diagnosed with MS, he was reassured that cognitive changes rarely occur and then only in very debilitated, end-stage patients. When Don's wife calls his doctor's office to renew a prescription for Lioresal®, she mentions off-handedly that she and Don are getting old, as shown by his failing memory. The nurse explains that although there are cognitive changes associated with age, people with MS frequently have memory problems even if they have only mild physical disability. Given this new information, Don and his wife decide to pursue the issue. Don's memory loss is confirmed through neuropsychological testing. He works for several weeks with an occupational therapist who helps him to learn compensatory strategies.

Not all stories have such a happy ending. However, it is often the nurse who is on the front lines and who may hear or see things that escape the notice of others. Sensitivity and quick action can often help people with MS get the intervention they need sooner rather than later.

Reasoning and Judgment

Abstract reasoning involves the internal manipulation of ideas, particularly symbolic representation of things existing in the real world. For example, "love" is an abstraction, a symbol that represents for the lover an entire set of thoughts and feelings. Mathematics is replete with abstractions such as "square root," something we cannot see or touch but which has an existence in our minds. Abstract reasoning can be impaired by MS but, because of its subtlety, impaired abstract reasoning may not be recognized as quickly as memory loss. At times the first sign of a problem with abstract reasoning may be a lapse in judgment. Anyone who engages in any sort of analysis or decision making may find that deficits in abstract reasoning get in the way. Here is an example:

Judy is 44 years old and has had MS since her mid-twenties. She has built a successful career as a securities analyst. During the last two years she has noticed mild memory impairment but has been able to compensate effectively using a notebook along with liberal use of the information management capabilities of computers. During the last six months she has had increasing difficulty in her work. She analyzes companies in order to develop recommendations concerning their investment potential. She now finds that she has trouble keeping straight the many facts that she must take into account in performing her analysis. Even worse, long known for having a "sixth sense" about investments, she now finds it hard to sort the more important from the less important factors in her analyses. Things came to a head recently when she submitted a positive report on a European telecommunications firm that the rest of the investment community had written off. About a week after she submitted her report, the company announced massive layoffs, huge fourth quarter losses, and the closure of several divisions. Fortunately, her report was still under internal review and had not been distributed to clients.

Judy is in a real bind. If MS has indeed affected her analytic skills to the extent suggested by this vignette, she will be confronting the need for a career shift. In addition to a good evaluation of her deficits, she is likely to need a lot of support as she goes through the process of accepting these new limitations, grieving for her loss, and adapting to the changes.

Other Cognitive Changes

Space does not permit a full discussion of all the ways in which cognitive functioning can be affected by MS. Memory and abstract reasoning were highlighted because they are often the initial cause of problems in work and family life. Here are some others:

⊃ Speed of information processing can be affected in MS and is often mentioned by those affected. A typical description might be, "I can still do everything I used to do, but now it takes longer. It's like my head is molasses." This problem can be particularly acute when people are called upon to process information that is coming at them quickly from many different directions, e.g., in a busy office or hectic household.

⊃ Word-finding problems may be the most socially mortifying of the MS cognitive changes. This refers to the "tip of the tongue" phenomenon in which the individual gets stuck in mid-sentence because she or he cannot think of a particular word. Unlike most other cognitive changes, this one is hard to hide and it occurs right where everyone can see it.

⊃ Attention and concentration may be affected in MS. Deficits here can be very disabling because they are essential steps in the use of most other intellectual functions. People with attention/concentration problems may be distractible or may have trouble concentrating or keeping their mind on a task. However, we tend to see these problems manifest in more subtle ways, such as when people are called upon to divide their attention. Much of life involves doing two things at once, e.g., preparing dinner while your 12-year-old tells you why she needs a new bomber jacket. People with MS sometimes find that they need to slow the flow of information and focus on only one channel at a time—otherwise dinner gets burned and the bomber jacket gets shot down!

⊃ People with MS often have problems with spatial organization, one of the skills you need in order to put together those toys that are labeled "some assembly required." An experienced auto mechanic who developed MS mentioned that he now has to think twice about which way to turn the wrench. This can be more devastating than memory loss for someone in a job that requires spatial skills. Many leisure activities also are dependent on these same skills—woodworking, sewing, etc.

So far we have discussed the cognitive functions more frequently affected in MS. The cognitive effects of MS, like its physical symptoms, can vary tremendously from person to person. Most language functions are preserved, so it is rare to find someone with MS having an expressive aphasia. Perhaps 90 percent of people with MS show either no cognitive changes (50 percent) or changes that are relatively mild (40 percent), interfering with daily activities to only a limited extent. However, because MS is variable and progressive, a minority (5–10 percent) may develop a severe global dementia, which in its most severe manifestations can resemble Alzheimer's disease. In such instances most cognitive functions are severely affected and the person may be unable to care for himself or manage his personal and financial affairs. When this happens, constant supervision will be needed as well as assistance with even simple tasks such as dressing, even if the person is physically able to perform them.

The Course of Cognitive Dysfunction

The cognitive symptoms of MS do not seem to relate very closely to the physical symptoms. There is little or no relationship between how long someone has had MS or how severely disabled they are physically and cognitive dysfunction. People with few physical symptoms may have fairly severe cognitive ones. Conversely, individuals who are unable to walk and have a host of physical symptoms may be cognitively intact. Although there is some evidence to suggest that people with a chronic progressive course are at greater risk for cognitive dysfunction, this relationship is extremely weak. Cognitive symptoms can worsen during an exacerbation and gradually abate as the person goes into remission. Sometimes these changes can be dramatic, but it is more common for cognitive symptoms to change slowly, perhaps progressing more slowly than physical symptoms. In one study cognitive symptoms showed little or no measurable progression over a three-year period (Rao, 1991). Given the generally mild severity of these symptoms and their slow progression, and the fact that many functions are intact, people with MS are generally excellent candidates for cognitive rehabilitation.

Intervention

At one time cognitive dysfunction was a taboo topic in MS, in part because the problem had no solution. We still do not have a cure, but many investigators and clinicians around the world are trying to address cognitive dysfunction. An error made by many family members, friends, and even professionals is to ignore these problems or try to dismiss them. Well-meaning but misguided people reassure the person with MS that "everyone is forgetful from time to time" or "I lose things all the time myself." The cognitive problems of the person with MS are generally not the same as the everyday forgetfulness experienced by others.

As discussed previously, the first step is recognition of the problem, followed by a thorough assessment. A good neuropsychological evaluation may cost close to $2,000. Thus, one should not undertake this testing unless there is a good reason to do so. Sometimes a short screening battery can determine whether or not something is wrong. However, the full-length battery will be needed to properly delineate the exact nature and severity of the deficits. People are naturally sensitive about these deficits. They may be afraid that others will consider them "crazy" or "stupid." Having cognitive changes does not mean that a person is stupid or has lost his or her intellectual abilities. Cognitive changes are generally specific, and the individual usually retains a good portion of his or her abilities and can use them in a rehabilitation program. Cognitive changes are neurologic manifestations of the disease, just like spasticity or optic neuritis, and do not imply craziness, stupidity, laziness, or any other misconstrued causes.

The most exciting development in this area has been the growth of cognitive rehabilitation for MS. In many parts of the world, psychologists, speech pathologists, and occupational therapists are working with people who have MS-related cognitive dysfunction. Such programs generally employ two complementary approaches. In the retraining approach, the brain is viewed as almost infinitely "plastic" and progressively more challenging exercises are used to strengthen impaired cognitive functions. The retraining approach to memory deficits might involve drills in which word lists are memorized. In the compensatory approach, the permanence of the impairment is taken as a given and the individual is taught how to perform specific functions in new ways using various aids and substitutions. The compensatory approach to memory deficits might involve use of a loose-leaf organizer book to record facts, tasks, and events that are likely to be forgotten. Retraining may be beneficial for some deficits, e.g., attention/concentration problems. However, based on clinical experience and the scientific literature in other disorders, the compensatory approach appears to be more productive.

Cognitive rehabilitation is routine in head injury but at this writing it remains something of a novelty in MS. Many people with MS are excellent candidates for cognitive rehabilitation: their deficits are usually mild to moderate; many abilities are intact; and their symptoms are not likely to progress rapidly. It thus seems likely that this area of treatment will grow rapidly during the next few years. Additionally, research is under way to look at possible pharmacologic interventions, including Cylert® (pemoline). Most of the major clinical trials that have begun during the last several years have included cognitive testing as part of their assessment batteries. In the next few years we will know whether the disease modifying agents that reach the market have any impact on the progression of cognitive symptoms.

IMPACT OF MULTIPLE SCLEROSIS ON THE FAMILY

When one member of a family is diagnosed with MS, it is almost as though a stranger has moved into the household and everyone must adjust or reorganize to make room. The central challenge facing the family is "to find a place for the illness while keeping the illness in its place" (Gonzales et al., 1989). In other words, family members have to learn how to incorporate MS into their individual and communal lives without sacrificing themselves, their family life, their interests and activities, and all of their energy to its demands. Clinical experience tells us that the family's adjustment to the intrusion of MS into their lives is an ongoing one that ebbs and flows over the course of the illness.

The impact of MS on the family is too pervasive and complex to describe in any detail within this chapter (For additional information, see Kalb and Scheinberg, 1992). Therefore, we highlight some of the major challenges to family life, including conflicting coping styles, role changes, the shared grieving process, family communication patterns, and parenting issues.

Conflicting Coping Styles

Even within a single family, people differ significantly in how they approach problems, deal with stress, and express feelings. Once MS is part of the household, each family member must try to understand and accommodate the changes brought about by the disease. One person may want to research MS and talk about it with others as a way of dealing with the stress and uncertainty associated with the disease. Another may be unable to talk or read about MS, and try to cope by busying him- or herself with other things. While there is no single "correct" coping style, family members with different or conflicting coping styles may misunderstand or misinterpret each other's behaviors.

Susan was recently diagnosed with MS following several months of mysterious but fleeting symptoms. Although she experienced some blurred vision, sensory changes, and occasional bouts of clumsiness, she is essentially symptom-free at the present time. She has called the MS Society to request literature and has checked out more than a dozen books from the library. She keeps trying to get her husband to talk and read with her about the disease and attend a support group meeting, but Jim does not seem interested. He has told her that he does not see any reason to spend a lot of time talking about MS because all of her symptoms have gone away. Susan is hurt by his lack of interest and has begun to worry that Jim may not be able to "handle" her MS.

Susan and Jim have different styles of dealing with their feelings. It is easy for Susan to interpret Jim's unwillingness to talk or read about MS as being insensitive to her feelings or uncaring about what is happening to her. Frequently, however, a spouse's reluctance to become educated about the disease has to do with fear of the unknown. Jim may also have concerns about his ability to deal with Susan's chronic illness and be afraid to learn what it might entail. Susan's anxiety about the diagnosis may be causing her to become overly focused on the disease to the exclusion of other things in her life, including her husband and their shared interests and activities.

Susan should be encouraged to invite Jim to visit the physician with her. This will help to ensure that they are both hearing accurate information about Susan's MS and have the opportunity to ask any questions they might have. The nurse is often in an ideal position to observe a couple's conflicting coping styles and determine if they might benefit from family counseling sessions to help them talk to one another about their concerns.

Role Changes

MS-related disability may gradually necessitate role changes within the family. If a man who has been the primary wage earner becomes too disabled to continue working, his wife may need to take on the role of breadwinner while he remains at home to care for the children and manage the household. A woman who has previously handled most of the housework may require the assistance of other family members for tasks she can no longer do. The teenage child of a severely disabled parent may suddenly be required to assist not only with household chores but also with the parent's personal care. These role changes within the family are always stressful and sometimes problematic. Some happen gradually and others occur in response to an abrupt deterioration of symptoms. In either case, the changes disrupt the commonly accepted roles and rhythms of everyday life that gradually develop in every family.

Because these changes typically occur in response to disease-related disabilities, most family members find them difficult to discuss. The family member with MS may feel guilty about being unable to fulfill his or her former role(s); other family members may be resentful about the changes that are required and then guilt-ridden about their resentments.

George has always prided himself on working hard and providing for his family. When he was forced to retire on disability a few months ago, his wife took a job at a local department store. George now has primary responsibility for running the household. He feels guilty that his wife, Ellen, has to work, having always believed that it was his job to support the family. He enjoys seeing his children more but cannot resign himself to doing chores that he always considered "women's work." He is embarrassed about his new role and has become moody and short-tempered with Ellen and the children. Ellen always kept a clean and orderly household. She is dissatisfied with the way George does things around the house but doesn't have the heart to criticize him or the energy after a long day on her feet to do any housework herself.

George and Ellen had always felt good about their chosen roles within the family and proud of their relative contributions to family life. When George's disability forced them to change these roles, they made the necessary adjustments but never found a comfortable way to share their feelings about them. A family therapist can help them support each other through these changes in their lives, perhaps focusing on their success as a team; while each has had to make a major role change, their effective teamwork has enabled them to run the household and take care of their children.

Shared Grief

Feelings of loss and grief accompany the family through each new symptom and change in functional ability. Each progression in the illness requires that the individual and family members adjust to the loss and redefine themselves accordingly. "Who are we as a family now that our roles have changed and our relationships to each other and the larger community are changing?" The family that once defined itself as "outdoorsy, athletic" may need to find a new identity. A family whose resources are being strained by medical costs or job changes may need to give up activities that once formed a core of their recreational time together and provided important connections with other members of the larger community.

The Jones family was always very active. Sid coached the kids' soccer and baseball teams and Sid and Mary belonged to a neighborhood tennis club. The whole family enjoyed hiking together during the summer. As Sid developed balance problems and severe fatigue, the family gradually started doing fewer and fewer of their sports activities. Sid felt like a burden, slowing everyone down all the time, and Mary and the children felt uncomfortable doing things that Sid once enjoyed so much. Both Mary and Sid stopped seeing their friends from the tennis club; they were worried about the club costs and Mary felt that Sid resented her playing tennis without him. The children, who previously had their dad with them at all their sporting events, found that they just didn't see him as much anymore. No one was happy—but no one knew what to do about it.

Although most people are familiar with the concept of grieving over the death of a loved one, many people do not realize that grief is a normal response to the loss of anyone or anything that is significant in their lives. When families are forced to give up activities that are important to them, they need to grieve over the loss before they can begin to find satisfying and meaningful alternatives. Sid and Mary need to talk with the children about the changes the family has experienced so that they can share the feelings of loss with one another. The children can encourage Sid to watch the games even if he is no longer able to coach. Sid might look into a mobility aid that would enable him to accompany the family on certain types of hikes. Sid and Mary might decide to learn to play bridge as an alternative way to meet other couples. Sid might encourage Mary to continue playing tennis even though he can no longer play with her. Many families need the help of a family therapist to recognize the grieving process and begin this type of problem-solving discussion.

Family Communication Patterns

Family communication patterns are complex under the best of circumstances. In times of increased stress and change, preexisting family patterns tend to become exaggerated. A family that has tended to talk little about their thoughts and feelings, either with each other or with others outside the family, may find it even more difficult to share their private fears and concerns about MS. Each lives with his or her own experience of the disease without attempting to share it with one another or with outside resources.

Another family that has been more comfortable with shared expressions of feelings and opinions may rely on this as their primary coping strategy when faced with the diagnosis of MS. As with conflicting coping styles, the family's communications become even more complex when individuals within the same family have different communication needs and styles.

Richard had already been diagnosed with MS by the time he and Joan got married. He was relatively symptom-free and MS was never a major topic of conversation. Richard was the quieter member of the couple. He enjoyed solitary activities like carpentry and gardening and never talked much with Joan or anyone else about MS or his feelings about it. Joan was the social member of the couple. She enjoyed being with people and talking with family or friends about anything and everything. As Richard's MS became more disabling, their lack of communication became more and more of an issue. Even when he was forced to give up his job, Richard felt no need to discuss the major changes confronting the family. In response to Joan's efforts to talk to him about the changes in their lives, Richard would respond, "What's to talk about? This is the way it is." Joan became increasingly resentful of her husband's inability or unwillingness to talk about their situation and finally mentioned her difficulty to Richard's neurologist, who referred them for family counseling.

A second communication issue that is frequently observed in families learning to live with MS involves a conspiracy of silence. Family members feel the need to keep their feelings and concerns to themselves in order to protect one another. The partner with MS may not want to talk about her symptoms or her feeling that the disease is getting worse for fear of being a burden to her spouse or frightening him away. Her spouse is resentful and overwhelmed by the increased responsibility and workload but feels guilty expressing these feelings in light of his wife's disability. Each is carrying a heavy emotional burden that could more easily be handled if they could learn how to share their feelings and support one another.

Couples locked in this type of silence may benefit from a couples' support group. In this setting, they may find it easier to share what they are feeling and ask for what they need from one another because each member of the couple has the support of the other group members facing similar issues. It is sometimes easier for people to understand and accept feelings expressed by their spouses when they realize that other spouses are expressing similar feelings.

A third communication issue has to do with talking about MS with children. Parents tend to tell their children about MS on a need-to-know-basis, and the parents' assessment of the child's need to know is frequently based on the severity or visibility of the physical symptoms of the parent with MS. The parent who needs an ambulation aid is more likely to tell the children than is a parent who has no apparent symptoms. However, recent studies involving children who have a parent with MS have strongly suggested that children are at least as concerned about, and affected by, the psychological changes in their parents—including both cognitive and emotional changes—as they are about balance or ambulation problems. In fact, children seem to be more affected by the emotional climate within the household than by the parent's physical limitations. Thus, children are aware that something is going on to cause a parent to be more upset, tearful, cranky, or forgetful than usual, but do not have the information they need in order to be able to understand and deal with the behavioral changes they are witnessing.

Parents are also hesitant to talk with children about the MS diagnosis if that diagnosis has not been shared with the parent's employer or other family and friends. They may think (correctly) that the children would not be able to keep this "secret." This is a complex problem with no simple solution. On the one hand, adults sometimes need to protect their privacy in order to avoid employment problems. Or a parent may not be ready to have people in the community know about the disease. On the other hand, the parent's need for secrecy interferes with important parent-child communication about MS-related issues in the household that might help everyone live more comfortably with MS. The notion that the MS is a "secret" cannot help but give the child some feeling that there is something shameful or bad going on in the household.

Parenting Issues

Multiple sclerosis is often diagnosed during that period of a person's life when important career and family decisions are being made. In prior years women diagnosed with MS were often told not to have children. In light of more recent evidence indicating no long-term risk of disease progression associated with pregnancy and childbirth (Birk et al., 1988; Birk & Kalb, 1992; Birk & Werner, 1996), couples are generally being encouraged to proceed with their families. This means that couples in which one partner has MS are faced with a decision that is essentially nonmedical. Today the issue is seldom whether it is "safe" to begin a family, but whether it will be manageable in the face of MS-related impairments.

The nurse is in a unique position to help couples think through this important decision. Couples need to be encouraged to (1) educate themselves about MS and think realistically about the problems it can pose; (2) evaluate their available economic, emotional, and family resources; (3) assess their ability to be flexible in their family and societal roles in the event that progressive disability requires a sharing or switching of anticipated parenting and breadwinning activities; and, perhaps most importantly, (4) think beyond the initial months of infancy to the big picture of parenting. Many prospective parents focus so intently on how they will hold, change, or carry a newborn that they forget how brief the period of placid immobility actually is.

Most adults begin parenthood with many preconceived ideas about what it means to be a "good" parent. Men frequently envision playing ball or coaching a soccer team as prototypical "father" activities. Women may picture themselves chauffeuring to lessons or play dates, baking cookies, and being a room mother or active in the PTA. Physical impairments that interfere with these activities shake a parent's confidence. The person wonders how he or she can be a good parent if these activities are not possible.

Fortunately, a variety of resources are available to help mothers and fathers deal with these concerns (Garee, 1989; Kalb & Miller, 1996). Family therapists experienced in disability issues, support groups, and parenting literature can help men and women think through their attitudes and preconceptions about parenting. People can be helped to redefine their parenting priorities, identify alternative ways of doing the things they want to do with their children and, perhaps most importantly, talk with their spouse and their children about their feelings and concerns. In recent studies, children have indicated quite clearly that open communication, emotional closeness, and shared time are more important than any particular parent-child activity.

CHALLENGES FOR NURSES

Nurses are involved in the care of people with MS in hospital inpatient services, outpatient treatment settings, and through community nursing services. Regardless of the setting in which the nursing activities take place, there are certain challenges that, although not unique to the care of MS patients, seem to be particularly common for health care professionals working with relatively young, chronically ill people.

Emotional Reactions to Working with Young, Progressively Disabled Patients

Most health care professionals view their work as a way to help people recover from illness and feel better. Nurses working with people who have MS are faced with the reality that their work, while necessary and important for maintaining a patient's optimal functioning and preventing unnecessary complications, will not help the person "get well." In fact, nurses in hospital settings and MS centers frequently encounter MS patients who are becoming increasingly disabled. This can be particularly distressing for the young nurse who meets a newly diagnosed MS patient of similar age and sex, with whom there is more of a tendency to identify.

The Dependent and Demanding MS Patient

Nurses often find that MS patients can be demanding and manipulative. Examples might include the person who packs a suitcase full of clothes for a four-day admission for high-dose corticosteroids—and demands nursing help for dressing and putting on make-up, or the person who calls the doctor's office every day with an endless list of questions and requests. In most cases, the patient is reacting either to the multiple losses imposed by the disease or to the anticipated loss of control and independence that can result from progressive disability. So many things in the person's life are out of his or her control that the effort to control the details of daily life becomes exaggerated.

Teaching Self-Care Skills to the Memory-Impaired Patient

In caring for people with MS, much of the nurse's skill is directed toward teaching patients how to manage their symptoms effectively. The nurse educates the patient about medications, bladder and bowel management, skin care, and important community resources. Given that some degree of cognitive impairment occurs in more than half of the MS population, it is not surprising that nurses often feel frustrated in their teaching efforts. Patients who ask the same questions repeatedly or fail to follow through with specific procedures may need written instructions to help them remember what they have been told.

These are just a few of the challenges facing nurses who work with MS patients. While it is important to keep them in mind, it is equally important to remember that it is precisely because of these challenges that the nurse's work in MS is so vital. Individuals living with a chronic, progressive illness need a unique and ongoing kind of support for their efforts to manage the disease effectively and live full, productive, and comfortable lives.

Acknowledgment. Preparation of this chapter was supported in part by grants from the National Institute on Disability and Rehabilitation Research: H133G10158; H133B80018; H133B30015.

REFERENCES

Beatty, W.W., Goodkin, D.E. (1990). Screening for cognitive impairment in multiple sclerosis: an evaluation of the mini-mental state examination. *Archives of Neurology, 47,* 297–301.

Birk, K., Kalb, R. (1992). Multiple sclerosis and planning a family: fertility, pregnancy, childbirth, and parenting roles. In R. Kalb, L.C. Scheinberg (eds.). *Multiple sclerosis and the family.* New York: Demos, 51–62.

Birk, K., Smeltzer, S., Rudick, R. (1988). Pregnancy and multiple sclerosis. *Seminars in Neurology, 8,* 205–213.

Birk, K., Werner, M. (1996). Fertility, pregnancy, childbirth, and gynecological care. In R. Kalb (ed.). *Multiple sclerosis: the questions you have—the answers you need.* New York: Demos Vermande.

Dalos, N.P., Rabins, P.V., Brooks, B.R., O'Donnell, P. (1983). Disease activity and emotional state in multiple sclerosis. *Annals of Neurology, 13,* 573–577.

DeLuca, J., Johnson, S.K. (1993). Cognitive impairments in multiple sclerosis: implications for rehabilitation. *NeuroRehabilitation, 3,* 9–16.

Fischer, J.S., Foley, F.W., Aikens, J.E., Ericson, G.D., Rao, S.M., Shindell, S. (1994). What do we really know about cognitive dysfunction, affective disorders, and stress in multiple sclerosis: a practitioner's guide. *Journal of Neurologic Rehabilitation, 8 (3),* 151–164.

Foley, F.W., Bedell, J.R., LaRocca, N.G., Scheinberg, L.C., Reznikoff, M. (1987). Efficacy of stress-inoculation training in coping with multiple sclerosis. *Journal of Consulting and Clinical Psychology, 55,* 919–922.

Foley, F.W., Miller, A.H., Traugott, U., et al. (1988). Psychoimmunological dysregulation in multiple sclerosis. *Psychosomatics, 29,* 398–403.

Foley, F.W., LaRocca, N.G., Kalb, R.C., Caruso, L.S., Shnek, Z. (1993). Stress, multiple sclerosis, and everyday functioning: a review of the literature with implications for intervention. *Neurorehabilitation, 3,* 57–66.

Franklin, G.M., Nelson, L.M., Filley, C.M., Heaton, R.K. (1989). Cognitive loss in multiple sclerosis: case reports and review of the literature. *Archives of Neurology, 46,* 162–167.

Garee, B.(ed.) (1989). *Parenting: tips from parents (who happen to have a disability) on raising children.* Bloomington, IL: Accent Press.

Gonzalez, S., Steinglass, P., Reiss, D. (1989). Putting the illness in its place: discussion groups for families with chronic medical illness. *Family Process, 28,* 69–87.

Kalb, R.C., Miller, D.M. (1996) Psychosocial issues. In R. Kalb (ed.). *Multiple sclerosis: the questions you have—the answers you need.* New York: Demos Vermande.

LaRocca, N.G. (1984). Psychosocial factors in multiple sclerosis and the role of stress. *Annals of the New York Academy of Sciences, 436,* 435–442.

Peyser, J.M., Edwards, K.R., Poser, C.M., Filskov, S.B. (1980). Cognitive function in patients with multiple sclerosis. *Archives of Neurology, 37,* 577–579.

Rao, S.M. (1986). Neuropsychology of multiple sclerosis: a critical review. *Journal of Clinical and Experimental Neuropsychology, 8,* 503–542.

Rao, S.M., Leo, G.J., Bernardin, L., Unverzagt, F. (1991). Cognitive dysfunction in multiple sclerosis. I. Frequency, patterns, and prediction. *Neurology, 41,* 685–691.

Schiffer, R.B., Herndon, R.M., Rudick, R.A. (1985). Treatment of pathologic laughing and weeping with amitriptyline. *New England Journal of Medicine, 312,* 1480–1482.

Warren, S., Greenhill, S., Warren, K.G. (1982). Emotional stress and the development of multiple sclerosis: case-control evidence of a relationship. *Journal of Chronic Diseases, 35,* 821–831.

CHAPTER 7

Sexuality and Family Planning

Rosalind C. Kalb and Nicholas G. LaRocca

INTRODUCTION

Sexual feelings and behavior are an important aspect of everyday life. Our culture bombards us with sexual stimuli and encourages us to be sexually active and open. Yet sexuality remains one of the most difficult topics for people to discuss, with the result that neither people with multiple sclerosis (MS) nor their physicians are likely to bring up the subject. Why is sexuality such a difficult topic? In spite of the modern emphasis on openness and sexual freedom, many people still feel that sex is too private, too mysterious, or even too shameful to discuss with anyone. The current emphasis on sexual performance or prowess makes it uncomfortable for men and women with MS to talk about the problems or changes they are experiencing. People frequently have no idea that these changes have anything to do with the disease and may be embarrassed to share their concerns for fear that the doctor or nurse will think less of them. If such questions and concerns are ignored in the early stages of the disease, it becomes less likely that they will be addressed as the MS progresses; the more disabled people become, the less likely it is that health care providers, caregivers, and even partners will think of them as sexual beings with sexual feelings or concerns.

One purpose of this chapter is to describe the ways in which multiple sclerosis can affect a person's sexual life, ranging from the problems caused directly by neurologic impairment (primary) to those caused by the debilitating physical symptoms of MS (secondary), and those resulting from the psychosocial sequelae of the disease (tertiary) (Foley & Iverson, 1992; Holland & Cavallo, 1993; Foley & Werner, 1996). While reports of the incidence and prevalence of sexual dysfunction in MS vary considerably (Lilius et al., 1976; Lundberg, 1978; Barrett, 1982; Valleroy & Kraft, 1984; Szasz et al., 1984), the consensus is that most men and women with MS experience sexual changes that are in need of far greater clinical attention than they have received in the past.

The goal of this discussion is to go beyond a simple description of symptoms and their management to a discussion of sexual problems within the context of each person's personality and lifestyle. The initial sections of the chapter describe the most common sexual problems and issues confronted by people with MS. The nurse is in a unique position to help people ask questions and seek appropriate solutions. The time spent with the nurse discussing general symptom management or bowel and bladder problems may be more relaxed or less pressured than the physician's appointment and therefore more conducive to discussion of sensitive topics.

Perhaps less difficult to discuss but just as emotionally loaded are the questions men and women have about the role of MS in family planning decisions. This chapter also addresses the most common concerns pertaining to childbearing and the early parenting role: the genetic risk for one's children; impact of MS symptoms on pregnancy, childbirth, and nursing; and the relationship between pregnancy and disease progression.

RECOGNIZING AND MANAGING SEXUAL PROBLEMS THAT OCCUR IN THE CONTEXT OF MULTIPLE SCLEROSIS

Primary Sexual Dysfunction

Neurologic changes caused by MS can directly alter sexual feelings and responses. In women, neurologic changes can result in decreased libido, reduced or unfamiliar genital sensations, decreased vaginal lubrication, and diminished orgasmic response (Lilius et al., 1976; Lundberg, 1978; Valleroy & Kraft, 1984; Kalb & LaRocca, 1987; Schover et al., 1988; Foley & Iverson, 1992; Foley & Werner, 1996). Men may experience diminished libido, changes or reduction in genital sensitivity, problems in achieving or maintaining an erection, and reduced ejaculatory force or inability to ejaculate (Lilius et al., 1976; Lundberg, 1978; Valleroy, & Kraft, 1984; Kalb & LaRocca, 1987; Kirkeby et al., 1988; Schover et al., 1988; Foley & Iverson,

1992; Foley & Werner, 1996). Both men and women can experience MS-related cognitive changes that affect the sexual response and/or the sexual relationship; hypersexuality, disinhibition, and sexual preoccupation have all been described in the MS population (Huws et al., 1991).

From the time of diagnosis onward, it is important to give patients the opportunity during routine office visits to talk about changes in their sexual functioning. One should never assume that a person with MS has no problems simply because he or she does not mention them to the physician or the nurse. Since a significant number of happily married couples in the general population of healthy adults will report occasional sexual dysfunction (Frank et al., 1978), problems or changes in neurologically impaired individuals are probably more the rule than the exception. Patients should be asked on a regular basis about any changes in their sexual feelings and responses. This matter-of-fact approach to the subject accomplishes two things: first, it alerts people with MS and their partners to the fact that changes they may be experiencing could be related to MS; second, the ease and regularity with which the subject is broached by the physician or nurse gives the message that sex is safe to talk about. Sometimes people need encouragement to bring up this difficult topic. Thus, for example, if a person denies any difficulties but is experiencing significant bowel and bladder problems of the type often seen in tandem with sexual changes, it is appropriate to let him or her know that these types of problems often coexist and that there is help for both.

Once the person with MS has expressed questions or concerns, it is appropriate to recommend a thorough evaluation by a health care professional who is knowledgeable about sexual dysfunction *and* multiple sclerosis. This may be a neurologist, urologist, nurse, sex therapist, psychologist, or some combination thereof. Evaluation and accurate diagnosis of the problem are essential to the formulation of an adequate treatment plan. This process should include a detailed medical evaluation, including a review of all medications being taken, since sexual functioning can be affected by many of the medications used to manage MS symptoms (e.g., anticholinergics) as well as those used for other common health problems (e.g., high blood pressure, depression). Specific tests of sexual function may be used. For example, the Dacomed Snap Gauge® Test, which provides a simple, at-home assessment of the frequency and rigidity of nocturnal erections, helps to determine whether erectile dysfunction is the result of neurologic impairment.

The evaluation must also include a detailed sexual history of the individual and, if the person is married or has a sexual partner, of the sexual relationship as well. The information elicited during this kind of detailed discussion is the best indicator of both the problems to be targeted and the individual's and couple's ability to talk freely in a mutually supportive way and to engage in sexual problem solving. Individuals or couples who have never been able to discuss sexual feelings and/or behavior in the past, or who have always been somewhat inhibited in their lovemaking, will not suddenly find it easy to explore and experiment with new sexual behaviors.

Treatment of Primary Sexual Dysfunction

Decreased libido in men and women can be distressing and problematic to treat. While there is no doubt that a person's interest in sexual activity and sexual responsiveness can be affected by the neurologic changes in MS, it is also true that they can be affected by a variety of emotional states that can come and go in the course of living with any chronic, progressive illness, including anxiety, grief, depression, and anger. Careful evaluation can determine the cause of the change in libido. Changes resulting from transient emotional states often respond well to individual and couple's counseling in which feelings can be explored and expressed in a supportive environment. Decreased libido resulting from a clinical depression is somewhat more complex because the antidepressants used may lift the depression and restore the libido while simultaneously interfering with the orgasmic response. When decreased libido seems to be the direct result of neurologic change, counseling can help to provide individuals and couples with ways to talk about the change and its effect on their relationship while also helping them to explore ways to heighten the sexual mood and enhance intimacy.

Changes in sensation for men and women can be confusing and frightening. Something that once felt good may now feel bad—even painful—or may hardly be felt at all. Treatment often involves a series of sensate focus exercises in which the person is encouraged to explore his or her own body, alone or with a partner, in order to discover what does and does not feel good, and to communicate that information to the partner. For many, the hardest part of the treatment is becoming comfortable with the idea of asking for what they want and need from their partner. Decreased genital sensation in both sexes often requires different, more intense stimulation; however, the introduction of oral stimulation, lubricants, or vibrators may initially be threatening to those who have never used them.

Decreased vaginal lubrication is managed most effectively with any one of a number of water-soluble lubricants now available (e.g., Replens®). Non-water-soluble products such as Vaseline® can cause urinary tract infections and should be avoided.

Several options are currently available for the treatment of erectile dysfunction. The choice of treatment should be guided by the nature and severity of the problem and by personal preference. Some men can achieve a reflex erection by stroking the penis or putting on a tightly fitting condom. A reflex erection, which may be only partial or of short duration, makes intercourse possible but seldom leads to ejaculation. The reflex erection will not restore sensations in the genital area once they have been reduced or lost, but it is a reasonable option for men who derive pleasure and satisfaction from pleasuring their partner and achieving the intimacy of intercourse. The same is true of vacuum suction devices, which induce blood flow into the penis. Once an erection has been achieved, a band is placed at the base of the penis to prevent venous return during intercourse.

Injections for the management of erectile dysfunction have been available for about 15 years (Kirkeby et al., 1988; Foley & Werner, 1996). Three medications are commonly prescribed at this time. Prostaglandin E1 is the newest of the medications and the only one that has been approved for this use by the Food and Drug Administration (FDA). The original drug used for this purpose, papaverine, is a safe and effective alternative for any man who has a problem using prostaglandin E1. The third drug, regitine, is never used alone but may be combined with either prostaglandin E1 or papaverine to enhance their effectiveness.

The penile injection produces a fully turgid erection that lasts for several hours. Men who retain their ability to ejaculate report natural and satisfying results. While this pharmacologic approach is safe, effective, and inexpensive, careful counseling and medical follow-up are required. Although men occasionally experience scarring at the injection site or slight discomfort, the most significant potential complication with these drugs is priapism. It is important for the man to be carefully instructed in the injection procedures and to use only the dosage prescribed for him.

Of equal concern is the fact that individuals and couples vary considerably in their reactions to the injection process. Some are happy to find this relatively simple solution to a difficult problem; others find the use of a needle so threatening and unpleasant that it interferes with the expression of intimate sexual feelings. Careful discussion and supportive counseling are particularly useful when a man and his partner react in opposite ways. As in all areas of sexual expression and sharing, pressure to participate in behaviors that are threatening or uncomfortable reduces the intimacy and mars the pleasure.

Surgical implants are also available to treat erectile dysfunction (Small, 1978; Massey & Pleet, 1978; Foley & Werner, 1966). While they do nothing to address sensory or ejaculatory problems, they do make intercourse possible. The noninflatable rod prosthesis consists of a sponge-filled rod that is implanted into the corpus cavernosum and produces a permanent semi-erection. A flexible version of this device allows for the penis to be bent upward to simulate an erection and downward for easier conceal-ment. The simulated erection is smaller than normal and sometimes awk-ward in its omnipresence, but the implant procedure is relatively simple.

The inflatable prosthesis mimics the natural erection process by allow-ing the normally flaccid penis to become erect through the manipulation of a pump or pressure transducer inserted in the scrotum. A fluid-filled reservoir is implanted in the abdomen; when an erection is desired, the man or his partner "pumps" the fluid from the reservoir into expandable cylinders implanted in the penis. The surgical procedure for this device is somewhat more complex and involves more potential complications. Manipulation of the pump requires a certain degree of manual dexterity and sensitivity.

While various interventions and strategies are available to address pri-mary sexual dysfunction in MS, they are effective only to the extent that individuals and couples are comfortable and competent with them. Health care providers can maximize this comfort and competence in several ways: first, by acknowledging the deep feelings of loss and embarrassment that can accompany changes in sexual function. It is not enough simply to hand someone a booklet about penile injections or implants. The loss of libido or genital sensations, changes in sexual responsiveness, and the inability to achieve or enjoy orgasm threaten a person's sense of self and sexual iden-tity. The recognition of this loss is a necessary preamble to any efforts to provide solutions.

Second, health care providers can enhance the effectiveness of their interventions by teaching/modeling important communication skills. The interventions will prove satisfactory only if the people using them are able to communicate comfortably and effectively with one another. An integral part of any therapeutic intervention is communication skills training to ensure that sexual partners are talking and listening to each other in mean-ingful ways.

Secondary Sexual Dysfunction

While primary sexual dysfunction in MS is the direct result of neurologic impairment, secondary dysfunction follows from the various physical symp-toms that can be part of the picture, including fatigue, spasticity, bladder and bowel problems, pain, and cognitive impairment. People with MS often report that they are simply too fatigued or uncomfortable to feel sex-ual or engage in physically exhausting sexual activities. One woman reported that the relatively short period of physical/emotional enjoyment associated with sexual activity was simply not worth the day that it took her to recover her energy.

Recommended Treatments for Secondary Sexual Dysfunction

Stiffness of the lower limbs and adductor spasms of the hips can make sexual activities awkward, uncomfortable, or even painful. Spasticity is usually managed quite effectively with baclofen (Lioresal®). Within reasonable limits prescribed by the physician, people can self-monitor their baclofen dosage schedule to maximize comfort and flexibility during sex. Individuals with intractable spasticity and those who cannot tolerate the oral medication can be treated with a surgically implanted pump that releases baclofen into the subarachnoid space at a slow, continuous rate. Chemical nerve blocks and surgery are additional treatments that can be used to relieve intractable spasticity.

MS-related bowel and bladder symptoms can have a significant impact on a couple's efforts to engage in stress-free, spontaneous sex. Concerns about loss of bladder or bowel control and the discomfort of constipation interfere with sexual activities and enjoyment. The presence of a urinary catheter or diaper does little to enhance feelings of sexual attractiveness or interest. Aggressive symptom management will help considerably when combined with open, honest discussion and some judicious planning and preparation. Bladder symptoms can be managed in a variety of ways. Reducing fluid intake for the previous several hours and urinating just prior to intercourse may enhance bladder control and alleviate anxiety about urinary incontinence. Those who manage their bladder by intermittent self-catheterization can catheterize just prior to intercourse. Women who use an indwelling catheter will need to hold or anchor the catheter to one side in any way that is least cumbersome and most comfortable for them. Medications for incontinence, including oxybutynin chloride (Ditropan®), propantheline bromide (Probanthine®), and imipramine hydrochloride (Tofranil®), relax the bladder so that it can fill up before the urge to urinate occurs, thus alleviating symptoms of urgency and frequency. Medication schedules can sometimes be arranged to enhance comfort during sexual activity. Since medications might also increase vaginal dryness, the use of a water-soluble lubricant is advised. Constipation is best managed with a careful dietary regimen and adequate fluid intake. Obviously, the need to increase fluid intake to reduce constipation can work at cross-purposes with the desire to control urinary incontinence; each individual needs to experiment and arrive at the management techniques best suited to his or her own needs. For those with little or no control or predictability of their bowel functions, a regular schedule can be artificially imposed via the carefully prescribed use of laxatives, enemas, and/or routine disimpaction. This schedule can be established in such a way as to create relatively stress-free times for sexual activity.

Fatigue in MS is best managed pharmacologically with amantadine (Symmetrel®—an antiviral/antiparkinsonian agent) or pemoline (Cylert®—a mild central nervous system stimulant) and a variety of energy conservation techniques, including the use of ambulation aids and motorized carts or wheelchairs. Unfortunately, most people with MS miss out on the valuable energy-saving benefits of these aids because they resist their use until ambulation is no longer possible. So much time and energy is consumed in the struggle to walk that little energy is left for anything else, including sex. Short naps or rest periods at different times during the day can also provide relief for most people. Since fatigue tends to build over the course of the day, many people find that sexual feelings are at their lowest ebb by evening. Again, a short nap late in the day may be helpful, but many find that sexual activity can be enjoyed more fully in the early morning before all their energy has been used up by the daily routine. Since sexual activity requires time and energy, both precious commodities for the person with MS, a certain amount of planning and prioritizing becomes important. While it necessarily involves some loss of spontaneity, planning for sexual activity allows a couple to give it the time, attention, and energy required to make it an enjoyable, relaxing, and intimate experience.

Various types of MS-related pain can also interfere with sexual interest and pleasure. Sharp, stabbing pains of the type experienced in trigeminal neuralgia are best treated with carbamazepine (Tegretol®) or phenytoin sodium (Dilantin®). Chronic, dull pain in the extremities usually responds well to the tricyclic antidepressants or to fluoxetine (Prozac®) for those individuals who cannot tolerate the tricyclics.

Unlike spasticity and incontinence, which can be obvious and visible, the symptoms of fatigue and pain are much less apparent to a sexual partner. Clear and open communication becomes more important than ever when the lack of sexual interest or responsiveness is due to causes that cannot be seen or felt. In the absence of open discussion, the partner may feel frustrated and rejected while the person with MS begins to feel pressured and resentful over the partner's lack of sensitivity; neither can read the other's mind.

Providers must also be aware of the role played by MS-related cognitive impairment in sexual dysfunction and its potential impact on treatment interventions. Cognitive impairment of the type often found in MS involves a variety of problems that include short-term memory loss, attentional problems, word-finding difficulties, and impaired judgment. These are discussed further under tertiary sexual dysfunction since their primary impact is on interpersonal communication. In general, however, MS-related cognitive dysfunction requires a thorough neuropsychological evaluation in order to assess the type and extent of deficits. Fortunately, remediation programs are becoming increasingly available to people with MS (Fischer, LaRocca, & Sorensen, 1996).

Another facet of MS-related cognitive impairment involves hypersexuality, sexual preoccupation, and inappropriate sexual acting out, which are best managed psychiatrically with small amounts of haloperidol (Haldol®) and a great deal of structure and limit-setting. The effects of this type of hypersexuality are devastating on a marital relationship because it completely removes sexual expression from the realm of emotional intimacy. The spouse (usually the wife) is pursued incessantly—poked, stroked, and fondled—in a childlike, nagging fashion that is unpleasant and uncomfortable. Relationships with health care aides in the home also become complicated by this innocent but unacceptable sexual acting out. Fortunately, this type of MS-related hypersexuality is relatively rare.

Tertiary Sexual Dysfunction

The tertiary effects of multiple sclerosis on sexual functioning encompass all of the complex feelings and attitudes people have about sexuality and its expression. The feelings and attitudes range from the more general, societal ones about the apparent incompatibility between illness/disability and sexuality to the more personal feelings and attitudes of individuals struggling to deal with the changes MS brings to their daily lives and personal relationships. We live in a culture that associates sexuality and sexual attractiveness with youth, vigor, and good health. Even if a disabled person continues to have all of the same sexual thoughts, feelings, and desires that he or she has always had, family members, friends, and even health care providers may cease to see the person as a sexual being. Not only is this a devastating blow to self-esteem, but it also affects efforts to relate in a sexual way and to gain needed help and information concerning sexual problems.

On a more personal level, each individual must reformulate his or her self-concept to incorporate whatever changes in sexual feelings or functioning have occurred. Our sexual roles and behaviors play an integral part in the way we define ourselves (Holland & Cavallo, 1993). As with all of the losses and changes caused by MS, these changes must be acknowledged and grieved over before the person can begin to reestablish a meaningful, satisfying sense of self. The same struggle to redefine oneself that follows the loss of ambulation or the termination of gainful employment can follow the change in sexual response. This cycle of loss-grief-redefinition is experienced to some degree by everyone going through these changes—whether married or single, heterosexual, lesbian, or gay. Health care providers must try to be alert and open to everyone's need for information and support in their efforts to cope with these changes.

In addition to the sexual symptoms that may be occurring within the individual, a variety of changes in individual and family functioning are probabaly occurring that can affect a sexual relationship. Primary among these are the changes in roles that family members undertake in response to the demands of the illness. The balance of partnership within a couple may shift periodically as the roles of wage earner, houseperson, or caregiver are hampered by worsening symptoms. As the partnership gradually shifts away from the familiar, agreed-upon role relationships, partners may find their sexual feelings changing as well.

A spouse who begins to feel more like a nurse than a husband or wife, or who is trying to juggle several roles and responsibilities at once, may feel too angry, tired, or resentful to be interested in sex. A spouse may find it difficult to feel sexually aroused by a partner with symptoms such as tremor, spasticity, or incontinence. As one husband described his situation, "I love my wife dearly, but it isn't very stimulating to hug someone whose body feels like a board." Similarly, the spouse may be afraid of hurting or tiring a partner who must cope with debilitating and uncomfortable symptoms. The partner with MS may find that dependency needs, fears of abandonment, or feelings of sexual inadequacy interfere with open communication about sexual feelings or problems. She or he may be afraid that discussion of physical symptoms or sexual problems will "turn off" the partner or drive the partner away completely. Or the person with MS may simply be less interested in sexual activity.

Partners also report that the cognitive and personality changes that can occur with MS interfere with sexual relationships. The person with MS may have problems with memory, attention, word-finding, or logical thinking, any of which can interfere with empathic communication. A husband or wife may find that the partner with MS thinks, behaves, or relates very differently—"is not the same person I married."

Recommended Treatment for Tertiary Sexual Dysfunction

Given all of the possible stresses that MS can bring to bear on a person's sexuality and sexual relationships—physical, emotional, and social—the need for adequate information and support is clear. Nurses can provide the link between people with MS and the resources they need, whether it be a medical evaluation, reading material, individual or couple's counseling, cognitive remediation, or communication skills training. Accurate, well-written materials about MS and sexuality are available from the National Multiple Sclerosis Society. Individuals and couples can derive important benefits from this kind of reading, such as feeling less alone as they read that others share similar problems, becoming more familiar and therefore more comfortable with the vocabulary used to describe their difficulties, and learning how to get help with the problems they are experiencing. By providing people with appropriate reading materials and offering to answer any questions that they might have, nurses and other professionals convey the message that it is just as appropriate and important to talk about sexual problems as it is to talk about any other MS-related symptoms.

Individuals and couples often find the relaxed atmosphere of an ongoing counseling relationship the most conducive to discussion of sexual questions or problems. The group therapy setting—whether it be for persons with MS, spouses of persons with MS, or couples—is also ideal for discussion of the impact of MS on sexual feelings and intimate relationships. By sharing with one another in a psychotherapy or support group, people can share the feelings of loss, strengthen the sense of self and adulthood that can be threatened by sexual changes, and exchange suggestions and ideas.

FAMILY PLANNING

Questions about family planning are very much on the minds of young men and women with MS. People have concerns about the effects of pregnancy and childbearing on a woman's disease progression, and about the impact of MS on a couple's ability to conceive, deliver, and ultimately nurture and raise children. Multiple sclerosis typically has its onset in the young adult years when people are trying to make plans and decisions about the future. The unpredictability of the illness can make planning for the future difficult and stressful, particularly regarding emotionally charged issues like childbearing and parenting. People with MS often look to their doctors and nurses to answer the unanswerable questions: Should I have children? How will it affect my MS? Will I be able to be the kind of mother/father I always wanted to be? Will my children develop MS? The following discussion describes the current thinking about these issues. However, it is important for patients and professionals to bear in mind that current opinion is based on research findings, which yield nothing more than probability statements about outcomes. Thus, we can say to a young couple that most women with MS have no long-term effects of pregnancy, or that the risk of their child developing MS is very small, or that most people with MS do not end up in a wheelchair, but these are only statements of probability. There are no guarantees. Each individual and each couple must be encouraged to make these decisions based on careful consideration of all possible outcomes.

The Genetic Factor in MS

Based on population and family studies of MS, it is the consensus among researchers that certain people are genetically predisposed to MS (Eastwood, 1992; Smith & Schapiro, 1996). This susceptibility, in combination with a set of other, as yet undetermined, environmental factors, results in the illness. In a population-based twin study (Ebers et al., 1986), monozygotic twins, who share identical genetic material, demonstrated a significantly higher concordance rate for MS (i.e., both members of the pair having the disease) than dizygotic twins, who have in common only one-half of their genetic material. The concordance rate for monozygotic twins was 25.9 percent versus 2.3 percent for dizygotic twins. In a study of 815 individuals with MS and 3,000 of their siblings and children, Sadovnick et al. (1988) found the relatives' risk of developing MS to be 3–5 percent, which is 30–50 times the .01 percent rate for the general population. While the risk factor is thus greatly increased for children of a parent with MS, it nevertheless remains relatively small.

Fertility

Because neither male nor female fertility is generally affected by MS, couples must make the same decisions and take the same precautions as anyone else. Any form of birth control is medically acceptable for someone with MS (Birk & Kalb, 1991; Birk & Werner, 1996) and should be selected on the basis of ease, comfort, and effectiveness. Oral contraceptives are safe, effective, and easy to use (Birk & Rudick, 1989). Since condoms and diaphragms require a certain amount of manual dexterity, significant hand tremor or weakness might make either of these methods unmanageable. However, couples can be encouraged to make the insertion of the diaphragm or fitting of a condom part of sexual foreplay, with the partner "doing the work." Women who have used antibiotics and/or immunosuppressive drugs for long periods of time should be aware that these can reduce resistance to infection, thereby compromising the safety and efficacy of an IUD (Birk & Kalb, 1991).

The erectile and orgasmic difficulties experienced at one time or another by most men with MS can interfere with fertility. Couples need to be aware that these difficulties are not necessarily related to a person's age or the duration or severity of his illness. They can occur at any time (even as an initial symptom of MS) and depend solely on the location of MS plaques (Birk & Kalb, 1991; Foley & Werner, 1996). Problems specific to the orgasmic phase have been reported by 44–77 percent of men with MS (Lilius, Valtonen, & Wikstrom, 1976; Minderhoud et al., 1984; Valleroy & Kraft, 1984; Schover et al., 1988). "Dry orgasms" are caused by the failure of seminal emission or by retrograde ejaculation into the bladder. Dry orgasms of either type can obviously impair fertility. Since these problems have been successfully treated with medication and/or electroejaculation, male patients should be encouraged to consult a urologist experienced in this area (Shaban, Seager, & Lipshultz, 1988; Birk & Werner, 1996)

Effects of MS on Pregnancy, Birth, and Lactation

Multiple sclerosis has no apparent effect on the course of pregnancy, labor, delivery, or lactation. There is no added risk of miscarriage, complications in labor or delivery, fetal malformations, or stillbirths (Tillman, 1950; Birk & Werner, 1996; Birk, 1995). In other words, MS does not affect a woman's physiologic capability of conceiving, carrying, delivering, or nursing a healthy infant. However, it is important for women and their partners to consider the following: (1) pregnant and lactating women must refrain from taking certain types of medications (See Birk & Kalb, 1992, and Birk, 1995, for precautions regarding the use of MS-related medications during pregnancy and lactation.) *In general, women of childbearing age should routinely be advised to alert their physicians as soon as they are considering becoming pregnant so that the doctor can make recommendations about discontinuing or substituting medications;* (2) women with MS-related fatigue may find pregnancy and lactation even more than normally tiring; (3) various MS symptoms (e.g., impaired ambulation, weakness, sensory changes, loss of coordination or balance) can make pregnancy, delivery, and infant care more than normally challenging. The sharing of parenting activities (particularly nighttime feedings) and utilization of all available resources (primarily helpful friends and relatives) will greatly reduce a woman's stress and fatigue in pregnancy and the postpartum period.

Effects of Pregnancy, Birth, and Lactation on MS

Of equal concern to couples are the effects of pregnancy and childbirth on the mother's MS. Many women with MS have read or heard from well-meaning friends or relatives (and even some physicians) that they should not have children because pregnancy causes the disease to worsen. Indeed, medical opinion prior to 1950 did advise against women with MS becoming pregnant. More recently, research findings have altered this view. In seven retrospective studies, reviewing a total of 925 pregnancies, only 10 percent of the women experienced any disease progression during pregnancy and 29 percent experienced *temporary* worsening of the illness in the six months postpartum (Tillman, 1950; Sweeney, 1955; Schapira et al., 1966; Ghezzi & Caputo, 1981; Poser & Poser, 1983; Korn-Lubetzki et al., 1984; Birk, 1995). The exacerbation rate during pregnancy was actually found to be lower than the average expected rate for women (Korn-Lubetzki et al., 1984), indicating that women with MS are somewhat protected during pregnancy by certain immunoactive proteins and pregnancy-related hormones (Runmarker & Andersen, 1995; Birk & Werner, 1996). Hence the wish expressed by some women with MS that they could stay pregnant forever because they feel so much better than they did prior to pregnancy. In a recent prospective study (Birk, Smeltzer, & Rudick, 1988), eight pregnant women were followed over a two-year period. Over the course of the pregnancies, one woman reported disease worsening that was attributable to disease activity while three of the women experienced improvement in their neurologic symptoms. Six women experienced exacerbations (usually mild) during the six-month period following delivery. In one retrospective study of 178 pregnant women (Thompson et al., 1986), no difference was found in the long-term disability levels of women with zero, one, or two plus pregnancies. The authors concluded that pregnancy does not have any long-term effect on disability level. However, the possibility that women with greater disability might have chosen to have fewer children makes the research findings somewhat difficult to interpret (Birk, Smeltzer, & Rudick, 1988).

In communicating these findings to concerned couples, one can say that a woman's condition is likely to remain stable or even improve during the nine months of pregnancy but that there is a 20–75 percent risk of temporary worsening of the disease in the six months following pregnancy (even if the pregnancy ends prematurely due to spontaneous or elective abortion). Most researchers also agree that pregnancy does not affect final disease outcome or disability level. Once again, however, it is important to make sure that a couple understands the meaning and implications of these statements of statistical probability. They need to think through their family planning decisions with an open mind, considering not only the probable (positive) outcomes but also the possible (negative) ones.

Multiple Sclerosis and Parenting

Men and women with MS often ask whether the disease will interfere with their parenting (Kalb & Miller, 1996). For the most part, they tend to focus their concerns on the early days and months of infant care. Like all other couples making family planning decisions, they need to consider their ability to provide long-term emotional and financial security for their children. If one or the other parent could no longer work at a salaried job, if one or the other parent could no longer provide the necessary hands-on child care, or if the parent with MS were to require costly medical treatment, would they be willing and able to make the adjustments necessary for coping with these changes? Because there is no accurate way to predict disease course or outcome, couples need to be helped and encouraged to think through these questions so that they will not be caught unawares and unprepared several years down the road. It is particularly important for a husband and wife to discuss these issues openly with each other in order to lessen future resentment and recriminations.

At one time or another, most fathers and mothers with MS need to modify their parenting behaviors to meet the demands of the illness. Fatigue or any of a variety of other physical limitations can interfere with parenting activities. They should be encouraged to approach their roles with an open mind and a certain degree of flexibility. To the extent that a parent feels there is only one right way to do the job, he or she will feel frustrated, inadequate, and guilty. Playing catch and being a soccer coach are not the only ways to be a father; there is more to being a mom than baking cookies and sewing Halloween costumes.

Health care providers have an important role in helping couples with the decisions and adjustments that MS forces on them. The uncertain and unpredictable nature of MS prevents us from giving people many of the answers they seek. Nevertheless, we can help them to ask the right questions, explore their options, and support them in their decisions. In so doing, we must recognize that any adjustment or compromise in one's sexual life, family planning decisions, or parenting roles involves a kind of loss. Whether it be a change in sexual interest or activity level, a decision to have no children or fewer children than one had anticipated, or a need to let go of certain parenting activities—any of these kinds of adaptations require the person to redefine himself or herself in accordance with the demands imposed by the illness. The process of redefinition can be slow and painful. Nurses and other care providers accompany people with MS through this process, supporting them as they grieve over their losses and work to identify satisfying options and alternatives.

REFERENCES

Barrett, M. (1992). *Sexuality and multiple sclerosis.* Toronto: Multiple Sclerosis Society of Canada.

Birk, K. (1995). Reproductive issues in multiple sclerosis. *Multiple Sclerosis: Clinical Issues 2(3)*, 2–5.

Birk, K., Kalb, R. (1992). MS and planning a family: fertility, pregnancy, childbirth, and parenting roles. In R. Kalb, L. Scheinberg (eds.). *Multiple sclerosis and the family.* New York: Demos, 51–62.

Birk, K., Rudick, R. (1989). Caring for the OB patient who has multiple sclerosis. *Contemporary Ob/Gyn, 34,* 58–63.

Birk, K., Smeltzer, S., Rudick, R. (1988). Pregnancy and multiple sclerosis. *Seminars in Neurology, 8(3),* 205–213.

Birk, K., Werner, M.A. (1996). Fertility, pregnancy, childbirth, and gynecological care. In R. Kalb (ed.). *Multiple sclerosis: the questions you have—the answers you need.* New York: Demos Vermande.

Eastwood, A. (1992). *Facts &issues: genes and MS susceptibility.* New York: National Multiple Sclerosis Society.

Ebers, G., Bulman, D., Sadovnick, A. (1986). A population-based study of multiple sclerosis in twins. *New England Journal of Medicine, 315,* 1638–1642.

Fischer, J., LaRocca, N., Sorensen, P. (1996). Cognition. In R. Kalb (ed.). *Multiple sclerosis: the questions you have—the answers you need.* New York: Demos Vermande.

Foley, F.W., Iverson, J. (1992). Sexuality and multiple sclerosis. In R. Kalb, L. Scheinberg (eds.). *Multiple sclerosis and the family.* New York: Demos, 63–82.

Foley, F.W., Werner, M.A. (1996). Sexuality. In R. Kalb (ed.). *Multiple sclerosis: the questions you have—the answers you need.* New York: Demos Vermande.

Frank, E., Anderson, C., Rubinstein, D. (1978). Frequency of sexual dysfunction in "normal couples." *New England Journal of Medicine, 299 (3),* 111–115.

Ghezzi, A., Caputo, D. (1981). Pregnancy: a factor influencing the course of multiple sclerosis? *European Neurology, 20,* 517–519.

Holland, N., Cavallo, P. (1993). Sexuality and multiple sclerosis. *NeuroRehabilitation, 3(4),* 48–56.

Huws, R., Shubsachs, A.P.W., Taylor, P.J. (1991). Hypersexuality, fetishism and multiple sclerosis. *British Journal of Psychiatry, 158,* 280–281.

Kalb, R., Miller, D. (1996). Psychosocial issues. In R. Kalb (ed.). *Multiple sclerosis: the questions you have—the answers you need.* New York: Demos Vermande.

Kirkeby, H.J., Poulsen, E.U., Petersen, T., Dorup, J. (1988). Erectile dysfunction in multiple sclerosis. *Neurology, 38,* 1366–1371.

Korn-Lubetzki, I., Kahana, E., Cooper, G., et al. (1984). Activity of multiple sclerosis during pregnancy and puerperium. *Annals of Neurology, 16,* 229–231.

Lilius, H.G., Valtonen, E.J., Wikstrom, J. (1976). Sexual problems in patients suffering from multiple sclerosis. *Journal of Chronic Diseases, 29,* 643–647.

Lundberg, P.O. (1978). Sexual dysfunction in patients with multiple sclerosis. *Sexuality and Disability, 1(4),* 218–220.

Massey, E.W., Pleet, A.B. (1979). Penile prosthesis for impotence in multiple sclerosis. *Annals of Neurology, 6,* 451–453.

Minderhoud, J., Leemhuis, J., Kremer, J., Laban, E., Smits, P. (1984). Sexual disturbances arising from multiple sclerosis. *Acta Neurologica Scandinavica, 70,* 299–306.

Poser, S., Poser, W. (1983). Multiple sclerosis and gestation. *Neurology, 33,* 1422–1427.

Runmarker, B., Andersen, O. (1995). Pregnancy is associcatetd with a lower risk of onset and a better prognosis in multiple sclerosis. *Brain, 118,* 253–262.

Sadovnick, A.D., Baird, P.A., Ware, R.H. (1988). Multiple sclerosis: updated risks for relatives. *Am J Med Genet, 29,* 533–541.

Schover, L., Thomas, A., Lakin, M., Drogo, K., Fischer, J. (1988). Orgasm phase dysfunction in multiple sclerosis. *Journal of Sex Research, 24(4),* 548–554.

Shaban, S., Seager, S., Lipshultz, L. (1988). Clinical electroejaculation. *Medical Instrumentation, 22(2),* 77–81.

Shapira, K., Poskanzer, D.C., Newell, D.J., et al. (1966). Marriage, pregnancy, and multiple sclerosis. *Brain, 89,* 419–428.

Small, M. P. (1976). Small-carrion penile prosthesis. *Mayo Clinic Proceedings, 51,* 336–338.

Smith, C.R., Schapiro, R.T. (1996). Neurology. In R. Kalb (ed.). *Multiple sclerosis: the questions you have—the answers you need.* New York: Demos Vermande.

Sweeney, W.J. (1955). Pregnancy and multiple sclerosis. *American Journal of Obstetrics and Gynecology, 66,* 124–130.

Szasz, G., Paty, D., Maurice, W.L. (1984). Sexual dysfunction in multiple sclerosis. *Annals of NY Academy of Science, 436,* 443–452.

Thompson, D., Nelson, L., Burns, A., et al. (1986). The effects of pregnancy in multiple sclerosis: a retrospective study. *Neurology, 36,* 1097–1099.

Tillman, A. (1950). The effect of pregnancy on multiple sclerosis and its management. *Res Publ Assoc Res Nerv Ment Dis, 28,* 548–582.

Valleroy, M.L., Kraft, G.H. (1984). Sexual dysfunction in multiple sclerosis. *Archives of Physical Medicine and Rehabilitation, 65,* 125–128.

CHAPTER 8

Women's Issues In Multiple Sclerosis

June Halper

Although the onset of multiple sclerosis (MS) ranges from 10 to 59 years, it usually begins during the reproductive period (Sadovnick et al., 1994). Population surveys prior to 1977 showed that MS was approximately 1.4 times more common in women than in men (Matthews, 1991). Several investigations since that time suggest that this may be an underestimate, with a sex ratio range between 1.9 and 3.1 (Matthews, 1991). Gender differences in the incidence of disease occur commonly but often fail to provide any strong clues about etiology. It is possible that the higher incidence of MS in women reflects a hormonal factor, but there may be many other equally possible explanations (Matthews, 1991). Many diseases with a known or alleged autoimmune etiology have an unbalanced sex distribution in which a majority of cases occur in women. Lupus erythematosus is nine times more frequent in women than in men; thyroid disease, myasthenia gravis, and rheumatoid arthritis occur more frequently in women than in men. Sex hormones are thought to influence immune responses although there has been no research to validate this theory (Duquette et al., 1992).

Many issues are unique to women in MS and numerous questions remain unanswered. For example, why does MS disproportionately affect women? Why do hormonally mediated events such as menses, pregnancy, the postpartum period, and menopause impact disease activity? How is disease activity affected? Are primary and secondary health care and rehabilitative services available to women with MS? What are the long-term implications of ancillary services such as assistance with child care and peer support in the course of MS? Is there is difference in the health state of women with MS who breast- or bottle-feed? The questions are many—the answers are few. There is a paucity of research on women's issues in multiple sclerosis. This chapter presents an overview of prominent issues and related research

MULTIPLE SCLEROSIS AND THE CONTEMPORARY WOMAN

The past three decades have resulted in the emergence of women in the workforce with full-time careers and roles and responsibilities within the home and the community. The diagnosis of multiple sclerosis can be viewed as a second or third career, almost another full-time job, which imposes alterations in lifestyles and adaptation to a changed body image. Multiple sclerosis, which in and of itself can cause loss of spontaneity and a sense of security about one's future, can also result in anxiety and insecurity in the woman juggling marriage, career, and parenting. The experiences of family planning, pregnancy, and childrearing are major life events for most couples. The diagnosis of MS makes events more complicated (Birk & Kalb, 1992). While multiple sclerosis does not appear to affect the course of pregnancy, labor, or delivery, the woman with multiple sclerosis faces an increased risk of an exacerbation three to six months postpartum (Davis & Maslow, 1992; Birk, Smeltzer, & Rudick, 1988). Pregnancy does not appear to alter the long-term course of the disease (Birk, Smeltzer, & Rudick, 1988).

The decision to start a family requires more than ordinary planning. Alterations in roles and responsibilities may be required for energy conservation. Parenting activities may have to be delegated or curtailed based on the mother's functional status. Spouses, care partners, family, or friends may have to be enlisted for assistance and relief during the postpartum period or during infancy or childhood. Nurses can play a vital role during the antepartum and postpartum period by assisting the patient to reassess their strengths and weaknesses; prioritize their activities; identify resources within the home and the community; and facilitate the patient's ability to parent effectively while caring for herself. As any new mother, the mother with multiple sclerosis requires education about bodily changes to expect along with signs and symptoms of potential problems. She should be particularly alert for signs and symptoms of infection, such as UTI or mastitis, since these might cause a pseudoexacerbation of her MS. It is important to emphasize the need for adequate nutrition and hydration as well as rest and sleep. The new mother should be encouraged to discuss her postnatal needs with her obstetrician.

Returning to work or to other prepregnancy activities also requires a great deal of thought and planning. Child care poses an added burden to a woman with MS who is working full-time. The nurse can guide the patient to identify child care options in the community. Choices of programs must include not only cost and quality but also location. Traveling great distances to day care programs and then on to her job will tire the woman before she begins her work day. Working with both partners is desirable whenever possible to lighten the mother's responsibility. Child care and childrearing are more difficult for the single parent and occasionally community resources may be necessary. Pediatricians—and, in some areas of the country, pediatric nurse practitioners—can be helpful to new parents with parenting concerns and other worries about chronic illness and disability

MENSES AND MENOPAUSE

While there have been a number of studies on pregnancy and multiple sclerosis (Sadovnick et al., 1994; Frith & McLeod, 1988; Birk, Smeltzer, & Rudick, 1988; Davis & Maslow, 1992), literature searches reveal very few studies on gender differences in multiple sclerosis and even fewer on the relationship of MS to the menstrual cycle and menopause. Anecdotally, many women report changes in their symptoms related to menstruation, and two unpublished pilot studies substantiated these reports (Holland et al., 1987; Giesser et al., 1990). Many women assert that their symptoms worsen two to three days prior to the onset of their period and improve once bleeding has started. Other women report that there are no changes in their condition related to their menses. This is an area that requires research in order to further understand the neuroendocrine connection.

Menopause, with its fluctuations in hormone levels and temperature swings, can cause functional problems for women in general. For women with multiple sclerosis, these changes can intensify symptoms or cause significant changes in functional status. Additionally, women with MS are at greater risk for osteoporosis because of gender, potential or real immobility, and corticosteroid use (Nieves et al., 1994).

The nurse can play a vital role during the perimenopausal period by counseling the patient to seek gynecologic care regarding hormone replacement therapy and guarding against risks such as cardiac disease, osteoporosis, and other well-known sequelae of this period. While women with MS may be limited in weight-bearing exercises, alternatives can be explored with the patient and family to guard against bone loss. Programs such as yoga, swimming, passive standing, and stretching can be effective in maintenance of function and prevention of complications of altered mobility or immobility (Witmer & Sweeney, 1992).

MANAGING BARRIERS

Women with physical disabilities face long-standing, substantial barriers, which may include the physical environment, the attitudes of society, and possibly abusive behavior of people close to them (Nosek et al., 1994). Women with multiple sclerosis must be assisted to develop a wellness perspective, and the nurse is in an ideal position to do so. Desirable outcomes are a positive self-concept, having productive relationships, managing barriers, and maintaining optimal health and physical and sexual functioning. The nurse can help the woman recognize her own vulnerability and then seek information and take action on her own behalf (Nosek et al., 1994). The nurse can help the woman with multiple sclerosis throughout her life span access and utilize services and programs addressing her dynamic needs. The goals of these interactions are the development of a rich knowledge base and practices capable of promoting advancement in all aspects of physical and psychological wellness (Nosek et al., 1994).

REFERENCES

Birk, K.A., Kalb, R. (1992). MS and planning a family: fertility, pregnancy, childbirth, and parenting roles. In R. Kalb (ed.). *Multiple sclerosis and the family*. New York: Demos Publications, 51–62.

Birk, K., Smeltzer, S., Rudick, R. (1988). Pregnancy in multiple sclerosis. *Seminars in Neurology. 8, 3*, 205–213.

Davis, R.K., Maslow, A.S. (1992). Multiple sclerosis in pregnancy: a review. *Obstetrical and Gynecological Survey*, 290–296.

Duquette, P., Pleines, J., Girard, M., et al. (1992). The increased susceptibility of women to multiple sclerosis. *Canadian Journal of Neurological Sciences, 19*, 466–471.

Frith, J.A., McLeod, J.G. (1988). Pregnancy and multiple sclerosis. *Journal of Neurology, Neurosurgery and Psychiatry, 51*, 495–498.

Giesser, B.G., Halper, J., Holland, N., et al. (1990). Symptoms of multiple sclerosis fluctuate during the menstrual cycle. Pilot study. Gimbel MS Center and Albert Einstein College of Medicine.

Holland, N., Giesser, B.G., et al. (1987). The effects of the menstrual cycle on MS symptoms. Pilot study. Albert Einstein College of Medicine.

Matthews, W.B. (1991). *McAlpine's multiple sclerosis*. Edinburgh: Churchill Livingstone, 9.

Nieves, J., Cosman, F., Herbert, J., et al. (1994). High prevalence of vitamin D deficiency and reduced bone mass in multiple sclerosis. *Neurology, 44*, 1687–1691.

Nosek, M.A., Howland, C.A., Young, M.E., et al. (1994). "Wellness models and sexuality among women with physical disabilities." Baylor College of Medicine, Houston, TX.

Sadovnick, A.D., Eisen, K., Hashimoto, S., et al. (1994). Pregnancy and multiple sclerosis. *Archives of Neurology, 51,* 1120–1124.

Witmer, J.M., Sweeney, T.J. (1992). A holistic model for wellness and prevention over the life span. *Journal of Counseling and Development. 71, 2,* 140–148.

CHAPTER 9

Interfacing
with Rehabilitation Services

Frances Francabandera and Patricia M. Kennedy

"Go home and live with it—there is nothing we can do." All too often people with multiple sclerosis have heard these words. However, experts in the field of MS know that providing rehabilitation as well as symptomatic treatment for existing problems can assist the person with MS to remain as independent as possible in an environment of his or her choosing (Rosner & Ross, 1992; Scheinberg & Smith, 1987). Although research has not demonstrated that rehabilitation has an impact on the pathologic process in MS, rehabilitation techniques are often highly effective in treating its symptoms. According to Lechtenberg (1988), "during remission, much of the weakness, speech difficulty, or incoordination that developed with the flare-up can be compensated for with physical or occupational therapy" (p. 187).

Larsen (1995) states, "rehabilitation is an approach to care, a philosophy, and an attitude, as much as it is a set of specialized techniques" (p. 536). Although there is no cure for MS, much can be done to alleviate its symptoms and assist the client to lead a relatively normal life to the optimum level possible within the limitations of the disease and within the least restrictive environment possible.

This chapter discusses the definitions and goals of rehabilitation, the rehabilitation team, the interdisciplinary approach to MS management, and the purpose and function of the rehabilitation team in the acute care, home care, and outpatient settings. The role of the nurse in rehabilitation is addressed relative to case management, data collection, and both preventative and restorative care.

DEFINITION OF REHABILITATION

To rehabilitate is defined by Webster (1980) as "to restore to a condition of health or useful and constructive ability" (pp. 966–967). According to Hickey (1992), rehabilitation is ". . . a dynamic process through which a person achieves optimal physical, emotional, psychological, social, and vocational potential and maintains dignity and self-respect in a life that is as independent and self-fulfilling as possible" (p. 178). In a broader sense, Holland, Wiesel-Levison, and Francabandera (1987) acknowledge that rehabilitation, as it pertains to multiple sclerosis, "includes all efforts to achieve optimal function in activities of daily living, within limitations of the disease or disability" (p. 144).

The American Nurses Association, Division of Medical-Surgical Nursing Practice, and the Association of Rehabilitation Nurses define rehabilitation nursing practice as "the diagnosis and treatment of human responses of individuals and groups to actual or potential health problems stemming from altered functional ability and altered style" (ANA & ARN, 1988, p. 4). McEachron states, "rehabilitation is teaching, learning. It is discovering teaching is good, learning better, but applying is best of all" (Dittmar, 1989, p. 10).

There are two types of rehabilitation, both of which are implemented in the care of MS clients. *Restorative* rehabilitation attempts to reestablish function that has been lost accompanying an exacerbation. *Maintenance* rehabilitation, although not well compensated for by most insurance companies, is an effort to keep a progressive disease process from causing unnecessary functional deterioration. The term *maintenance* has been mostly replaced by *preventative* since the latter reflects a dynamic process.

GOALS OF REHABILITATION

Bauer (1977), in *A Manual on Multiple Sclerosis,* identifies significant guidelines in setting goals: "In every rehabilitation program, the patient must be treated as a whole, the best physical and psychological condition under the circumstances must be achieved, complications eliminated as far as possible and realistic motivations exploited. This can only be accomplished by the well-coordinated teamwork of doctors, nurses, physiotherapists, occupational therapists, clinical psychologists, social workers, the patient and his family and friends, and organizations with a genuine interest and sense of responsibility for him" (p. 34).

It is disheartening to realize that some nurses (and doctors) do not have a rehabilitation focus, particularly toward patients with chronic illness. Chronic illnesses are rarely cited in the rehabilitation literature. The nurse manager of a rehabilitation unit stated, "My staff and I don't like to work with multiple sclerosis patients. They usually don't improve. It's very frustrating." Nurses working with MS patients in the acute care, home care, and outpatient settings need to be cognizant of the benefits of rehabilitation and identify the need for rehabilitation protocols to improve function and quality of life for their patients. Many schools of nursing have incorporated well-defined rehabilitation content in their curriculum, preparing nurses to specialize in this area. Exposure of nursing students to rehabilitation concepts and practices fosters incorporation of a rehabilitation perspective across all specialty areas, focusing attention on maximizing function in all areas of daily life. Growth in the field of rehabilitation is escalating, as evidenced by the increased membership of nurses in such organizations as the Association of Rehabilitation Nurses, which is now approaching 10,000.

The goals of rehabilitation, as expressed by Dittmar (1989), are ". . . to prevent further disability, maintain existing ability, and restore maximum levels of function within the limits of the client's impairment" (p. ix).

The goals of rehabilitation for the patient with MS are to restore optimum function in the self-care activities of daily living, assist the patient and family to adjust to the disability, maximize the potential of each individual, and foster a lifestyle of wellness.

THE REHABILITATION TEAM: AN INTERDISCIPLINARY APPROACH

Unlike many other neurologic impairments, people with MS exhibit a wide variety of symptoms, often differing over time. Classically, the patient with a spinal cord injury knows the level of impairment and a rehabilitative plan of care can be developed based on the location of the severance of the cord. Due to the variability of symptoms caused by multi-level lesions, there can be no set rehabilitation plan of care or regimen for the person with multiple sclerosis. Each is unique and, depending on the location of plaques, dysfunction may vary widely among patients. Indeed, an ongoing, goal-oriented program of varying intensity, rather than a one-time rehabilitation program, is recommended by Coville (1983). Cobble and Burks (1985) and Maloney (1985) stress that rehabilitation goals in MS must be developed from careful functional assessment and the patient's ongoing response to treatment, taking into account past, current, and expected disease activity.

An interdisciplinary model is required by both the Joint Commission on Accreditation of Health Care Organizations (JCAHO) and the Commission on Accreditation of Rehabilitation Facilities (CARF). In this model, the patient is viewed as the center or core of the team, which may offer the patient control over his or her illness, i.e., the experience of living with the disease. This model encompasses professionals from various fields working together to achieve a desired outcome. Inherent in this concept is a comprehensive, nonfragmented, consistent approach that fosters optimal client outcomes and provides the team with a holistic view of client needs while reducing health care costs and improving client outcomes (Kipnis, 1993; O'Toole, 1992). A multidisciplinary approach, on the other hand, includes the same professionals working individually toward a desired outcome.

Members of the interdisciplinary team include health professionals who meet regularly and engage in problem solving beyond the confines of their own discipline to reach a common goal (Diller, 1990). Weekly or biweekly team meetings afford the opportunity to share information and discuss progress toward goals. A key component of the interdisciplinary model is the concept of working together to unify individual treatments into a comprehensive plan (Diller, 1990; O'Toole, 1992; Cobble & Burks, 1985; Kipnis, 1993). According to Frankel (1990), ". . . the overriding principle in setting rehabilitation goals [for the patient with MS] is to maximize independence, self-determination, and quality of life within the context of the individual's life-style and abilities" (p. 544). The team works together to meet the physical, emotional, social, economic, and vocational needs of people with MS and their families.

The person with MS and his or her family are an integral part of the rehabilitation team and must be active participants in the rehabilitation process. They need to attend team meetings and must be included in identifyng goals and developing a plan of care. According to Dittmar (1989), "the client and family are the core members of the rehabilitation team and the reasons for its existence" (p. 31).

Inherent in the effectiveness of the rehabilitation team is the relationship between the person with MS and the health care provider based on open communication, establishing trust and rapport, sharing information, respect for the feelings of the patient, ability to listen, clear and concise information transferral, freedom to ask questions, providing available resources, realistic goal-setting, and periodic evaluation.

The following disciplines are most commonly represented on the MS rehabilitation team, both facility- and community-based (these are referenced from Cobble & Burks, 1985; DeLisa, Martin, & Currie, 1993; Cobble, Dietz, Grigsby, & Kennedy, 1993; Hoeman, 1996; Schapiro, 1991; LaRocca, Kalb, & Kaplan, 1987).

Nurse

The nurse involved in rehabilitation of the person with MS functions as a "change agent" and patient advocate empowering a patient and family to know, envision, and evaluate options and to work together formulating problem-solving strategies and behaviors to achieve outcomes. In addition to providing direct physical care, the nurse evaluates the health status of the patient, helps determine short- and long-term goals, interprets medical terms, acts as a resource for community services, and provides education for the patient and family. Often the nurse can provide fellow team members with valuable insights regarding the patient's motivation, problem-solving skills, and family process. The nurse effectively functions as a coordinator of care/case manager, overseeing cost-effective, efficient, and beneficial coordination of therapies.

The patient who is experiencing neurogenic bladder with "failure to empty" may be advised to learn self-catheterization. The nurse provides teaching to the patient and family in the inpatient, home, or outpatient settings, often enlisting the services of the visiting nurse. The physical therapist assesses for bathroom mobility, including the ability to transfer from wheelchair to toilet. The occupational therapist assesses the patient for hand coordination and hand ability. Problems with dexterity, decreased sensation, and/or tremors may make insertion of the catheter difficult. At times the assistance of a family member may facilitate this process. During team conference each discipline contributes to the overall process in formulating a plan of care, which will be coordinated by the nurse from the primary care setting.

Physiatrist

The physiatrist has special skills in the evaluation of the neuromuscular, musculoskeletal, and cognitive systems and usually leads the team. The physician assumes primary responsibility for the medical and rehabilitative evaluation and treatment and may work with the nurse in coordinating and integrating an often complicated rehabilitation program.

Physical Therapist

The physical therapist assists the patient to achieve or maintain functional restoration and predominately concentrates on the lower extremities. A person with lower extremity weakness or other difficulty with mobility may benefit from exercise to maintain general conditioning and reverse or prevent disuse atrophy. Consideration needs to be given to the temperature of the environment in which physical therapy takes place, as a cooler environment will reduce the risk of elevating body temperature, which leads to fatigue. Gentle, sustained stretching exercises are beneficial in the management of spasticity.

Historically, the role of exercise in MS has not been clear. Schapiro (1995) reminds us that numerous research studies have demonstrated that exercise, when performed regularly, is beneficial for the heart, lungs, skin, bones, and psyche. Exercise helps to increase an individual's general health, with or without multiple sclerosis. Petajan et al. (1996) reported that individuals with multiple sclerosis participating in 15 weeks of aerobic training achieved a substantial increase of maximal aerobic capacity independent of the level of neurologic impairment. In addition to improved fitness, exercise training had a positive impact on factors related to quality of life. Significant reductions in fatigue, anger, and depression, improved ambulation, mobility, and body care and movement were reported. A sense of control over one's destiny, while fostering empowerment, can be created through exercise. When properly performed, exercise should alleviate fatigue rather than increase it. Studies at the Jimmie Heuga Center in Vail, Colorado, and the Fairview MS Center in Minneapolis, Minnesota (as cited in Schapiro, 1995) demonstrated that individuals with MS were capable of engaging in serious exercise. The outcome of the study revealed that their MS did not worsen; indeed their general well-being improved and there was an improvement in their ability to exercise. It is clear that individuals with multiple sclerosis can exercise and although their disease may not show improvement, their hearts, lungs, skin, and mental awareness can benefit with no fear of loss to their neurologic function (Schapiro, 1995).

Keep in mind that there are different kinds of exercises and the choice of type depends on the desired goal. Types of exercise include aerobic exercises such as swimming and running, which build endurance. Stretching and range of motion exercises are helpful in the management of spasticity and the prevention of contractures, while relaxation exercises such as visualization, yoga, and biofeedback can be effective in stress reduction (Schapiro, 1995).

Exercise facilitates improvement of the psyche, improves physical conditioning, allows for expression of a positive attitude, and permits individuals with multiple sclerosis control over some aspects of their lives (Schapiro, 1995).

Patients with stable neurologic impairment benefit from a preventative or maintenance exercise program, such as therapeutic swimming, to limit functional deterioration and foster a sense of well-being. This activity is often helpful both psychologically and physically (Cobble & Burks, 1985).

Mobility Aids

Mobility aids are not useful in all instances. When the patient is disabled primarily because of fatigue rather than from weakness or spasticity, other measures need to be introduced. Ambulation aids may assist the patient to improve function and remain walking as long as possible. The appropriate use of an aid, specific to the needs of the patient, can increase endurance, decrease energy cost, and improve safety while ambulating. The nurse needs to be aware that the use of assistive devices may raise complicated emotional issues for the person with MS as they represent increasing disability and may be perceived as also increasing dependence. It is important to stress that while use of a wheelchair for mobility may feel like a threat to self-esteem, the conservation of energy and increase in access permit more diverse activities that outweigh the psychological need to ambulate. Keep in mind that the goal is to improve function and that whatever "tools" it takes to improve the quality of life for the patient is paramount.

Common ambulation aids include one or two canes, a quad cane, lightweight forearm crutches, ankle-foot orthoses, and walkers. Proper fit of the aid to the patient, teaching safe and efficient use, and subsequent evaluation of the method of use are of vital importance. Using a wheelchair, often on an "as needed" basis, can be effective for the patient who tires easily. The nurse needs to be cognizant of the fact that impaired walking is not always the primary consideration in determining the need for a wheelchair or scooter, but that fatigue may be the main factor driving this decision. For example, a wheelchair allowed a woman with MS and her husband to take a long-anticipated trip to London, successfully taking in all the sights and the theater. Motorized wheelchairs and/or scooters can also increase a patient's independence, sense of freedom, and mobility. Ideally, wheelchair design and use will be evaluated by the team, including occupational and physical therapists, rehabilitation engineer, physiatrist, nurse, psychologist, and social worker. Environmental factors—such as doorway and bathroom dimensions in the individual's home and workplace—are a consideration (Schapiro, 1991; Hoeman, 1996).

Occupational Therapist

The occupational therapist focuses more specifically on functional activities and is concerned with how one is "occupied" in life, particularly with respect to activities of daily living. Emphasis is on the upper extremities in such areas as maintaining and improving joint range of motion, muscle strength, coordination, endurance, and dexterity. Fatigue, for example, can be disabling to the patient with MS and not easily recognized by others as such. The occupational therapist may assess how the patient plans the day relative to activities of daily living and may simply suggest that the patient do more activities in the morning when the energy level is higher. The patient experiencing tremors may find that weighted eating utensils and cups are helpful in decreasing tremors during eating.

Speech-Language Pathologist

The speech-language pathologist evaluates and treats patients with neurogenic disorders such as dysarthria (speech difficulties) and dysphagia (swallowing difficulties) that may occur in MS. Dysarthria may vary from a slight slur to a more severe condition such as scanning speech, in which understanding speech may be difficult. Therapy is ideally initiated when symptoms first appear and focuses on teaching and training techniques that compensate for reduced neuromuscular function, such as the use of pauses between one or two words and exaggeration in articulation.

Social Worker

The social worker assesses the patient and the family's total living situation and assists in such areas as financial arrangements, community resources, and alternative living situations, as well as facilitating discharge planning. In many settings the social worker is also the primary counseling professional.

Psychologist

The psychologist (or social worker) assists the patient and family to prepare psychologically for active participation in rehabilitation. In an MS care center, as well as in some other settings, the psychologist can be involved in a number of activities that include assessment of psychological status, coping styles, problem-solving skills, testing of cognitive function in areas such as intelligence, memory and perceptual functioning, and clinical research. Through counseling, the psychologist assists the patient with MS to develop or strengthen the tools necessary for coping with periods of extra stress and turmoil. Counseling in the following areas may be needed: dealing with the diagnosis, adjustment to body changes, development of problem-solving skills, anxiety/uncertainty about the future, loss of self-esteem, secondary problems caused by the disease and its disability, adjustment to changes in sexual functioning and viable alternatives, and family upheaval. This support may come in various forms based on the needs of the patient, e.g., orientation/counseling groups and individual, group, and family counseling.

Recreational Therapist

The recreational therapist utilizes recreation as an intervention to bring about a desired change in physical, emotional, or social behavior while promoting the growth and development of the patient. Therapeutic activities include the assessment of the patient's capabilities and interests and development of a program plan based on the patient's needs. These activities include leisure activities, increased concentration or maintenance of physical strength, social skills and motivation, as well as assisting in adjustment to disability and increasing independence.

Vocational Rehabilitation Counselor

The vocational counselor assists the patient with MS in identifying, developing, and attaining realistic vocational goals. Efforts should focus on continuing work activities with whatever modifications are needed, as maintenance of employment is much more easily achieved than reemployment. Modifications might include staggered work hours, lunchtime naps, locating the workspace closer to restrooms, or providing enlarging capacity for the computer screen. For those who are unable to work or choose not to work, the vocational counselor will help identify other activities, such as volunteer work or homemaking, to support the need for productivity.

Depending on individual patient needs, other professional team members may include an orthotist, neurologist, respiratory therapist, urologist, chaplain, and others.

The following is an example of how the rehabilitation team may function interactively when dealing with bladder dysfunction, a problem common in MS and discussed in Chapter 4. According to Holland and Francabandera (1987), "urinary symptoms are common in multiple sclerosis (MS), with as many as 80 percent of individuals affected at some time during the course of the disease" (p. 147). Although bowel problems frequently occur, it is important to treat bladder problems first because of the risk of urinary tract infections and the potential for kidney damage. Also, the necessary high fluid intake needed to treat constipation is unlikely to occur when urinary symptoms are present. The physician, urologist, nurse, and occupational and physical therapists will collectively work toward a mutual goal for the patient to be free from infection and incontinence. The plan should include assessment, evaluation, medication if indicated, and teaching a bladder program to patient/family members, including intermittent self-catheterization if indicated. In addition to assessing bladder function, hand function, transfers, and sitting/standing, balance might need to be evaluated by the occupational and physical therapist. A critical health need is determining and treating the underlying pathology, as well as treating urinary infections, and creating an overall intervention plan for management of urinary symptoms. Evaluation on an ongoing basis is inherent in this process.

Ideally, a relationship between the person with MS and team members should be based on open communication, willingness to share, flexibility, trust, clear and concise transferral of information, realistic goal-setting, and periodic evaluation. At times team members may identify with patients as peers, e,g., age, educational background. Consequently, feelings of identification could surface, such as "this could be me or my daughter," as well as discomfort and/or frustration. Such feelings should be addressed openly by the team with support from its members or, if indicated, from outside. Conflict within the team is a normal part of the process. An atmosphere in which members are permitted to agree to disagree can be a stepping-stone to growth.

THE REHABILITATION TEAM IN THE ACUTE CARE, HOME CARE, AND OUTPATIENT SETTINGS

The mission of rehabilitation is to treat the multiple needs of the individual as a whole. Ideally, rehabilitation should begin at the time of diagnosis, with evaluation early in the disease process and reevaluation as changes in condition or function warrant. Team emphasis should focus on wellness because people who perceive themselves as being well may extend themselves to a full range of activities within the rehabilitation process and gain a sense of control over their lives. The World Health Organization (WHO) defines health as ". . . the state of complete physical, mental and social well-being, and not merely the absence of disease or infirmity" (WHO Constitution, 1946). According to Holland (1992) and Francabandera (1992), the contemporary view of health is not strictly the absence of disease as this is not always a possibility. When viewed as a goal for everyone, health is the optimal level of function and well-being within possible limitations imposed by an emotional or physical impairment.

The following factors are important if rehabilitation is to succeed: a motivated patient, attainable goals, a team effort, and on-going emotional support. Keep in mind that the desired outcome of rehabilitation for the patient with multiple sclerosis is primarily an improved quality of life.

There is a developing shift away from inpatient settings toward the delivery of rehabilitation services in the home and other community-based settings. The current economic climate offers limited availability of financial resources for health care. This has given impetus to regulatory systems such as Diagnostic-Related Groups (DRGs) and Medicare Prospective Payment, which have resulted in intense scrutiny of the need for and length of hospitalization. At this time, inpatient rehabilitation is exempt from DRGs in some states. Increased financial incentives are being offered to hospitals to reduce costs and discharge patients more quickly. In some instances patients will receive their entire rehabilitation program in the home (Hoeman, 1996).

State-run Medicare policies are extremely fluid. Medicare, Medicaid, and HMOs are looking at the care delivered and subsequent outcomes and will not reimburse for anything unless results can be demonstrated. Documentation is an absolute must. It is imperative that the nurse record all relevant data and state the results obtained. This is true in home care rehabilitation as well as inpatient facilities. Progress must be shown, and outcomes must be proven, or the insurance companies will not pay.

Subacute units are emerging as a kind of "step-down unit" from the acute care hospital, bridging the gap before returning home. Rehabilitation can be initiated on a short-term basis in a controlled setting while allowing for more patient independence. The unit is often freestanding but connected to an acute care facility, with considerably less cost than the acute care hospital. Medicare will generally reimburse for two to three weeks of therapy, whereas other insurance types usually will approve a seven to ten day stay with a review each week to ascertain realistic goals. The patient usually receives about three hours of therapy (PT, OT, bladder management, counseling) daily as needed, but often at a slower pace than in the acute care setting. The key to a successful program is family involvement. Upon discharge the patient often continues with home care or outpatient rehabilitation services.

RESEARCH STUDIES

Feigenson (1981) reported that patients who have not responded to outpatient rehabilitation benefit functionally from intense inpatient therapies, usually requiring a longer commitment. However, an untreated control group was not used in the study.

Fox and Aisen (1994) also conducted an uncontrolled study composed of a retrospective chart review with follow-up phone calls. Results again suggested that inpatient rehabilitation was associated with significant functional improvement for MS patients, which was maintained in part following discharge.

Francabandera et al. (1988) examined the effects of inpatient vs. outpatient rehabilitation using comparison groups, with early reports corroborating Feigenson's findings. Initial reports at three-month follow-up indicated that the inpatient group showed less disability on the Incapacity Status Scale (ISS) than the outpatient group. The ISS is similar to the Barthel Index and looks at activities of daily living such as mobility and self-care. However, both groups showed a gradual worsening of their disability over the next nine months. By the twelve-month evaluation, both groups were back where they had started with no difference between them. The results of the study suggested that while inpatient rehabilitation might have some initial advantage over outpatient treatment, any such advantage was indeed short-lived. The implication of these findings is that patients with MS may need a course of rehabilitation periodically, perhaps every twelve months or so, in order for any gains to be preserved. (LaRocca & Kalb, 1992).

THE FUTURE OF MS REHABILITATION

As noted previously, the future of rehabilitation appears to lie in the outpatient setting, and inpatient rehabilitation may largely disappear except for selected cases. It is projected that the acute care setting will provide a brief rehabilitation period, almost an orientation for the outpatient arena. Increasing emphasis is on outpatient modalities that are monitored closely. Outpatient settings meet the needs of some patients and can provide a "refresher course" of skills previously learned, providing for reevaluation and perhaps a redefinition of treatments and skills. This method of rehabilitation tends to be short term, since fatigue, difficulty traveling, and limited availability of family members may be limiting factors. Frequent recertification is required with demonstrated progression toward documented goals. Insurance companies such as HMOs do not generally pay for what is considered "maintenance" therapy. Chances for reimbursement are improved when it can be reconceptualized as "preventative" therapy, with specific goals defined. Home care has the advantage of providing skills learning in a familiar setting in which the patient is comfortable. The patient may feel more in control of his or her environment and have the support of family and friends who are willing and available to participate in the rehabilitation process. Also, skills can be directly practiced in the environment where they will need to be used on a long-term basis. A well-coordinated team effort with definite goals and coordination by the nurse is imperative for successful implementation. The cost of this rehabilitation setting is generally less than for the inpatient setting.

At any point in time, people with MS may need services in inpatient (acute care), home care, or outpatient settings. The best approach to rehabilitation is a system in which patients can utilize a variety of services based on their needs at that particular time, with rehabilitation concepts incorporated into the plan of care regardless of the setting. Even the obstetrical nurse needs to initiate a plan for the postpartum MS patient to resume maximal function as quickly as possible.

QUALITY IMPROVEMENT

Health care providers can no longer *say* that an intervention has "good outcomes" but must *prove* it to inquiring patients, families, third-party intermediaries, risk managers, and the professionals involved in the care. The processes of assessment, management of programs, and patient care problems must be looked at in an effort to demonstrate that care is effective and efficient. The health care provider must prove the efficacy of care and services provided through quality assurance activities and program evaluation (Patterson, England, & Glass, 1989).

Components of a quality improvement (QI) program should encompass activities that enhance the effectiveness of patient care, improve the delivery of health care, and result in reaching expected outcomes. External regulatory bodies such as the Joint Commission on Accreditation of Healthcare Organizations (JCAHO), the Commission on Accreditation of Rehabilitation Facilities (CARF), and nursing organizations such as the American Nurses Association (ANA) and the Association of Rehabilitation Nurses (ARN) are instrumental in setting standards for determining quality of care. JCAHO identified "quality assurance monitoring and evaluation" standards while CARF identified "program evaluation" standards. Two quality assurance models have been identified by Kipnis (1993) as being of value to nurses involved with QI at the unit level. The ANA's conceptual model promotes quality improvement utilizing a cyclic process that is concordant with the nursing process. The JCAHO ten-step operational model is an organized process used to monitor, evaluate, and improve the appropriateness and quality of care provided to patients. Quality improvement and quality assurance depict philosophical commitments to the notion of "doing the best you can." Quality improvement challenges health professionals to measure and monitor quality enhancing, ever-improving methods in the provision of patient care throughout the continuum of care. In an effort to prove that a health care organization can make a positive difference in the lives of the individuals it serves, the organization demonstrates its commitment to the measurement of quality patient care services (Patterson, England, & Glass, 1989; Kipnis, 1993).

ROLE OF THE NURSE IN REHABILITATION

Case Management

In the complex world of medical care, care for MS patients can easily become fragmented. In the 1980s, the need for case management was identified and research into various models was instituted, resulting in its now widespread use by facilities, governmental agencies, insurance carriers, and health care programs. Third-party payers also retain case managers to coordinate services provided to clients (McBride, 1992). With proposed health care reforms in the 1990s, there is a national mandate for efficiency and quality in health care delivery, as well as the prudent use of health care resources. Nurses who deal with MS patients in rehabilitation settings, both inpatient and outpatient, are in an ideal position to serve as case managers for their care.

Various models of case management are described in the nursing literature. The concept has been implemented in a variety of settings with differing patient populations, but is best suited for patients who are classified as high risk or high cost (McBride, 1992). These include people with MS, who often have complex health care needs.

Regardless of the model, case management is a way to systematically organize care. In MS, it provides a system to identify areas that need coordination, helps provide a framework to define unmet needs, and guides the selection of providers to meet those needs. It organizes the formulation of specific treatment plans to improve the quality and efficiency of services provided. This, in turn, serves as a framework to measure outcomes and quality of care.

Through case management, nurses can identify when treatment approaches become so complex that they increase frustration or confusion in the patient. Nurses also communicate and clarify the plan to other providers as well as to the patient and family. Nurses can assist the patient in gathering information from all involved providers and participating in a comprehensive treatment plan.

Data Collection

Case management is both a process and a system. The process of case management closely follows generic nursing process theory of assessment, planning, implementation, and evaluation. Case management involves the identification, coordination, procurement, implementation, and evaluation of an integrated series of formal and informal services and support systems provided in a timely and cost-effective manner (McBride, 1992). In rehabilitation settings, the nurse is constantly in a position to assess the MS patient. This assessment should be documented in writing for the rest of the team and communicated verbally at team meetings. The more the team understands about a patient's strengths and limitations, the more effective the interactions with that patient will be.

Physiologic Assessment

The physiologic status of patients entering or returning to a rehabilitation system must be evaluated by the nurse. Attention must be paid to all systems, not just the neurologic. Problems are often missed if they are not directly related to MS. A thorough history should be taken about current problems related to neurologic function as well as a review of systems. In specialty care, less attention is paid to general physiologic status, and the nurse is frequently the one who identifies other problems. Particular attention should be directed to subtle changes in bladder, bowel, sexual function, swallowing, speech, vision, and skin. While sometimes considered insignificant by the patient, problems in these areas can indicate more serious neurologic/physiologic problems. Patients may fail to mention these subtle changes because they are unaware of their importance or the fact that they are related to MS.

Reporting these changes to the other members of the rehabilitation team will be helpful in their assessments. Nurses can use this information to formulate their teaching plans and expected outcomes of performance by the patient. No information or finding is too trivial, nor should it be assumed that someone else is aware of it. As the professional who spends the most time with the patient, the nurse can observe a great deal. Careful attention to written documentation of the nursing assessment is critical to the team process.

Psychological Assessment

In some settings the rehabilitation team has a psychological professional who can perform a formal assessment; in other settings this resource is not readily available. All members of a rehabilitation team are constantly observing psychological status. The nurse needs to assess on an ongoing basis for symptoms of clinical depression, observing or obtaining history of significant changes in behavior and obtaining a history of suicidal thoughts. Being sensitive to expressions of helplessness, hopelessness, anger, sadness, and lack of motivation will help in assessing the emotional state. Nurses need to be critical observers and hear what patients are really saying, not what they want the medical staff to hear. Family input is vital in evaluating emotional status since patients often deny or are unaware of emotional changes in themselves. Attention should be paid when there are discrepancies between a patient's self-assessment and that of the family.

Cognitive Assessment

Patients and families may not always be aware of cognitive changes resulting from MS. These changes may be misinterpreted as stubbornness, acting out, not listening, not paying attention, and irritability. Nurses can perform a bedside mental status exam but unless changes are significant, patients tend to do well with this testing. It is the subtle changes that are the most telling. Patients who do not concentrate well, have difficulty following directions, have short-term memory problems, or experience confusion if doing more than one task at a time may be manifesting symptoms of cognitive dysfunction. People who fear job loss but do not know why may be experiencing cognitive problems that interfere with their performance. Patients who are concerned because they are more irritable, struggle in relating to family, or are withdrawing may be demonstrating behavior changes related to cognitive status or reflecting a psychological response to the illness.

When performing physical assessment, the unspoken observations are as important as the historical data collected. Patients with MS may demonstrate difficulty in recall, staying on a topic, following directions, or selecting words or ideas.

When nurses obtain history indicating cognitive or behavioral dysfunction, this information must be shared with the rest of the team. Evaluation by a neuropsychologist is desirable if resources are available. With formal assessment, patients and families can be educated about the problems and offered strategies to lessen their impact. Holland (1992) and Francabandera (1992) acknowledge that family members of individuals with multiple sclerosis play an important role in providing support and assistance to the patient. However, their need for information regarding the disease and the rehabilitation process is frequently overlooked by the health care system. Nurses and other team members can use this information to modify teaching and treatment plans to be more effective.

Social Assessment

Part of the nursing assessment may be obtaining a thorough social history, particularly if a social worker is not part of the team. In other settings, team members who identify social needs communicate this information to the social worker as part of the referral process. The nurse continues ongoing social assessment for feedback to the team. In order to implement plans, social supports must be identified. Financial resources need to be explored for food, housing, equipment, help in the home, and transportation to appointments. Patients who live alone must be evaluated for safety, ability to perform personal and household tasks, and access to help in the home. When a patient lives with family or friends, the entire support system needs to be evaluated to determine how it can be integrated into the plan of care. A patient's geographic location is important in determining what services are available in the community. It is important to evaluate the educational level of both the patient and the family to tailor education or treatment plans. Determining their level of understanding and belief system and communicating that information to the team will help establish realistic goals.

Family Assessment and Input

Patients who are in close contact with their families have a greater chance of positive outcome from rehabilitation measures. Rehabilitation teams have a better chance of making inroads when there is family involvement in providing information as well as formulating the treatment plan. Nurses can assist the team by gathering information about the family and from the family. Close alliances are often formed between patients, families, and nurses. Information that no one else can elicit may be shared with nurses. It is often this information that cements an intervention or treatment plan (Watson, 1992; Watson, 1989).

Question patients about their families. Are they supportive? Do they help too much or too little? Who has the primary financial responsibility, and is this a change? How does the patient feel about that? What is expected of the patient at home? What does the patient expect of his family? Who is the primary care provider for the children? What do the children understand about MS? How often does the extended family visit? Does the family provide financial help? Who does the majority of the household tasks?

Question the families about existing roles. What is their perception of the patient? Do they think the patient has the ability to do more than he or she does? Do they think the patient does activities that are unsafe? Are they experiencing burnout? Do they need respite? What is their understanding of MS? How willing are they to learn or do more? Are they willing to change roles or tasks?

Communication Assessment

Speech and language encompass a broad area. People with MS can have limitations from dysarthria that make intelligible speech difficult. This includes articulation disorders, voice disorders, vocal tremor, and loudness control.

Those with cognitive impairment also demonstrate problems with word finding, tangential speech, loss of ability to complete verbalization of ideas, and/or paraphasic errors. Some patients experience problems with verbosity and have difficulty interacting with others. Patients are sometimes easily distracted and struggle with interactions if they are in a busy or noisy area.

If MS has caused significant weakness that affects respiratory function, the ability to produce and sustain enough airflow to speak effectively will be impaired. Weakness may also decrease the ability to communicate in writing, push a call light, dial a phone, or call for help.

While the speech-language pathologist on the rehabilitation team will do a formal assessment, information gathered by the nurse can be used to initiate interventions that will enhance communication among patient, family, and staff and decrease frustration. Speech-language pathologists often use information from the nursing assessment to direct their work-up.

Work and Productivity (Vocational) Assessment

Whether you are dealing with an MS patient in the clinic, home, or rehabilitation facility, the subject of "work" usually comes up. Work can be a paid position, a volunteer task, or a role in the family. In our society, many people believe they "are what they do." When a disease such as MS threatens their usual activities, they experience problems with self-esteem, fear of economic hardship, role reversals, and grief over what they have lost. It is not uncommon for patients to set unrealistic goals regarding their ability to work safely and effectively at their usual employment. Others prematurely make a decision that they cannot perform their usual activities when they experience an impairment before they have explored their actual abilities. When working with patients, it is important to assess work history, attitudes about work, perception of what their work is, and educational level. Using this information, various members of the rehabilitation team can be alerted to further evaluate any identified problems. The rehabilitation counselor is the primary professional relating to vocational issues, but often many disciplines are involved, such as occupational therapy, physical therapy, social work, speech-language pathology, and psychology. Check the state vocational rehabilitation office, your local chapter of the National Multiple Sclerosis Society, independent living centers, and publications such as *Employment Issues and Multiple Sclerosis* (Rumrill, 1996) to identify services and resources for the MS patient (see Appendix A).

Recreation Assessment

It is also important to assess recreational interests. Knowing what a patient enjoyed doing previously may help set goals for what can be done with remaining abilities. Any patient facing loss of employment or change in role can be encouraged by the nurse to develop new interests or rediscover old ones. The nurse can make a referral to a therapeutic recreational therapist for assistance or to other community resources such as the National Multiple Sclerosis Society.

Educational Needs Assessment

As in any patient education scenario, before a plan can be formulated, the nurse needs to determine the educational level of the patient, what he needs to know, what he wants to know, and what the gaps in his knowledge are. Some patients self-educate about MS from a variety of sources, some of which are more accurate than others. In order to move forward with new education, corrections may need to be made to the old. When the nurse identifies areas in which education would be appropriate, she can convey this to specialized team members or devise a plan of teaching to do herself.

Adult Education

Holland, Wiesel-Levison, and Francabandera (1987) identify the nurse as an educator and interpreter, one who can ". . . explain the disease process and what to expect from it, as well as provide a better understanding about the various symptoms and what causes them" (p. 129).

In considering the learning process of both patients and family members, Orr (1990) believes that individuals are endowed with a natural process, the ability to learn, a natural curiosity that allows one to view new, often difficult situations as challenges rather than as defeats. The nurse can offer support and education to patients and families in this effort to acquire essential new information.

It is important that patients and families learn that two-thirds of people with MS do not become severely disabled, that one does not die from MS but can expect to lead a reasonably normal life, and that most disabilities are usually temporary or mild to moderate in severity, with all MS-related problems being manageable to some degree. Assessment of the readiness of patients and family members to learn is an integral part of the process since a better comprehension about MS is related to better health management (Cobble, Dietz, Grigsby, & Kennedy, 1993).

Education about MS can occur through interaction with each therapist in addition to formal education such as reading, videotapes, and the like. Another important aspect of education and communication is the participation in regular team/family conferences providing the opportunity to address past progress, time frame, and future plans in a supportive environment (Cobble & Burks, 1985).

According to Holland (1992) and Francabandera (1992), both learner- and content-centered approaches are necessary for acquiring MS-related information and skills. Certain content is considered essential for optimal adaptation to this chronic illness requiring content focus. However, the adult education principle of learner-focus is also necessary for pursuit, acquisition, and implementation of the critical learning information.

Knowles views adult education as a "process" by which the "activity" of learning takes place. Knowles (1980) describes adult education: "In its broadest sense, the term describes a process—the process of learning" (p. 25). Six principles of adult learning have been selected from *Workplace Education and the Principles and Practices of Adult Education* (Lawler, 1986), as they are relevant here.

1. *Adult education includes and builds on the experience of the participant.*
   Most patients and family members do not have prior knowledge about the disease upon which to build; however, all adults have had experiences that required coping behavior.
2. *Adult education fosters critically reflective thinking.*
   Issues such as self-esteem and self-image, which are important to people with MS and their families, can be addressed by the process of critical self-reflection, leading to critical analysis of assumptions (attitudes, values, beliefs, orientations).
3. *Problem posing and problem solving are fundamental aspects of adult education.*
   Multiple sclerosis can present problems in all aspects of daily living. Therefore, the process of looking at problems, analyzing their components, and deriving solutions is crucial for people with MS and their families and is relevant to the self-directed learning process.
4. *Learning for action is valued in adult education.*
   Learning that can be translated into action is important to address the physical, emotional, and interpersonal problems presented by multiple sclerosis.
5. *Adult education empowers the participant.*
   Brookfield (1985a) defined "genuine" adult education as including activities that assist adults in their efforts to establish a sense of control over their lives, within their interpersonal relationships and societal roles.
6. *Self-directed learning is encouraged and enhanced in adult education.*
   Encouragement of independence in action and thought is believed by some to be a crucial component of adult learning activities. (Holland, 1992; Francabandera, 1992).

The advent of computers has opened up a new arena for learning and communication. There are over 150 sites on the Internet related to MS. "Chat rooms" exchange experience and information about multiple sclerosis. It is interesting to participate but important to differentiate between personal experiences and factual information from other WEB sites such as the National Multiple Sclerosis Society's Home Page. This is useful for patients with MS to participate in their own home in an independent manner.

Chart Review

Because nurses work in a variety of settings, the type and availability of records may vary. Whenever possible, they should obtain prior records that provide historical information including past assessments and indicate functional changes that may be more objective than those provided by the patient and family. Previous goals set by the patient may contribute to current goal-setting, as well as response to previous medications and interventions.

Input from Community Agencies

If a patient receives help in the home from a home health agency, any information obtained from the staff about how they view the patient in that setting can be exceedingly helpful to others in outpatient or inpatient settings. The nurse can request, compile, and communicate that information to the team. Communication from the rehabilitation team to the home health staff about proposed plans and goals can be facilitated by nurses.

Data can also be collected from other community agencies such as vocational rehabilitation agencies, social services and community mental health if the patient signs a release to do so. At times, it is appropriate to contact an employer (if requested to do so) to enable the team to address pertinent issues in the workplace.

Discharge Planning

Discharge planning is an integral component of rehabilitation and should occur as a parallel process, with ongoing coordination and reassessment. Modifications may be in the home or place of employment, new equipment may be needed, and community agencies may become essential to successful functioning of the patient and family. Excellent rehabilitative care will have less impact if patients are sent home or discharged from home services without support systems in place.

Help in the home is often needed when leaving an inpatient setting; it should be arranged prior to discharge and should be in place when the patient arrives home. Family education should have occurred throughout hospitalization. The patient and family should be able to demonstrate understanding of discharge instructions. Because of cognitive impairments or the stress of hospitalization, patients and families may indicate understanding of information but may not fully comprehend it, so succinct written plans for follow-up should be in place. A home health nurse often will make follow-up visits and report the patient's status to the primary care provider. Medications should be clearly explained and instructions written. Ideally, the team has fostered independence when appropriate, but patients and families need to be encouraged to call a contact person with questions and concerns. Going through a rehabilitation stay with all of its help, support, and structure is different from being home alone or with a family member.

As an outpatient involved with a team or part of a team, the patient is discharged when goals are met or measurable improvement has plateaued. Planning is directed at individual issues and needs. A nurse functioning as the case manager will coordinate efforts and plan follow-up.

Patients who receive care in the home are sometimes discharged from this care. The home health nurse is charged with educating the patient and family in self-care and providing clear plans for follow-up. Discharge plans need to be coordinated with the primary care provider to facilitate continuity of care.

Patient Safety

Opportunities for patient education abound in caring for individuals with MS. As mentioned in Chapter 11, an emphasis on wellness and self-care is desired for this population. This is an ongoing process, and all disciplines should coordinate their recommendations with the process in mind. In the face of disabilities, however, function changes and adaptations are needed to promote safety. Patients and families must be aware of risks and know measures they can take to reduce those risks.

For patients who interact with the community through employment, volunteerism, or recreation, health and safety risks also need to be evaluated in those settings and communicated to appropriate members of the team. Problem solving by the person with MS can be done individually with therapists or by team members going to the workplace or recreation setting to evaluate adaptation needs. The team can also work directly with employers to educate, advise, and facilitate change. The nurse should continue to encourage the patient to access this type of assistance when problems arise.

Barriers in the Community

People with any type of disability face social and physical barriers. Socially, our society continues to discriminate against people who are different.
Those who are newly diagnosed often are reluctant to tell others of the
diagnosis for fear of their response. Regrettably, these fears are often well-
founded. Nurses are taught to advocate for their patients, but it is more
important to prepare patients to advocate for themselves. As nurses, we
can be supportive. We can educate patients, families, and the community.
We can participate in the national advocacy efforts of the National Multiple Sclerosis Society by calling 1-800-FIGHT MS and accessing the local
chapter. We can write to our representatives in Congress to educate them
about issues facing the disabled and request their support on specific legislation.

The Americans with Disabilities Act of 1992 provides guidelines to the
community for making adaptations for people with disabilities. It is hoped
that this will lessen the physical barriers experienced by people with MS. If
a nurse recognizes a noncompliant situation, she needs to make the patient
and family aware of the law. Patients and families may be able to advocate
for themselves or may need assistance from the legal community.

CONCLUSION

The authors believe that the following concepts should be inherent in the
successful rehabilitation process for an individual with MS. The nurse
should recognize the patient as a unique, total human being while emphasizing wellness. The nurse should foster the inquisitiveness of the patient
and his or her family while striving for improved quality of life.

These suggestions are made to assist the experienced nurse to work
successfully with a patient who has multiple sclerosis. Unless nurses work
with many patients with this disease, the nuances may be missed. Whether
he or she works in a setting with an existing team of rehabilitation specialists or works independently and has to network to create a team, the quality will be enhanced by teamwork.

The authors believe this excerpt from a definition of rehabilitation by
McEachron, a rehabilitation nurse, has special meaning (truth) for the
patient with multiple sclerosis: "Rehabilitation is a dynamic process of
planned adaptive change in lifestyle in response to unplanned change
imposed on the individual by disease or traumatic incident. The focus is
not cure, but on living with as much freedom and autonomy as possible at
every stage and in whichever direction the disability progresses" (Dittmar,
p. 8).

REFERENCES

American Nurses Association and the Association of Rehabilitation Nurses (1988). *Rehabilitation nursing: scope of practice; process and outcome criteria for selected diagnoses.* Kansas City, MO: American Nurses Association.

Bauer, H. (1977). *A manual on multiple sclerosis.* Vienna: International Federation of Multiple Sclerosis Societies.

Bower, K. (1992). *Case management for nurses.* Washington, DC: American Nurses Publishing.

Brookfield, S.D. (1985a). A critical definition of adult education. *Adult Education Quarterly, 36, (1),* 44–49.

Cobble, N.D., Burks, J.S. (1985). The team approach to the management of multiple sclerosis. In F.P. Maloney, J.S. Burks, S.P. Ringel (eds.). *Interdisciplinary rehabilitation of multiple sclerosis and neuromuscular disorders.* New York: J.B. Lippincott.

Cobble, N.D., Dietz, M.A., Grigsby, J., Kennedy, P.M. (1993). Rehabilitation of the patient with multiple sclerosis. In J.A. DeLisa (ed.). *Rehabilitation medicine: principles and practice,* Second Edition. Philadelphia: J.B. Lippincott.

Cohen, E., Cesta, T. (1993). *Nursing case management from concept to evaluation.* St. Louis: C.V. Mosby.

Coville, P.L. (1983). Rehabilitation. In J.F. Hallpike, D.W.M. Adams, W.W. Tourtellotte (eds.). *Multiple sclerosis: pathology, diagnosis and management.* Baltimore: Williams & Wilkins.

Dean-Barr, S. (1987). Purpose and function of the rehabilitation team. In C.M. Mumma (ed.). *Rehabilitation nursing: concepts and practice,* Second Edition. Evanston, IL: Rehabilitation Nursing Foundation.

DeLisa, J.A. (ed.). (1993). *Rehabilitation medicine: principles and practice,* Second Edition. Philadelphia: J.B. Lippincott.

DeLisa, J.A., Martin, G.M., Currie, D.M. (1993) Rehabilitation medicine: past, present, and future. In J.A. DeLisa (ed.). *Rehabilitation medicine: principles and practice,* Second Edition. Philadelphia: J.B. Lippincott.

Diller, L. (1990). Fostering the interdisciplinary team, fostering research in a society of transition. *Archives of Physical Medicine and Rehabilitation, 71,* 275–278.

Dittmar, S.S. (1989). *Rehabilitation nursing: process and application.* Baltimore: C.V. Mosby.

Ethridge, P. (1991). A nursing HMO: Carondelet St. Mary's experience. *Nursing Management, 22 (7),* 22–27.

Feigenson, J.S., Scheinberg, L., Catalano, M., Polkow, L., Mantegazza, P.M., Feigenson, W.D., LaRocca, N.G. (1981). The cost-effectiveness of multiple sclerosis rehabilitation: a model. *Neurology, 31 (10),* 1316–1322.

Fox, N., Aisen, M.L. (1994). Predictors of outcome in multiple sclerosis rehabilitation. *Neurology, 44 (Suppl 2),* April, A313.

Francabandera, F.L., Holland, N.J., Wiesel-Levison, P., Scheinberg, L.C. (1988). Multiple sclerosis rehabilitation: inpatient vs. outpatient. *Rehabilitation Nursing, 13 (5),* 251–253.

Francabandera, F.L. (1992). "Self-directed learning by family members of individuals with multiple sclerosis." (Doctoral Dissertation, Teachers College, Columbia University, 1992). *UMI Dissertation Abstracts,* 5305, 1361.

Frankel, D.I. (1990). Multiple sclerosis. In D.A. Umphred (ed.). *Neurological rehabilitation*, Second Edition. Philadelphia: C.V. Mosby.

Hickey, J.V. (1992). *The clinical practice of neurological and neurosurgical nursing*, Third Edition. New York: J.B. Lippincott.

Hoeman, S. (1992). Community-based rehabilitation. *Holistic Nursing Practice, 6 (2)*, 32–1.

Hoeman, S.P. (1996). *Rehabilitation nursing: process and application*, Second Edition. New York: C.V. Mosby.

Holland, N.J., Francabandera, F. (1987). Bladder and bowel management. In L. Scheinberg, N.J. Holland (eds.). *Multiple sclerosis: a guide for patients and their families*, Second Edition. New York: Raven Press.

Holland, N.J., Wiesel-Levison, P., Francabandera, F. (1987). Nursing care. In L. Scheinberg, N. J. Holland (eds.). *Multiple sclerosis: a guide for patients and their families*, Second Edition. New York: Raven Press.

Holland, N.J., Kaplan, S.R., Hall, H.L. (1987). Vocational issues. In L. Scheinberg, N.J. Holland (eds.). *Multiple sclerosis: a guide for patients and their families*, Second Edition. New York: Raven Press.

Holland, N.J. "Self-directed learning by individuals with multiple sclerosis." (Doctoral Dissertation, Teachers College, Columbia University, 1992).

Kipnis, N.D. (ed.) (1993). The rehabilitation team: composition, models, function and issues. In A.E. McCourt (ed.). *The specialty practice of rehabilitation nursing*, Third Edition. Skokie, IL: Rehabilitation Nursing Foundation.

Knowles, M. (1980). *The modern practice of adult education: from pedagogy to andragogy.* Chicago: Follett.

LaRocca, N.G., Kalb, R.C., Kaplan, S.R. (1987). Psychological issues. In L.C. Scheinberg, N.J. Holland. (eds.). *Multiple sclerosis: a guide for patients and their families*, Second Edition. New York: Raven Press.

LaRocca, N.G., Kalb, R.C. (1992) Efficacy of rehabilitation in multiple sclerosis. *Journal of Neurological Rehabilitation. 6 (3)*, 147–155.

Larson, P. (1995). Rehabilitation. In I.M. Lubkin (ed.). *Chronic illness: impact and interventions*, Third Edition. Boston: Jones and Bartlett.

Lawler, P. (1988). "Workplace education and the principles and practices of adult education." Unpublished doctoral dissertation, Columbia University, Teachers College, New York.

Lechtenberg, R. (1988). *Multiple sclerosis fact book*. Philadelphia: F.A. Davis.

Maloney, F.P. (1985). Rehabilitation of patients with progressive and remitting disorders. In F.P. Maloney, J.S. Burks, S.P. Ringel (eds.). *Interdisciplinary rehabilitation of multiple sclerosis and neuromuscular disorders*. Philadelphia: J.B. Lippincott.

McBride, S. (1992). Rehabilitation case managers: ahead of their time. *Holistic Nursing Practice, 6 (2)*, 67–75.

McCourt, A.E. (1993). *The specialty practice of rehabilitation nursing: a core curriculum*, Third edition. Skokie, IL: Rehabilitation Nursing Foundation.

Orr, R. (1990). Illness as an educational opportunity. *Patient Education and Counseling, 15*, 47–48.

O'Toole, M.T. (1992). The interdisciplinary team: research and education. *Holistic Nursing Practice, 6 (2)*, 76–83.

Patterson, C.H., England, B., Glass, R.M. (1989). What is quality rehabilitation? In B. England, R.M. Glass, C.H. Patterson (eds.). *Quality rehabilitation: results oriented patient care.* USA: AHA, American Hospital Publishing.

Petajan, J.H., Gappmaier, E., White, A.T., Spencer, M.K., Mino, L., Hicks, R.W. (1996). Impact of aerobic training on fitness and quality of life in multiple sclerosis. *Annals of Neurology 39 (4),* 432–41.

Rosner, L.J., Ross, S. (1992). *Multiple sclerosis: new hope and practical advice for people with MS and their families.* New York: Simon & Schuster.

Rumrill, P.D., Jr. *Employment issues and multiple sclerosis.* New York: Demos Vermande, 1996.

Schapiro, R.T. (1991). *Multiple sclerosis: a rehabilitation approach to management.* New York: Demos Publications.

Schapiro, R.T. (1995). Rehabilitation. Exercise and multiple sclerosis. *MS Management, 2 (2),* 35–38.

Scheinberg, L., Smith, C.R. (1987). Rehabilitation of patients with multiple sclerosis. Neurologic Rehabilitation. *Neurologic Clinics, 5 (4),* 585–600.

Thurgood, A. (1990) Seven steps to rehabilitation. *Nursing Times, 86 (25),* 38–41.

Watson, P. (1989). Indicators of family capacity for participating in the rehabilitation process: a report of a preliminary investigation. *Rehabilitation Nursing, 14 (6),* 318–321.

Watson, P. (1992). Family issues in rehabilitation. *Holistic Nursing Practice, 6 (2),* 51–59.

Woolf, H.B., et al. (eds.). (1980). *Webster's new collegiate dictionary.* Springfield: G. & C. Merriam.

World Health Organization Constitution. (1946, June 19–22). Adopted at the International Health Conference, New York, NY.

CHAPTER 10

Disease Modifying Agents and Nursing Implications

June Halper

During the past decade, clinical trials into effective treatments for multiple sclerosis have proliferated. Agents that can reduce central inflammatory demyelination are of particular interest (Fang & Lublin, 1995). Of the many agents that have claimed therapeutic benefit, only a handful have actually been effective in multiple sclerosis. As also noted in Chapter 2, spontaneous remissions of the disease along with a strong placebo effect shown to be present in MS have frequently fooled investigators (Fang & Lublin, 1995). Most disease-altering therapies act by interfering with immune function. Three new agents listed in Table 10-1 are current treatment options in disease courses in which patients experience relapses.

Each of these regimes involves injectable medications and thus requires extensive patient and family education about drug reconstitution, self-injection (or with family assistance) with site rotation, and the need for regular laboratory testing to monitor for side effects.

Nurses are confronted with a number of challenges when educating patients about injectable treatments in multiple sclerosis. Unlike the insulin-dependent diabetic who is able to monitor glucose levels in blood and urine for treatment effectiveness, patients with multiple sclerosis cannot expect to see such dramatic results. In fact, some patients may initially feel worse with treatment because of side effects of the medications. The health care team (physicians and nurses) initially must determine who is eligible for which medication based on research data, the patient's clinical course, and his physical and cognitive capabilities. Since these medications are injectable and may or may not be covered by health insurance,

TABLE 10-1. Comparison of Key Aspects of Clinical Trial Results from Betaseron®, Avonex™ and Copaxone™

	Interferon beta-1b (Betaseron)	Interferon beta-1a (Avonex)	Copolymer 1 (Copaxone)
Dose/Route of Delivery	1.6 MIU (50µg) or 8MIU (250µg) every other day subcutaneous self-injection	6MIU (30µg) weekly intramuscular injection by health professional	20mg daily subcutaneous self-injection
Type of MS Studied	relapsing-remitting, male and female 18–50 years	relapsing-remitting or relapsing progressive, male and female 18–55 yrs	relapsing-remitting male and female 18–45 years
Inclusion Criteria & Entry Disability Rating (EDSS)	2 or more relapses in prior two years; stable for 1 month: EDSS 0–5.5	2 or more relapses in prior 3 years; no relapses for 2 months: EDSS 1–3.5	2 or more relapses in prior 2 years; first relapse 1+ years prior to enrollment: stable for 1 month: EDSS 0–5.0
Trial Duration	24 months: 1 year extension	up to 24 months	24 months
Number of Patients Studied	372 (125 low dose, 124 high dose, 123 placebo)	301 (158 treated, 143 placebo)	251 (125 treated, 126 placebo)
Number of Centers in Trial	11 (U.S.A. & Canada)	5 (U.S.A.)	11 (U.S.A.)
Trial Design	3 arm, low dose v high dose v placebo; randomized double blind; exams 4x/yr with 2 MD protocol; intent to treat analysis	2 arm, treatment v placebo, randomized double blind; exams 2x/yr, with 2 MD protocol; intent to treat analysis	2 arm, treatment v placebo, randomized double blind; monthly adverse reactions, exams 4x/yr with 2 MD protocol; intent to treat analysis
Primary Outcome Measures	annual relapse rate, proportion of relapse-free patients	time to sustained progression of EDSS 1.0 persisting at least 6 months	mean number of relapses in 24 months

Secondary Outcome Measured	time to first, second relapse; relapse duration/severity; change in disability from baseline; hospitalizations and steriod use; MRI lesion burden and activity	amount of progression; number and rate of relapses; time to first relapse; MRI lesion burden and activity; upper/lower extremity function; physician global assessment; quality of life; change in disability for 2-year completers	time to first relapse; time to progression of EDSS 1.0 persisting for 3 months; difference in patients showing progression; change in base disability, neuropsychological profile
Reported Results, *primary outcome*	34% reduction in relapse rate: 1.27 placebo, 1.17 to dose, 0.8 high dose; relapse free; 18 placebo, 23 low dose, 36 high dose	lower 2 year progression rates and predicted median time to sustained progression	29% reduction in 2 year relapse rate: 1.68 placebo, 1.19 treated
Reported Results *secondary outcome*	significant delay to 1st, 2nd relapse; reduced moderate/severe relapses: reduced hospitalizations; reduced accumulation of new MRI lesion burden and activity	32% reduction in relapse rate: 0.9 placebo, 0.62 treated; significant difference in % patients with sustained worsening; reduced number and volume of enhanced MRI lesions; reduction in multiple relapses	statistically more treated patients improved by 1.0 EDSS and more placebo patients worsened
Safety	flu, injection site reactions, decreasing over time; depression; slight liver function, white blood cell abnormalities	mild flu, mild anemia	Injection site reactions, systemic reaction including, rarely, chest tightness, shortness of breath

Reprinted with permission from *MS Management*, Vol. 2, No. 2, September 1995.

patients must be assisted to obtain coverage under their insurance plans. The most daunting endeavor is educating patients and their families about the proper use of the prescribed product: storage, reconstitution, injection, site rotation, and monitoring for side effects. Training, education, and support—all of which promote an informed patient and family—have been shown to improve adherence to a protocol and reduce noncompliance.

THE PSYCHOEDUCATIONAL APPROACH

The psychoeducational approach to patient and family education differs from teaching methods that impart didactic material and then respond to the learner's needs (see Table 10-2). Psychoeducation, which is currently employed by many MS centers throughout the United States and Canada, is a rather complex procedure that has been found to be effective in promoting adherence to medication regimes and treatment protocols (Marciniak et al., 1991). Current literature suggests that adherence is a dynamic process that implies a partnership between the patient and the health care team, whereas compliance is a patient's unquestioning fulfillment of a physician's instructions (Brooks, 1985). Today's health care consumers, particularly patients with multiple sclerosis, tend to be more informed and cautious about new procedures. Therefore, innovative approaches are strongly indicated in educational activities that involve self-care and self-responsibility. Additionally, culturally sensitive interventions along with the attitude of health care providers have been shown to improve adherence (Elliott, 1994).

The psychoeducational approach begins with the health care professional determining the goals and expectations that the patient has for the prescribed treatment. By eliciting this perspective, the nurse then has the

TABLE 10-2. Psychoeducation Versus Traditional Learning Model

Psychoeducation	Traditional Learning
Learner's perspective is determined before teaching is initiated.	Teaching is initiated based on material to be learned.
Goals and objectives are explained in light of learner's expectations.	Goals and objectives are predetermined by learning material.
Teaching is dynamic and individualized.	Teaching is standardized for each person.
Teaching is reinforced with additional learning material and hands-on activities.	Teaching may include other learning activities such as additional material and hands-on activities.

opportunity to clarify perceptions and clear up misconceptions of anticipated outcomes. For instance, if a treatment is seen as a cure rather than
as a palliative intervention, the patient and family will be disappointed
about outcomes and the patient is likely to discontinue therapy fairly quickly. Should the treatment bring the additional burden of side effects, disappointment will be compounded and one may expect a more abbreviated
treatment program. The patient's educational and cultural background
along with his or her previous experience with health care providers must
be taken into consideration when providing health care education and
information. Patient and family education may be enhanced with printed
material, media support, such as audiotapes or videotapes, and written
instructions tailored to the patient's needs. Psychoeducation is consistent
with an emerging concept in chronic illness: comprehensive care that is
proactive and whose goal is empowerment and patient involvement
(Halper & Burks, 1994). This model has proven to be valuable for a regimen that presumes patient responsibility, self-monitoring, and accurate
feedback to the health care team.

Current treatment options in multiple sclerosis are complex and can
be frightening to patients since they involve self-injection. The psychoeducational design includes a care partner who can coach, assist, and occasionally substitute for the patient. The teaching program can be divided
into a number of sessions to reduce information overload and allow for
absorption of the new material. During the first meeting, the nurse may
determine the patient's expectations of the treatment and his or her concerns about side effects, insurance coverage, self-injection, and the prior
experiences of other patients. The nurse should discuss goals for treatment, expected side effects, and previous research outcomes with potential
relevance to the patient. The nurse, patient, and care partner can, at this
time, simulate the injection technique using an orange or another convenient device. At the end of the session, the patient should be given educational material to study prior to the next visit.

At the second visit, previous material may be reviewed and the
patient's goals and objectives for treatment may be discussed once more.
Technical skills may be developed at this time, including site rotation,
reconstitution, and the injection itself.

The third, and most likely final teaching visit, should consist of another discussion of the patient's perceptions about the treatment. At this time,
the patient will demonstrate drug reconstitution and actually inject the
medication. Additional visits may or may not be required but patients
should be encouraged to call regularly until they feel comfortable with the
procedure. Following the initial injection, patients are usually seen every
three months for the first year, and laboratory studies are performed at
each visit (usually CBC and liver profile).

COMMUNICATING AND CARING

A vital part of the psychoeducational approach is clear and effective communication (see Table 10-3).

Due to its variety of courses and unpredictable symptoms, multiple sclerosis imposes uncertainty into the lives of patients (Bansil, Troiano, & Dowling, 1993). Current treatment options have not to date resulted in the cure for MS that is the hope of patients and families. This painful reality can lead to disappointment and frustration unless potentially positive outcomes are pointed out at the onset of treatment. Thus, the nurse is not only faced with the challenge of technical education and development of skills, but the responsibility to clarify what patients can expect. Complicating this process is the fact that some patients have problems with cognition, as evidenced by difficulty in understanding and learning new tasks (Rao, 1986). It is important to include written material to reinforce learning. Currently, manufacturers of injectable medications are providing both written and audiovisual support to assist with patient education and will supply them to the nurse upon request. Including a care partner in the learning process may increase the patient's comfort level and provide him or her with a backup if difficulties occur with self-injection. These strategies will assist the nurse to promote a successful integration and retention of learned material in order to achieve patient adherence to the prescribed protocol.

OUTCOMES OF THE PSYCHOEDUCATIONAL MODEL

The psychoeducational approach to patient and family education has proven to be very effective in promoting patient adherence to complex procedures. Utilizing psychoeducational interventions, important skills are taught in a psychotherapeutic rather than a didactic setting. By responding to individual needs and concerns regarding a complex injectable protocol, one can realistically assess the patient's understanding of anticipated side effects and his or her skill development for the injection process. Through continuous communication regarding questions or concerns, the nurse is able to impart caring and concern and provide the support that is required for new treatment options.

TABLE 10-3. Key Points for Effective Communication

⊃ Be brief and succinct.

⊃ Ask that patients repeat instructions in their own words to clarify misunderstandings.

⊃ Supplement verbal instructions with written instructions.

REFERENCES

Bansil, S., Troiano, R., Dowling, P., et al. (1993). Advances in the pharmacological and neurological treatment of patients with multiple sclerosis. *NeuroRehabilitation, 3 (4)*, 1.

Brooks, N.A. (1985). Opportunities for health promotion: including the chronically ill and disabled. *Social Science Medicine, 19 (405)*.

Elliott, W.J. (1994). Compliance strategies. *Current Opinions Nephrology Hypertension, 3 (3)*, 271.

Fang, J.Y., Lublin, F.D. (1995). Altering the course of multiple sclerosis. *Internal Medicine, 16 (1)*, 13.

Halper, J., Burks, J.S. (1994). Care patterns in multiple sclerosis. Principal care, comprehensive team care, consortium care. *NeuroRehabilitation, 4 (2)*, 67.

LaRocca, N.G., Kalb, R.C., Foley, F.W., et al. (1993). Psychosocial, affective, and behavior consequences of multiple sclerosis: treatment of the "whole" patient. *NeuroRehabilitation, 3 (4)*, 30.

Marciniak, M., Johnson, B., Foley, F.W., et al. (1991). The use of the Levo chair in the management of multiple sclerosis. Presented at the Consortium of Multiple Sclerosis Centers Conference. June 15–17, 1991. Halifax, NS, Canada.

Platt, F.W., Tippy, P.K., Turk, D.C. (1994). Helping patients adhere to the regimen. *Patient Care*, 30–43.

Rao, S.M. (1986). Neuropsychology of multiple sclerosis: a critical review. *J Clin Exp Neuropsychology, 8 (5)*, 503–42.

CHAPTER 11

Alternative Therapies

June Halper

Interest in alternative medical therapies has been steadily increasing. A 1990 Harvard study revealed that of 1,539 people surveyed one out of three had used some kind of alternative medical therapy during the past year (Eisenberg et al., 1993). Based on this survey, it was calculated that 425 million visits were made to alternative practitioners versus 388 million visits to primary care physicians (Eisenberg et al., 1993). Alternative therapy can be defined as any approach to solving a health problem that is different from approaches used by practitioners of Western medicine (Fugh-Berman, 1996). It might be more accurate to call some of these therapies *complementary*, since they are designed to complement rather than replace conventional medical practice (Fugh-Berman, 1996).

The percentage of patients with chronic illnesses using alternative therapies is even higher than that of the general population. In a survey of 184 HIV-positive patients in Philadelphia, 40 percent reported using alternative therapies; another study found that 55 percent of Alzheimer's caregivers had tried at least one alternative therapy to improve their patient's memory (Eisenberg et al., 1993). A study conducted by the National Multiple Sclerosis Society revealed increased utilization of alternative therapies by more educated patients with multiple sclerosis (Pignotti, 1996). Thus, it is important for nurses to be aware of issues relating to alternative or complementary therapies that may be raised by their patients with multiple sclerosis. Many private foundations are interested in alternative therapies and the NIH has established an Office of Alternative Medicine. The following is an overview of therapies frequently mentioned in contemporary literature.

ACUPUNCTURE

Acupuncture is the insertion of hair-thin needles into specific points on the body to prevent or treat illness. It is one component of traditional Chinese medicine (TCM), an integrated system that has been used for over 2,000 years (Fugh-Berman, 1996). There is a great deal about this treatment that we do not clearly understand, and there have been no definitive studies of its use in multiple sclerosis. There have been some anecdotal reports that acupuncture may be beneficial for some symptoms of multiple sclerosis, particularly pain (Kraft & Catanzaro, 1996).

HYPNOTHERAPY AND IMAGERY

There are two contemporary schools of hypnosis. Traditional hypnosis works with enhanced suggestibility, which occurs in formal trances (Fugh-Berman, 1996). In the approach pioneered by Erickson, hypnosis is an altered state of mind and behavior that is affected by the everyday trances that we all experience (Fugh-Berman, 1996). Imagery is often used in hypnosis and has been shown to increase blood sugar, affect gastrointestinal activity, and alter skin temperature. Guided imagery is used with relaxation, biofeedback, hypnosis, meditation, or behavioral therapy (Fugh-Berman, 1996). Many symptomatic benefits have been attributed to hypnosis but there is no evidence that it alters the course of MS (Kraft & Catanzaro, 1996).

MASSAGE AND BODYWORK

Massage was a part of many ancient cultures, including those of China, Persia, Arabia, and Greece. In the United States, there are four major categories of bodywork, the best known of which is European massage. Swedish massage is the most popular of these (Fugh-Berman, 1996). The others are deep tissue technique, which includes structural integration or rolfing; pressure-point techniques such as reflexology, acupressure (Shiatsu); and polarity therapy, Reiki, jin shin jyutsu, and jin shin do. Therapeutic touch is a related approach to the latter therapy (Fugh-Berman, 1996). Another category, movement integration, includes Feldenkrais and Alexander techniques, which teach better ways to move one's body to reduce stress (Fugh-Berman, 1996). Some people with multiple sclerosis find these modalities effective, particularly for symptoms like spasticity or pain. It is more difficult to treat a global symptom such as fatigue, although patients report increased relaxation, which indeed can lessen fatigue (Kraft & Catanzaro, 1996). Massage can relieve muscle tightness and facilitate joint mobility but it has no effect on the course of multiple sclerosis. It has been reported to alleviate pain in some patients but not in others (Kraft & Catanzaro, 1996).

BIOFEEDBACK

Biofeedback translates skin temperature, muscle contractions, blood pressure, pulse, brain waves, or other bodily functions into audio or video signals. By learning to control the pitch of a sound, the rate of a series of beeps, or an image on a computer screen, the patient can learn to control the bodily process that is being monitored (Fugh-Berman, 1996). Biofeedback has been shown to be effective in teaching a person to reduce muscle tension associated with certain types of pain such as muscle tension headaches. Biofeedback has also been used to manage spasticity but studies have not substantiated its effectiveness in this area (Kraft & Catanzaro, 1996).

TAI CHI

Sometimes called a moving meditation, Tai Chi is a Chinese blend of exercise and energy work. Its arm movements are slow, circular, continuous, smooth, and controlled, and weight is shifted regularly from one foot to the other (Fugh-Berman, 1996). The program may provide the health benefits of more strenuous exercise without straining the muscles of the heart, and may improve coordination, physical agility, and speed (Kraft & Catanzaro, 1996). Many chapters of the National Multiple Sclerosis Society have organized Tai Chi programs, which provide both physical and social benefit to participants.

CHIROPRACTIC THERAPY

Chiropractic was invented by Daniel David Palmer in the late nineteenth century. He was influenced by spiritualism during that period and performed his first spinal adjustment in September 1895. The word *chiropractic*, coined by a patient a year later, is derived from Greek and means "done by hand." Chiropractors generally only manipulate the protruding parts of the spinal vertebrae (short lever manipulation) (Fugh-Berman, 1996).

The maintenance of health in multiple sclerosis is very important. People with MS can have a variety of problems that can be treated by a variety of health care providers including chiropractors. It is important to find a practitioner who is qualified and experienced in the specific problem the patient is experiencing and who also understands MS (Kraft & Catanzaro, 1996).

CONCLUSION

Because alternative therapies are often cost-effective, third-party payors are beginning to reimburse for these services. Medical education is also changing and many medical schools are incorporating alternative medicine into their curricula. Both recognized and complementary treatment options may be the wave of the future as we enter the twenty-first century, a new era of therapy in multiple sclerosis.

REFERENCES

Eisenberg, D.M., Kessler, R.D., Foster, C., et al. (1993). Unconventional medicine in the United States: prevalence, costs, and patterns of use. *New England Journal of Medicine, 328,* 246–52.

Fugh-Berman, A. (1995). *Alternative medicine: what works.* Tucson, AZ: Odonian Press, 5.

Kraft, G.H., Catanzaro, M. (1996). *Living with multiple sclerosis: a wellness approach.* New York: Demos Vermande.

Pignotti, M. (1996). "Multiple sclerosis: choosing alternative treatments." Fordham University, Unpublished Master's Thesis.

CHAPTER 12

Patient and Family Education

Nancy J. Holland

Nurses are increasingly emphasizing wellness and quality of life over disease orientation. This is especially important for individuals with a chronic disease or disability, who face a lifetime of dealing with its ramifications. Unlike acute illness leading to either recovery or death within a brief period of time, chronic conditions have long-term implications for all aspects of living.

The quality of life perspective moves the person with MS out of the "patient" role, which identifies the medical team as leader and expert. Instead, the individual is seen as the controlling force of his or her life, with the ultimate decision-making power over proposed health-related and life-planning strategies. Quality of life is important to individuals with chronic disease, their families, and health care/service providers because it represents the individual's judgments about how the illness and related interventions affect everyday life (Stuifbergen, 1992).

The quality of life construct has been interpreted as having several different but related meanings by various authors. Life satisfaction and well-being are prominent suggestions (Klemmack et al., 1974; George et al., 1985; and Padilla & Grant, 1985). Salamon (1988) contends that there is universal acceptance of life satisfaction as a valid measurement of quality of life. A recent concept analysis of quality of life identified a positive view as encompassing satisfaction with one's life and acceptance of one's life circumstances (McDaniel & Bach, 1994). A new "functional assessment of MS quality of life" instrument has been validated and will be a likely component of future MS intervention outcome studies (Cella et al., 1996).

QUALITY OF LIFE GOALS

Through a consensus-building process, the National Multiple Sclerosis Society identified three main areas that contribute to quality of life: MS KNOWLEDGE, HEALTH, and INDEPENDENCE.

These categories extend thinking beyond the physical and emotional well-being of the person to also encompass changes that might be necessary in the environment. An MS employment specialist may be needed to perform a job analysis and partner with the employer and employee with MS to make job accommodations essential for continued employment. Legal assistance may be needed in this area or to facilitate removal of environmental barriers in the community. The disability community criticizes the "medical model" for only working to "fix" what is wrong with the person, not realizing the missing piece needed to complete the picture—"fixing" the environment and attempting to impact societal attitudes that prevent full functioning of the disabled person outside the general medical or rehabilitation setting.

Acquisition of the MS KNOWLEDGE base needed to deal effectively with the disease is the focus of this section. HEALTH issues related to physical management, emotional needs, and family relationships/social support are addressed in many sections throughout the book. INDEPENDENCE—Independent Living, Long-term Services, Employment, and Accessibility—is addressed through chapter programs and community referrals.

Patient Education

The need for factual information about MS is the most basic element for enhancing quality of life for the person with MS and is crucial to the success of all other quality of life goals. The dissemination of information through educational programs can often have a major impact on the person with MS and his or her family. Such programs can effect the desired behaviors that will support health and minimize the negative features of a chronic, potentially disabling disease (Mazzuca, 1982).

In the dissemination of such knowledge, the nurse often has the primary interaction with patients and family members. A survey of people with amyotrophic lateral sclerosis at the University of Kansas Medical Center demonstrated that patients saw the role of information provider as one of the major roles expected of a nurse (Beiseckler, Kuckelman Cobb, & Ziegler, 1988).

To assure that the patient will continue to acquire necessary information and skills on a lifelong basis, the nurse needs to facilitate an independent learning orientation, which can be achieved through self-directed learning techniques. Self-directed learning emphasizes empowerment and suggests fairly independent activity. Gilroth (1990) notes that although the process is not well defined, most patient education programs do encourage patients to be actively involved in decision making and care delivery.

Duchin and Brown note that "patients with diabetes are ultimately responsible for their disease management, but many patients with diabetes do not have the necessary knowledge or skill" (Duchin & Brown, 1990, p. 255). This statement pertains to individuals with MS as well.

Patient education goals for individuals with MS include:

1. Understanding the diagnosis and successful coping with its potential impact on one's life;
2. Planning regarding critical areas such as relationships, parenting, employment, and lifestyle; and
3. Preventing potentially disabling outcomes, with specific goals related to new symptoms.

As the disease progresses, the process needs to be adjusted so that appropriate goals are developed relative to the person's changing condition. DeSouza and Ashburn (1988) note that planning, which begins at diagnosis, must be consistently followed throughout the course of the disease.

The task of assuring that people with MS have adequate information about MS and how to live most effectively with its limitations is facilitated by the desire to learn shown by many individuals with MS. A needs survey of 630 members of the National Multiple Sclerosis Society's New York City chapter indicated that respondents ranked first the need for more information about MS, with 41 percent reporting a great or very great need for more information (Genevie, Kallos, & Streuning, 1987). Orr (1990) described the perspective of viewing illness as an educational opportunity. He notes that, "it is our ability to learn that helps individuals who suffer from diseases to find innovative ways to cope with them" (p. 47).

An important learning tool utilized by people with MS is the newsletter. The National Multiple Sclerosis Society sends a quarterly newsletter/magazine called *Inside MS* to 460,000 members, including 220,000 who have MS. Each of the Society's 88 chapters throughout the United States is required to send a newsletter to chapter members at least quarterly. A study conducted at the Veteran's Administration in Buffalo, New York, evaluated the benefit of a patient newsletter for persons with peripheral vascular disease. Sixty-five percent of respondents reported that the information obtained from reading the newsletter stimulated a positive change in their behavior (Ventura et al., 1990). The authors also noted that the flexible structure of a newsletter allows current events to be used as topics or themes as a way of presenting information.

Other techniques people with MS have found helpful for learning include targeted reading, experiential learning, questioning physicians and other health professionals, and lectures and meetings.

Adult Education

When providing information to the person with MS, principles applicable to adult education can facilitate the learning experience (Lawler, 1986). Six principles that have relevance to working with people with MS are as follows:

1. *Adult education includes and builds on the experience of the participant.* Most people with MS do not have prior knowledge about the disease upon which to build. However, all adults have had experience that required coping behavior. These existing styles should be considered in learning activities relative to coping with MS. According to Knowles (1980), ". . . adults have a richer foundation of experience to which to relate new experiences (and new learnings tend to take on meaning as we are able to relate them to our past experience)" (p. 50).

2. *Adult education fosters critically reflective thinking.* Critical reflection, according to Mezirow (1990), is "assessment of the validity of the presuppositions of one's meaning perspectives, and examination of their sources and consequences" (p. xvi). A component of this— self-reflection—describes one of the three domains of learning (Mezirow, 1981). Critical self-reflection is defined as "assessment of the way one has posed problems and of one's own meaning perspectives" (Mezirow, 1990, p. xvi). Issues such as self-esteem and self-image, which are particularly important to people with MS, can be addressed by the process of critical self-reflection, leading to critical analysis of assumptions (attitudes, values, beliefs, orientations).

3. *Problem posing and problem solving are fundamental aspects of adult education.* According to Lawler (1988), problem posing and problem solving refer to "learning which involves examination of issues and concerns, transforms content into problem situations and necessitates analysis and development of solutions" (p. 48). In relation to adult education, Knowles (1980) points out that the motivation of most people who seek out adult education comes from the desire to improve their ability to cope with the problems they currently face in life. Therefore, their frame of mind is problem- or performance-centered.

   Multiple sclerosis can present problems in all aspects of daily living. Therefore, the process of looking at problems, analyzing their components and deriving solutions is crucial for people with MS and their families, and is relevant to the self-directed learning process.

4. *Learning for action is valued in adult education.* Action is often a direct consequence of problem solving, and therefore closely related to the preceding principle. Learning that can be translated into action is important to address the physical, emotional, and interpersonal problems presented by MS.

5. *Adult education empowers the participant.* Lawler (1988) stated that adult education designed to empower the participant is "learning which facilitates an awareness that one possesses the means to influence or change his or her environment" (p. 50). Brookfield (1985) defined "genuine" adult education as including activities that assist adults in their efforts to establish a sense of control over their lives, within their interpersonal relationships and societal roles.

6. *Self-directed learning is encouraged and enhanced in adult education.* Encouragement of independence in action and thought is believed by some to be a crucial component of adult learning activities (Lawler, 1986).

Some view these adult education principles as having greater application within a more formal classroom setting with a facilitator present. However, in the education of persons with MS, the health professional often fulfills the role of a facilitator. An understanding of these principles by the patient can also help shape subsequent educational activities, particularly self-directed learning efforts.

WHAT DOES A PERSON WITH MS NEED TO KNOW?

Living "optimally" with a chronic illness such as multiple sclerosis involves several levels of awareness and adjustment, both for the person diagnosed with the condition and for the family members who experience the illness as part of the family unit. These levels include:

1. emotional/psychological;
2. physical; and
3. interpersonal/social.

Emotional factors are identified first since a minimal level of acceptance must be present before information will be assimilated and acted upon. Beyond acceptance is the ongoing process of adjusting and coping which, according to LaRocca & Kalb (1987), ". . . is not a simple, one-time event. For each individual, adjustment gradually evolves during the course of the disease" (p. 210).

Successful adjusting or coping permits the individual to explore additional areas of information or pursue new skills that will support psychological growth, reduce symptoms, prevent disabling and/or life-threatening complications, and continue to develop satisfying interpersonal and social relationships and activities.

To reach emotional, physical, and interpersonal levels of awareness involves learning by the individual. According to Mezirow et al. (1990), "learning may be defined as the process of making a new or revised interpretation of the meaning of an experience, which guides subsequent understanding, appreciation, and action" (p.1).

Understanding certain underlying concepts is key in the ability to learn needed behaviors and skills. Such concepts include the disease process; symptoms and therapies; prevention of complications; nonmedical therapies; coping strategies; family issues; work issues; equipment and services; community resources; financial aid and arresting disease progression.

A STUDY OF LEARNING AND MS

A small study was done to see if there was any relationship between stages of MS, degree of disability, what topics the participants' learning included, and what areas they thought were most important (Holland, 1992). The sample consisted of 18 women and 8 men who were clients at an MS clinic in New York City. The purpose of the study was to identify possible trends, realizing that the sample was not representative of people with MS in the general population. There was some difference in areas addressed at different time frames in the disease process. The topics pursued by the majority of people with MS in the early stage (five years or under since diagnosis) included the disease process, symptoms and therapies, prevention of complications, coping strategies, and community resources. Interest in the disease process remained high for intermediate duration (six to ten years) and moderate for long-term MS (more than ten years). The majority in the intermediate and long-term stages sought to learn about halting disease progression, and almost all sought information about symptoms and therapies and the prevention of complications. Coping and community resources were high in the early stages, and coping again was high in long-term MS.

Questioning health professionals and reading were by far the most frequently used modes, regardless of the stage of MS. Self-directed learning about the disease process was mostly accomplished by reading, while arresting disease progression was pursued with health professionals. Information about coping strategies and family issues was obtained mainly through informal (experiential) learning, and individual and group counseling. Individual and group counseling and agencies were more utilized by those with early and intermediate MS, while people with intermediate and advanced MS used videos more often than their counterparts with early MS. This pattern may be changing due to increased use of videos by all groups, as home video viewing continues to increase in the population at large.

Coping and family issues were most notably pursued by those with severe disability. Otherwise, little difference was found in learning content as a function of degree of disability. This highlights the need to promote coping and family content areas with those newly diagnosed, at a time when this information might guide efforts in these areas rather than later in the disease course, when potentially avoidable problems may have already developed. Another area of concern is the low amount of self-directed learning in the areas of equipment and services by people with moderate disability. Again, the nurse must be especially attentive to the patients' knowledge and pursuit of information about appropriate assistive techniques.

Relevant previous coping was identified more frequently as MS stages advanced, suggesting a greater understanding of coping as the duration of MS increased. Regardless of the stage of MS or the degree of disability, people engaged in self-directed learning for the purpose of action and to gain a sense of empowerment.

During the course of the study, three themes emerged:

1. the value of experiential learning;
2. avoidance of others more disabled; and
3. the doctor as embodiment of the MS care team.

1. *Experiential learning.* While experiential learning can refer to planned classroom activities, for the purposes of this study it was defined as learning from experience, through sometimes unintentional but most often intentional trial and error activities. Study participants spoke about trial and error, relying on oneself to understand or master necessary concepts, and being an expert on the personal experience of living and coping with MS. Participants alluded to trial and error as an important way of experiencing a sense of control over the learning activities. This kind of informal learning involves learning from mistakes, learning by doing, and learning from interpersonal interactions, all of which were reported by participants in the study.

Kolb's (1984) model of experiential learning has two factors: emphasis on here-and-now concrete experience to test abstract concepts, and the role of feedback. These features were reflected in the statements of the subjects who applied actual experience to the abstract concepts of coping and symptomatic management, and applied the feedback of successful vs. unsuccessful measures.

Linda explained that much of her coping came from a personal decision to be more independent. She explored various routes of public transportation to select the most accessible.

Fran was discouraged from pursuing exercise by her previous physician: "He said I shouldn't. 'It makes you get tired. It will make you get worse.' And I kind of disagreed with that so I started doing it on my own."

Norma speaks about her own experience relative to coping: "So it's just been a gradual learning over the past fourteen years. What to do and what not to do for coping. If you don't know in fourteen years what MS is all about, you'll never know."

In a discussion of coping and independence, Henry stated, "I try to be as creative as possible."

Sue gave an example of her self-learning coping: "This is a very simple thing, I just learned it. When you go shopping, you don't go to the supermarket and then bring everything in. I learned that I just take in the stuff for the refrigerator . . . leave the rest in the car and the next day just bring it in."

Experiential learning is an important component of the coping scheme for people with MS. The trial and error aspect of experiential learning is a practical approach to problem solving and empowers the individual to perform an activity or function in a more effective or efficient manner.

2. *Avoidance of others who are more disabled.* A popular method of providing information and support for people with MS throughout the course of their illness is the group format. This may take the form of lectures sponsored by the National Multiple Sclerosis Society, counseling groups or self-help or other mutual support networks. Such groups are considered homogeneous since members share a common problem or diagnosis (Seligman, 1982). The benefits of such group experiences are well-documented. People feel less isolated and have the opportunity to develop mutual support networks with others going through a similar distressing experience. However, when questioned about the various learning modes that use a group format, a surprising number of people interviewed for the study were totally opposed to any kind of group interactive experience with others who have MS.

SUMMARY

The themes that emerged from the NMSS study on quality of life goals—MS KNOWLEDGE, HEALTH, AND INDEPENDENCE—add to an understanding of the self-directed learning process used by people with MS to learn about their disease and about ways to deal with it most effectively. Experiential learning strongly enhances empowerment but can limit access to important information if it is used as the exclusive learning mode. Avoidance of others who are more disabled needs to be considered by programmers during the planning process and should also be addressed as a potentially negative coping device. Overall, the themes that emerged will add to some unique perspectives in the MS educational program development for both clients and health professionals.

REFERENCES

Beisecker, A.E., Kuckelman Cobb, A., & Ziegler, D.K. (1988). Patients' perspectives of the role of the care providers in amyotrophic lateral sclerosis. *Archives of Neurology, 45.*

Brookfield, S.D. (1985). A critical definition of adult education. *Adult Education Quarterly, 36 (1)*, 44–49.

Campbell, A. (1981). *The sense of well-being in America: recent patterns and trends.* New York: McGraw Hill.

Cella, D.F., Dineen, K., Aranson, B., et al. (1996). Validation of the functional assessment of multiple sclerosis quality of life instrument. *Neurology, 47,* 129–139.

Counte, M.A., Bieliauskas, L.A., Pavlau, M. (1983). Stress and personal attitudes in chronic illness. *Archives of Physical Medicine & Rehabilitation, 64,* 272–275.

DeSouza, L.H., Ashburn, A. (1988). Knowledge of multiple sclerosis: implications for rehabilitation. *Clinical Rehabilitation, 2,* 139–142.

Duchin, S., Brown, S. (1990). Patients should participate in designing diabetes educational content. *Patient Education and Counseling, 16,* 155–267.

Genevie, L., Kallos, J., Struening, E. (1987). An overview of patients' perceptions of their needs: multiple sclerosis as a paradigm. *Journal of Neurologic Rehabilitation, 1, (1).*

George, L., Okun, M., Landerman, R. (1985). Age as a moderator of the determinants of life satisfaction. *Research on Aging, 7,* 209–233.

Giloth, B.E. (1990). Promoting patient involvement: educational, organizational, and environmental strategies. *Patient Education and Counseling, 15,* 29–38.

Holland, N. (1992). "Self-directed learning by individuals with multiple sclerosis." Unpublished doctoral dissertation, Columbia University, Teachers College, New York.

Klemmack, D., Carlson, J., Edwards, J. (1974). Measures of well being: an empirical and critical assessment. *Journal of Health and Social Behavior, 15,* 267–270.

Knowles, M. (1980). *The modern practice of adult education: from pedagogy to andragogy.* Chicago: Follett.

Kolb, D. (1984). *Experiential learning: experience as the source of learning and development.* New Jersey: Prentice Hall.

LaRocca, N.G., Kalb, R.C. (1987). Psychological issues. In L. Scheinberg, N. Holland (eds.). *Multiple sclerosis: a guide for patients and their families,* Second Edition. New York: Raven Press.

Lawler, P. (1986). Principles and practices of adult education, Adult Education Guided Independent Study IV Dissertation Committee, Columbia University, Teachers College, New York.

Lawler, P. (1988). "Workplace education and the principles and practices of adult education." Unpublished doctoral dissertation, Columbia University, Teachers College, New York.

Lechtenberg, R. (1988). *Multiple sclerosis fact book.* Philadelphia: F.A. Davis.

McDaniel, R.W., Bach, C.A. (1994). Quality of life: a concept analysis. *Rehabilitation Nursing Research,* Spring.

Mazzuca, S.A. (1982). Does patient education in chronic disease have therapeutic value? *Journal of Chronic Diseases, 35,* 521–529.

Mezirow, J. (1981). A critical theory of adult learning and education. *Adult Education, 32 (1),* 3–24.

Mezirow, J. et al. (1990). *Fostering critical reflection in adulthood: a guide to transformative and emancipator learning.* San Francisco: Jossey-Bass, Inc.

Orr, R. (1990). Illness as an educational opportunity. *Patient Education and Counselling, 15,* 47–48.

Padilla, C., Grant, M. (1985). Quality of life as a cancer nursing outcome variable. *Advances in Nursing Science, 8,* 45–54.

Rosner, L.J., Ross, S. (1987). *Multiple sclerosis: new hope and practical advice for people with MS and their families.* New York: Prentice Hall.

Salamon, M. (1988). Clinical use of the life satisfaction in the elderly scale. *Clinical Gerontology, 8,* 45–54.

Sheinberg, L., Holland, N. (1987). *Multiple sclerosis: a guide for patients and their families,* Second Edition. New York: Raven Press.

Seligman, M. (ed.). (1982). *Group psychotherapy and counseling with special populations.* Baltimore: University Park Press.

Stuifbergen, M. (1992). Quality of Life for Individuals with Multiple Sclerosis. Health Services Research Report, National Multiple Sclerosis Society.

Ventura, M.R., Todd, K., Burch, K., Grace, M.L., Crosby, F., Lohr, G. (1990). Patient newsletter: a teaching tool. *Patient Education and Counselling, 15,* 269–274.

Wolf, J.K. (1987). *Mastering multiple sclerosis: a guide to management,* Second Edition. Rutland: Academy Books.

CHAPTER 13

Advocacy*

Gail B. Price**

Nurses have always been patient advocates. From the battlefields of the Crimea to the halls of Congress, advocacy for individual patients rights and health care policy changes have been, and always will be, integral parts of nursing practice.

Nurses are uniquely qualified to be patient advocates. The person who enters nursing usually is one who is caring, supportive, and compassionate, and nursing education and training shape, mold, and expand on those characteristics by providing the knowledge necessary for understanding health care needs and human behavior.

Nursing opportunities in the late 1980s and 1990s have multiplied, and work environments have become substantially more diversified. Nurses work in health care facilities, government agencies, corporations, the media, and private consulting. Thousands of nurses are professors, teachers, and researchers in academic institutions. Because of the broad range of options now available, the nurse advocate role is ever increasing as nurses function in positions that influence societal changes and impact the future of health care.

Nurses working with the multiple sclerosis (MS) population frequently face issues of patient advocacy.

---

* Parts of this chapter have been adapted with the permission of the publisher from *A Guide to Legal Rights for People with Disabilities,* by Marc D. Stolman. New York: Demos, 1994.
** Deceased.

The nature of MS—chronic, often progressive, with erratic symptoms—is complicated by its unknown cause, an elusive cure, and the inability to predict its prognosis with any degree of certainty. The age of the person affected—most commonly a young adult—and the emotional, psychosocial, and financial impact of this disease on individuals, families, primary social support systems, communities, and society as a whole present enormous challenges to the nurse as an advocate.

The nurse who advocates for patients with multiple sclerosis confronts many more complex issues than would normally be seen in an acute care setting. The multiplicity of needs of the MS population leaves several avenues for a potential advocacy role. These are:

1. Championing individual patient rights;
2. Supporting changes in institutional or agency rules and regulations;
3. Fostering health policy reform; and
4. Promoting the rights of the disabled.

INDIVIDUAL PATIENTS RIGHTS

Patient self-determination, informed consent, autonomy, dignity, and quality care are fundamental to all health care, but with a chronic illness such as MS, spanning decades of life, these principles become vulnerable to external influences and are tested repeatedly. Circumstances often change as the disease fluctuates, necessitating the frequent reinforcement of individual patient rights. This is accomplished through advocacy.

One major theme remains a constant in all advocacy efforts and it is best described in one word—empowerment.

The nurse advocate recognizes the critical need to empower patients, their families, and their support systems to become self-advocates and provides the encouragement and education needed to help and guide them through the process. With empowerment as a primary goal, the nurse advocate can have a dynamic effect on rights of all patients and fulfill one of nursing's most vital roles.

There are many advocacy opportunities for nurses working with the MS population. When dealing with the relapses and progressive disability that can occur in multiple sclerosis, where unproven, sometimes highly experimental therapies may be prescribed or tested, the advocacy role of the nurse may take on new and complex dimensions that challenge every aspect of nursing practice.

The allocation of limited resources and how these should be apportioned across the spectrum of needs raise difficult questions for nurse advocates working with the chronically disabled. Programs that seek to ration health care are threatening to the person with MS, and nurses are often called upon to be patient advocates when such situations arise.

ADVANCE DIRECTIVES

The importance of empowerment has been underscored in recently enacted laws assuring individuals the right to devise their future medical care. Federal regulations explicit in the Patient Self-Determination Act (effective December 1, 1991) require all health care facilities receiving federal funds to create formal procedures for the use of advance directives such as the living will and health care power of attorney. As advocates, nurses must be knowledgeable about the laws applicable to these documents in the specific states in which they practice.

Most people are reluctant to think about their own death or incapacitation. Since planning for the disposal of one's property after death or incapacitation requires *thinking* about it, many people do not make sufficient financial plans for their demise. However, everyone should make plans for his or her passing to avoid added pain and confusion for their loved ones.

Wills

The first thing to encourage clients to do is to make a valid will. Without a valid will, property passes by the laws of intestacy. This means that the individual has no control over the disposition of property after death; laws determine who will receive it.

Each state has different laws governing the division of property for people who die intestate (without a valid will). In most states property is divided between spouse and children. Some states may give 50 percent of property to the surviving spouse, with 50 percent divided equally among the children, whereas others may give the major portion to the children.

A will, which must be signed and witnessed, is a document that outlines how property (estate) is to be distributed. The will appoints a person known as the executor to govern the distribution of property. Some wills, known as holographic wills, are handwritten and are not witnessed. They are not recommended because courts often do not consider them valid. A will is the most common device that people use to control the disposition of their property after death.

Trusts

The second most common device used for estate planning is the trust, which is more complicated than a will and generally costs more to create. Trusts are gaining in popularity because they can sometimes reduce legal fees after death.

A trust has three components:

- ⊃ a *trustee,* who holds the trust property and manages it for the benefit of another;
- ⊃ a *beneficiary,* for whose benefit the trustee has the responsibility to deal with the trust property; and
- ⊃ *trust property,* which is held by the trustee for the beneficiary.

The person or group holding the trust property is known as the trustee. A trustee can be an individual or a corporation and needs only the legal capacity to take and hold the trust property. Trustees are required to use the utmost loyalty to control and preserve the property of the trust and to meet its objectives.

Durable Power of Attorney

If the patient worries about becoming incapacitated and wishes to appoint someone else to make decisions about finances and health care while he or she is still alive but unable to make such decisions, he or she may wish to have a Power of Attorney, which is a written document that appoints another person to act in place of the person who signs the document. An ordinary power of attorney becomes invalid if the person who signs it later becomes unable to care for his or her own welfare. However, a *durable* power of attorney is effective after the person who signs the document becomes incapacitated. Such a document gives another person the power to make decisions in financial or health care matters, or even the right to order that life support machines be discontinued in the event of complete incapacitation.

SYSTEMS ADVOCACY

Nurses working with MS patients can be instrumental in defending patients' rights before federal regulatory agencies such as the Social Security Administration (SSA), Health Care Financing Administration (HCFA), and the Department of Veterans Affairs (DVA). State Medicaid, vocational rehabilitation, and social service agencies have a direct impact on the MS population, and support from nurses is often vital in dealing with these entities. Local health departments and the programs they administer need to hear from health professionals who work with multiple sclerosis.

Dealing with complicated bureaucracies may present new challenges to nurses but they are challenges that will benefit both patients and providers.

HEALTH POLICY REFORM

Broader problems such as the lack of available, affordable, and accessible health insurance and long-term care services for people with multiple sclerosis are critical areas in which politically active nurses can make a difference. Elected officials on the local, state, and federal levels are generally responsive to grassroots efforts in their community and often look to health care professionals among their constituents for advice and guidance on health reform legislation.

DISABILITY RIGHTS

No discussion of nurse advocacy would be complete without including the role of nurses and other health professionals in supporting the rights of people with disabilities.

Reaching beyond the medical needs of individuals, disability rights extend into areas of accessibility in employment, education, transportation, avocational activities, and community socialization. The latter includes places that are part of daily living such as movie theaters, supermarkets, restaurants, parking facilities, voting booths, religious institutions, retail stores, and others.

Since the passage of the Americans with Disabilities Act in 1990, the issue of disability rights has had the force of the law behind it. However, it is society's negativism toward the disabled population that is now being recognized as an attitudinal barrier far more difficult to overcome than an existing physical barrier. Nurses can, and must, advocate for the breakdown of physical obstacles to independence and work toward positive attitudinal changes in society so that equal rights of the disabled become a reality.

THE PROCESS—WHERE DO YOU BEGIN?
WHAT DO YOU NEED TO KNOW?

All instructional books on nursing procedure start with a section on gathering equipment. In advocacy, your facts are your equipment.

Nurses should understand the function of federal, state, and local government and be aware of and support state laws, hospital or agency regulations, and codes of ethics that address the rights of patients. Nurses should vote in all elections, know who their elected representatives are, and stay informed about current health care issues by following general media coverage, reviewing professional journals, and actively participating in professional nursing organizations.

All of today's health care standards stress patient advocacy, empowerment, and consumerism. Professional nurses' associations and state practice acts clearly define the role of nurses in advocating for the health and social needs of the public, and groups such as the Joint Commission on Accreditation of Health Organizations (JCAHO) and the Commission on Accreditation of Rehabilitation Facilities (CARF) place increasing emphasis on patients' rights.

Advocating for people with multiple sclerosis requires the nurse to have a full understanding of MS. This includes the physical, emotional, psychosocial, and financial impact, and the medical, health, personal, and social implications of the disease. Knowledge of available community resources is also important, along with special services and programs available from the local or national offices of the National Multiple Sclerosis Society.

Some major issues facing the MS population are fertile ground for nursing advocacy on either an individual or a policy level. These include:

1. Assuring accessible, available, and affordable health and long-term care services for people of all ages;
2. Supporting health and long-term care services and programs that are based on need, not on ability to pay;
3. Expanding health care reimbursement (Medicare, Medicaid, private insurance, health maintenance organizations, etc.) levels;
4. Establishing eligibility for Social Security or veterans' benefits;
5. Supporting vocational rehabilitation programs; and
6. Promoting basic, clinical, and health services research funding.

Depending on the particular advocacy need, you may have to write or meet with a specific person and, most often, this requires written materials. Whether you are advocating for an individual patient with a physician, writing to the President of the United States, or delivering testimony before a Congressional committee, facts are the key to a professional presentation and will help you get the attention of your audience. Patient experiences should be included in a factual manner. Some tips are:

1. State your purpose at the outset.
2. Back up your opening statement with facts on:
   a. The incident, policy, or program being addressed.
   b. An example of the effects of the incident, policy, or program.
   c. Information on multiple sclerosis, including the medical, health, and social aspects of the disease and the impact of the incident, policy, or program on an individual or group of patients.
3. Keep your letter or presentation short but provide additional materials that can be retained for reference purposes.

SELF-ADVOCACY

Self-advocay is probably the most difficult aspect of advocacy for nurses. Self-advocacy is something that nurses neglect. In many corners, the image of the nurse as a self-sacrificing caregiver remains. Until this perception changes, nurses will continue to be ineffective in patient advocacy and shaping health care reform. This perceptual change must start with each individual nurse and how he or she views the nursing role and profession.

No group of health care professionals is more aware of advocacy issues that stem from patients' rights to dignity, self-determination, and informed consent than those in nursing. Through promotion of self-advocacy nurses can use that awareness to help make essential changes in the future of health care delivery. Nurses can have a powerful positive impact, but they must first recognize the power they possess, understand how to use that power, and welcome the role of advocate.

"Information and knowledge are power. Visibility is power. A sense of timing is power. Personal energy is power; so is self-confidence," Hedrick Smith said in his landmark book, *The Power Game, How Washington Works.* He could just as easily have been describing nurses as advocates, nurses who have the information and knowledge, the visibility, sense of timing, personal energy, and self-confidence to make a difference in the lives of millions of Americans.

CHAPTER 14

Hope: A Unifying Concept for Nursing Care in Multiple Sclerosis

Linda A. Morgante

"Learn from yesterday
live for today
hope for tomorrow"

(Anonymous, 1993, p. 15)

INTRODUCTION

Empowering hope in persons with multiple sclerosis (MS) is a prime aspect of caring. Hope is a multidimensional and dynamic process that energizes people and enables healthy coping (Farran, 1992; Miller, 1992; Herth, 1991; Hinds, 1988; Dufault, 1985). Hope is experiencing a sense of unlimited possibility and potential. It is a resource within each person that can be illuminated to promote healing.

This is an optimistic time in the field of multiple sclerosis. New drug treatments that can alter the course of the disease in a positive way are available. But MS remains incurable, and the disease has no boundaries. Symptoms of MS manifest differently in each person and are changeable over time. People who have MS experience its variability on a day-to-day basis and have difficulty living with uncertainty. There is a high incidence of depression, helplessness, and hopelessness in the MS population (Fischer, 1994; Long, 1991).

BACKGROUND

The study of hope by theologians, philosophers, sociologists, and psychologists provides underpinnings for the use of the concept in nursing (McGee, 1984). The Old Testament is filled with passages that reveal anticipation and hope for the coming of the Messiah. The New Testament reflects the teachings of Jesus, which promise a glorious life after death for those who follow His path. The contemporary philosopher Marcel (1962) viewed a person as having unending potential to be expansive and to transcend boundaries to become a fuller being. This implies the presence of hope within all of us.

Sociological evidence of hope can be found in Martin Luther King's famous "I have a dream" speech, which expressed his vision of equal rights for African Americans and the preservation of civil liberties for all. The existence of hope can also be found in our own ancestors and in the anticipation of a better life for every immigrant. Ellis Island is a moving tribute to those ideals and reminds us of past and present dreams that exist for those seeking a new home in America.

Psychologists documented hope in their studies of prisoners of war. They found that the idea of getting out and being reunited with loved ones sustained many of the prisoners (Korner, 1970). In her work with the terminally ill, Elisabeth Kubler-Ross (1969) found that hope for a cure or remission of illness helped people through difficult times. She noted that it was a sign of imminent death when people stopped expressing hopeful ideas.

People with MS cling to hope. They hope for a cure, hope that their condition will stabilize or improve, hope that they will not be abandoned, and hope that they will be able to endure the physical, emotional, and spiritual distress that accompanies MS.

The experience of hope is limitless. Redirecting peoples' attention to a fuller meaning for hope in their lives offers "greater flexibility in maintaining an authentic, reality-based hope despite changing circumstances." (Callan, 1989, p. 42). Hope then centers not only on tangibles like "a cure," but also taps previously unexplored dimensions of the self. Weaving a tapestry of hope while untangling a web of false hope becomes a nursing challenge when caring for those with MS and their families.

DEFINITION

The *American Heritage Dictionary* (1992) defines hope as a wish or desire accompanied by confident expectation of its fulfillment. Stotland (1969) defined hope as "an expectation greater than zero of achieving a goal" (p. 2). Lynch (1965) defined hope as a sense of the possible, "the best resource of man, always there in the inside making everything possible when he is in action, or waiting to be illuminated when he is ill. It is [our] most inward possession and is rightly thought of according to the Pandora story, as still there when everything else has gone" (p. 31).

Miller (1992) defines hope for nurses: "Hope is a state of being, characterized by an anticipation of a continued good state, an improved state or a release from a perceived entrapment. The anticipation may or may not be founded on concrete, real world evidence. Hope is an anticipation of a future that is good and is based upon: mutuality (relationships with others), a sense of personal competence, coping ability, psychological well-being, purpose and meaning in life, as well as a sense of the possible" (pp. 413–14).

Hope is often defined in relation to hopelessness or despair; when hope is lost, one becomes despondent and loses energy necessary for hopefulness. Fromm (1968) identified the loss of the ability to dream as a response of one who is hopeless. Dreaming takes place in sleep but is also an important part of wakefulness and being able to imagine better times. Talking about dreams can be comforting psychologically and emotionally. Disruption of sleep is a clue to possible hopelessness.

Lynch (1965) defined hopelessness as not having "the energy for either imagining or wishing. It is deeply passive, not in any of the good sense of the word, but in its most unhappy sense. Its only fundamental wish is the wish to give up. In a particular situation it cannot imagine anything that can be done or that is worth doing. It does not imagine beyond the limits of what is presently happening" (p. 50).

Although hope is often seen as the absence of hopelessness, no experience is static. It is just our language that limits our vision to an either/or situation. A person moves from hope to hopelessness from moment to moment, and recognition of this ever-changing process can inspire hope even in moments of despair (Figure 14-1). Hope can be a song, a poem, a painting, a flower arrangement, a smile, or a joke. Hope is the smallest or largest expression of the spirit of optimism (Morgante and McCann, 1992).

FIGURE 14-1

Hopeful	Hopeless
Able to verbalize future goals	Sadness
Motivated to achieve goals	Loss of interest
Positive attitude; energized	Negative attitude
Utilizes support and energy of others	Unable to achieve goals
Expands boundaries; is not limited	Lack of energy
	Unable to utilize resources

Nurses who care for people with MS and their families are in a position to provide the resources needed to promote hope and prevent hopelessness. Nursing care includes assessing behaviors that reflect hope (Table 14-1), identifying variables that make an impact on the process of hoping in order to plan care, and creating interventions for inspiring, sustaining, or restoring hope.

CASE STUDY

Catherine is a forty-four-year-old woman with a ten-year history of MS. She is married, has two children (aged twelve and ten), lives in Brooklyn, and works full-time as an audiologist in Manhattan. She initially had a relapsing-remitting course of MS, with symptoms of fatigue and sensory loss in her left leg and hands.

After her diagnosis, Catherine expressed a need to "wait and see" and did not wish to learn about the disease. She would not take any of the literature offered, but asked if she could phone with questions. The nurse offered her support and availability, but recognized the important protectiveness of denial when first learning that one has MS.

Denial is a mechanism that may protect hope for those acutely ill or newly diagnosed with an illness. O'Mailley (1988) determined that denial during the initial phase of an acute event protects people from perceptions that are hopeless in nature (such as the long-term threat of severe illness). Miller (1989) also suggested that denial plays a role in maintaining a person's sense of hope during a crisis.

Denial helps a person process upsetting information, such as learning that one has MS. It does not usually take a person long to experience the

---

TABLE 14-1. Behaviors That Reflect Hope Are:

1. Verbalizes future goals
2. Shows motivation to reach goals
3. Expects to accomplish goals
4. Imagines a brighter tomorrow
5. Reminisces about past successes
6. Sees options for self
7. Maintains a sense of control
8. Anticipates positive outcomes
9. Relates to family, friends, or caregivers in supportive and reciprocal ways
10. Feels connected to a higher being
11. Displays humor
12. Relaxes with imagery and visualization

realities of MS, even when symptoms are mild. Fatigue is a particularly common symptom that cannot be overlooked and usually triggers a call to the nurse for help.

Three months after her first visit, Catherine phoned because fatigue was limiting her at home and at work. She could not accomplish the tasks she needed to complete. She was feeling defeated.

Fatigue was discussed in relation to MS, and ways to manage the symptoms were reviewed. The silence on the other end of the phone was the telling sign that reality had begun to set in.

Catherine spent the next several years in remission, occasionally experiencing sensory signs and intermittent visual disturbances. She learned to manage fatigue by ensuring restful sleep, low impact exercise, and finding time for rest periods during the day. She was taught deep breathing and relaxation techniques and practiced them regularly. She became active in the local MS Society's fund-raising efforts and was a peer counselor for people newly diagnosed with MS. Catherine was a spirited fighter who had the inner strength to turn a negative experience into a positive one and was able to expand her own boundaries with support and reassurance.

Studies have shown that qualities such as hardiness (personal competence) and morale are important adjuncts to hopefulness. Hinds and Martin (1988) studied adolescents with cancer and found that feeling hopeful was not enough to sustain them through the long-term course of the illness. Feeling hopeful in conjunction with feeling personally competent helped these adolescents through the healing process. In an earlier study, Rideout and Montemurom (1986) looked at hope and morale as variables for adapting to chronic heart failure. Their findings raised the possibility that hoping alone cannot sustain a person through a long-term illness and that factors such as morale or hardiness should be considered as adjuncts to hope.

Barton, Magilvy, and Quinn (1994) explored the experience of living with MS among a group of veterans. Their study described "common threads" to support what they call a "fighting spirit" and includes a "personal ideology" that comes into play to help the person "cope with the uncertainty and unpredictability in MS" (p. 88). Learning about a person's past coping abilities provides clues to hope. A more hopeful outlook for the present and future can be determined by how hopeful one was in the past. Helping a person reminisce about previous experiences can provide valuable information for planning interventions to sustain hope.

In 1990 Catherine began a two-year period of more frequent relapses of MS. During this time she had four flare-ups of MS, two requiring intravenous steroids, and all but the last resulting in nearly complete remission. She was left with sensory deficits in her legs and mild ataxia. She was able to walk several blocks without a cane but carried one for reassurance and safety.

In January 1992 Catherine visited the MS Center to inquire about treatment options. She had obtained underwriting from dear friends who would finance trips overseas to obtain treatment. She remained stable on the drug and in July 1993 transferred to an approved treatment center in New York City.

In March 1993 Catherine experienced an exacerbation of MS that did not remit completely. Another exacerbation in October 1993 also did not remit completely. She now had severe sensory loss and mild weakness in her legs, more ataxia, urinary urgency and hesitancy, and bowel urgency. She needed to use her cane at all times. She was urged to switch to another drug therapy in January 1994.

The new arsenal of drug treatments for MS has been a great source of hope in the community. People with MS have the opportunity to try treatments that significantly alter the course of the disease. There are clinical trials and treatments available for people with progressive MS as well. If one treatment fails to be effective, a person can seek other options. Drug treatments and trials renew faith and hope and give people with MS and their families something to look forward to. There is a sense of control over their own destiny because they are participating in decisions about which treatment option or clinical trial is best for them.

At a recent visit to the MS Center, Catherine had clearly changed. She was progressing slowly now, showing evidence that all her symptoms had worsened and included new but rare bowel incontinence and mild upper extremity intention tremors. She decided she did not want another course of steroids. Her doctor suggested she stop the current drug therapy and consider entering a double-blind placebo controlled clinical trial that would test a new drug for people with secondary progressive MS.

The transition from relapsing-remitting disease to progressive disease is very difficult in the course of MS. People are faced with what MS takes away but does not give back. It is a time when hope dwindles and vulnerability and despair become apparent. Treatment options are limited for this group of people with MS.

The goal of nursing to empower hope takes on a new challenge. The nurse can provide the support to help a person maintain normalcy and maximize abilities. But first the person needs to be able to grieve the losses that accompany progressive MS. "Grief resolution may be needed to prevent the accumulated losses from becoming overwhelming, thereby causing hopelessness" (Miller, 1992, p. 416).

Catherine was always able to handle the changes in her body and the losses in her life caused by MS, but the slow worsening without improvement was dispiriting. She sat slumped in the chair, looking down at the floor.

Body language reflects hopefulness or despair. Eye contact is an example of a positive, nonverbal means of communication. It is likely that a despairing person avoids eye contact, whereas a hopeful person makes eye contact. People express hope in what they wear, how they interact, what they design and construct, how they experience the five senses, even how they enjoy humor. Nurses can assess hope by observing the presence or absence of these expressive behaviors.

Catherine and her family needed supportive counseling to counteract their overwhelming sadness. A referral was made for individual and family counseling.

Working with people with MS and their families closely and over long periods of time allows nurses a unique opportunity to form important connections. Nurses provide a healing presence for people with MS simply by virtue of their nurturing care, empathy, and unconditional support. Nurses are trusted with intimate details of people's lives. They are the "comforters" whose common sense, expertise, and openness give people an opportunity to be authentic.

Nurses inspire hope when they have hope. People with MS and their families constantly borrow from the nurse's wellspring of hope.

It is important to recognize the personal pain and grieving a nurse may experience when a favorite patient declines. The interdisciplinary team approach can provide the support needed to plan ahead and develop interventions that help keep hope alive. Peer support and self-care (Table 14-2) are other important energizers to foster personal hope.

TABLE 14-2. Self-Care Strategies for Nurses Who Care for People with MS

⊃ Savor each moment
⊃ Exercise regularly
⊃ Eat nutritiously
⊃ Network with peers
⊃ Rely on others for guidance when in doubt
⊃ Use your confidant
⊃ Nurture supportive and reciprocal relationships
⊃ Know your limitations
⊃ Expand your knowledge base
⊃ Be inventive
⊃ Share your expertise
⊃ Pamper yourself – massage, facials, manicures, pedicures, etc.
⊃ Try deep breathing, relaxation, yoga, and meditation
⊃ Give yourself something to look forward to each day
⊃ Take vacations

Catherine was scheduled to return to the MS Center one month later. Her plan of care needed revision to include new strategies to empower and sustain hope. She phoned the nurse to say she felt she had made progress with the help of the therapist and was ready to participate in her plan of care. She had stopped taking the injectable drug in order to be considered as a possible participant in a new clinical trial.

Assessment (September 6, 1995)

"I'm afraid I am going to be a burden to my family."

Catherine was guided to think about the things she wanted for herself and her family. She verbalized the importance of her role as a wife and mother and her need to continue to care for her family ("I want my home to be a normal place, and I want my husband and children to be able to count on me"). She also reinforced her commitment to her work and its importance to her sense of self, as well as its financial benefits ("I feel good about what I do, and the salary helps to pay the mortgage").

Foote et al. (1990) looked at hope, self-esteem, and social support as factors that affect well-being in people with MS. The results of this study support a relationship between hope and self-esteem, hope and social support, and self-esteem and social support. The interesting demographic data that emerged from this study showed that those who were employed had higher levels of self-esteem and hope than those who were unemployed. This information suggests the positive effect working can have on the MS population. Nurses can consider ways to help people to remain employed in order to enhance hope.

Supportive and reciprocal relationships with family, friends, and caregivers, as well as feeling connected to a higher being, are hope-sustaining factors that are consistently cited in the literature (Ponce, 1994; Byrne, 1994; Miller, 1992, 1989, 1985; Farran, 1992, 1989; Hinds, 1988; O'Mailley, 1988; Rideout, 1986; Dufault, 1986). Relationships are vital to hope. People center hope on others in order to feel more hopeful or to borrow hope. A small improvement in MS instills hope in the individual as well as in those touched by the illness.

Spiritual well-being inspires hope. People find comfort in religious beliefs and rituals. Spiritual well-being is manifested in expressions of love and trust in oneself, a higher being, or anticipation of a life after death.

Catherine was not practicing a traditional religion, but her spirituality was expressed in her belief in her own power and the power of the love of those around her. She believed in her ability to maintain her roles as a career person, wife, and mother. She valued these roles as crucial aspects for her self-esteem. Her family was bonded by love and trust and were willing participants in her plan of care.

Nursing Diagnosis

Effective Coping: Hope

Catherine was able to see options for herself and was an active participant in her care, which helped to preserve her sense of control. She was motivated to achieve her goals and expected that, with help, she would accomplish her goals. Catherine was open to possibilities for herself, was willing to work for a brighter tomorrow, and cherished her relationship with her family.

Nursing Actions

Education, counseling, and referrals are specific nursing tools to enhance hope in people with MS and their families. Teaching intermittent catheterization to Catherine and her husband in conjunction with medically prescribed anticholinergic drugs would help to eliminate her emptying problem. It would also alleviate the symptoms of urinary urgency and incontinence. A bowel regimen included a high fiber diet in addition to a high fiber supplement taken every night to ease the bowel problems and give her a hopeful sense of being able to live a normal life. These instructions would enable Catherine to work more comfortably, feel more in control of her bladder and bowels, enhance her self-esteem, and free her to concentrate on other matters.

The nurse's counseling was aimed at supporting Catherine's hopeful expressions for the future and guiding her energy toward realistic goals. A family approach capitalized on the hope-sustaining energy of relationships. Catherine and her husband were unsure about how to approach their sexual experience. Sexuality was discussed in terms of intimacy, and they were guided through alternative ways to heighten sexual pleasure, such as touch and oral stimulation. Intimacy is enhanced by touch, and an aura of hopefulness results when touch happens. The nurse suggested that Catherine catheterize about a half an hour before engaging in sexual intercourse in order to prevent incontinence and to heighten her sense of comfort and relaxation. Guided imagery techniques were used to help the couple visualize and fantasize to enhance their sexual experience.

Referrals were made for adaptive equipment for Catherine's use at home and at work. A motorized scooter was ordered so she could "soar" through the shopping sprees that she enjoyed so much. An occupational therapy referral was made for home and work adaptations for easier access. A physical therapist was called to help Catherine with gait training and exercises to maintain strength in the lower and upper extremities. A referral to the local MS Society's water therapy program was made for a class once a week after work. A referral was also made to the New York City's paratransit system, Access-A-Ride, in order to provide Catherine with transportation to and from the workplace.

Expected Outcomes

The outcomes anticipated for Catherine's plan of care were as follows:

- ⊃ Learn to catheterize self in the nurse's office, demonstrate the procedure, and continue performing this intermittently three to four times a day using clean technique.
- ⊃ Experience episodes of urinary incontinence less than once a month.
- ⊃ No incontinence during sexual intercourse.
- ⊃ Bowel pattern normal within one week.
- ⊃ Use relaxation and guided imagery techniques with partner to enhance intimacy.
- ⊃ Verbalize feelings of comfort while experiencing sexual intimacy.
- ⊃ OT to visit home within three days.
- ⊃ OT to visit workplace within one week.
- ⊃ PT to visit home within three days.
- ⊃ Order motorized scooter within two days and deliver in one week.
- ⊃ Attend water therapy sessions once a week beginning October 2, 1995.
- ⊃ Join a peer support group within one month.
- ⊃ Adaptations at the workplace to be completed within one month's time.
- ⊃ Access-A-Ride arranged within next three weeks.
- ⊃ Adaptations in the bathroom (grab bars and shower bench) within two weeks.
- ⊃ Modifications and adaptive devices for the kitchen within two weeks.

Evaluation

Catherine learned to self-catheterize at the MS Center and showed excellent clean technique. Her husband also demonstrated an ability to catheterize successfully using clean technique. Catherine is experiencing rare episodes of urinary incontinence (less than one time per month) and wears a protective pad to insure dryness. She is able to catheterize herself three to four times a day and reports being free of incontinence during sexual intercourse. Catherine verbalizes comfort with relaxation and imagery techniques and reports enhanced joy when being intimate with her husband. Catherine's bowel pattern was regular within three days of her visit and the symptoms of bowel urgency and incontinence subsided with the regimen recommended.

Catherine's bathroom was adapted with grab bars and a shower bench the week after her visit, making bathing easier and safer. Kitchen modifications were in place two weeks later and included rearranging cupboards for easier access, adding a cutting board table so she could sit to prepare meals, and a reacher to grab items that were difficult to reach.

Catherine's workplace was modified by converting the office next-door into a testing room to limit the distance she was walking. Her employer and co-workers have been supportive and open to learning more about MS and ways to help Catherine continue at her job. A representative of the MS Society arranged a class and presented information about MS to Catherine's boss and co-workers. Access-A-Ride was implemented and has been reliable in getting Catherine to and from her Manhattan office. A motorized scooter was ordered and Catherine was taught how to operate the device by the OT.

Catherine and her husband have become members of a peer support group that meets for an hour once a week. Through this network they have expanded their social support and met others who have prevailed despite the difficulties imposed by MS.

Catherine is able to express more confidence in herself and believes she can go on with her life despite the limits imposed by MS. She will be screened for a new study, which she sees as an opportunity to help not only herself, but also others with MS. Her outlook is a hopeful one that is shared by other members of this very special family. Nursing care will continue to search for creative and innovative ways to insure Catherine a hope-filled life with MS.

Acknowledgment. The author wishes to thank Mary Ellen McCann, MA, RN, for her inspiration and support.

REFERENCES

Anonymous (1993). *Hope.* Fort Worth, TX: Brownlow Publishing Co.

American heritage dictionary of the English language, Third edition. Boston: Houghton Mifflin Co., 1992.

Barton, J., Magilvy, J., Quinn, A. (1994). Maintaining the fighting spirit: veterans living with multiple sclerosis. *Rehabilitation Nursing, 3 (3),* 86–96.

Byrne, C., Woodside, H., et.al. (1994). The importance of relationships in fostering hope. *Journal of Psychosocial Nursing, 32 (9),* 31–34.

Callan, D. (1989). Hope as a clinical issue in oncology social work. *Journal of Psychosocial Oncology, 7 (3),* 31–46.

Dufault, K., Martocchio, B. (1985). Hope: its spheres and dimensions, *Nursing Clinics of North America, 20,* 379–91.

Farran, C., McCann, J. (1989). Longitudinal analysis of hope in community-based older adults. *Archives of Psychiatric Nursing, 3 (5),* 272–76.

Farran, C., Wilken, C., Popovich, J. (1992). Clinical assessment of hope. *Issues in Mental Health, 13,* 129–38.

Fischer, J., Crawford, P. (1994). Emotional aspects of multiple sclerosis. *Multiple Sclerosis Clinical Issues, 2 (1),* 6–9.

Foote, A., et al. (1990). Hope, self-esteem and social support in persons with multiple sclerosis. *Journal of Neuroscience Nursing, 22 (3),* 155–59.

Forsyth, G., Delaney, K., Greshan, M. (1984). Vying for a winning position: management style of the chronically ill. *Research in Nursing and Health, 7,* 181–88.

Fromm, E. (1968). *The revolution of hope – toward a humanized technology.* New York: Harper and Row.

Herth, K. (1991). Development and refinement of an instrument to measure hope. *Scholarly Inquiry for Nursing Practice, 5 (1),* 39–56.

Hinds, P., Martin, J. (1988). Hopefulness and the self-sustaining process in adolescents with cancer. *Nursing Research, 37 (6),* 336–40.

Korner, I. (1970). Hope as a method of coping. *Journal of Consulting and Clinical Psychology, 34 (2),* 134–39.

Kubler-Ross, E. (1969). *On death and dying.* New York: Macmillan.

Long, D., Miller, B. (1991). Suicidal tendency and multiple sclerosis. *Health and Social Work, 16 (2),* 104–109.

Lynch, W. (1965). *Images of hope.* Baltimore: Helicon Press.

Marcel, G. (1962). *Homo Viator* (E. Craufard, trans.). New York: Harper and Row.

McGee, R. (1984). Hope: a factor influencing crisis resolution. *Advances in Nursing Science, 6 (4),* 34–44.

Miller, J. (1985). Inspiring hope. *American Journal of Nursing, 85 (1),* 23–25.

Miller, J. (1989). Hope—inspiring strategies of the critically ill. *Applied Nursing Research, 2 (1),* 23–29.

Miller, J. (1992). *Coping with chronic illness: overcoming powerlessness,* Second Edition. Philadelphia: F.A. Davis Company.

Morgante, L., McCann, M.E. (1992). "The energy and power of hope." (unpublished manuscript.)

O'Mailley, P., Menke, E. (1988). Relationship of hope and stress after myocardial infarction. *Heart and Lung, 17 (2),* 184–90.

Poncar, P. (1994). Inspiring hope. *Journal of Psychosocial Nursing, 32 (1),* 33–38.

Rideout, E., Monterurom, M. (1986). Hope, morale and adaptation in patients with chronic heart failure. *Journal of Advanced Nursing, 11,* 429–38.

Stotland, E. (1969). *The psychology of hope.* San Francisco: Jossey-Bass.

APPENDIX **A***

Resources

There is a vast array of resources available to help you to assist your patients with multiple sclerosis. This list is by no means a complete one; it is designed as a starting point in your efforts to identify the resources you need to help your patients.

Nursing Organizations

American Academy of Nurse Practitioners, (Capitol Station LBJ Bldg., P.O. Box 12846, Austin, TX 78711, tel: 512-463-6930); American College of Nurse Practitioners (2401 Pennsylvania Avenue N.W., Suite 900, Washington, DC 20006, tel: 202-466-4825. National Alliance of Nurse Practitioners, 325 Pennsylvania Avenue S.E., Washington, DC 20003, tel: 202-675-6350.

Three national organizations representing nurse practitioners. Activities include legislative awareness, advocacy, professional education, and certification and/or recognition of advanced practice nurses.

American Association of Neuroscience Nurses (224 N. Des Plaines, Suite 60, Chicago, IL 60661, tel: 312-993-0043). This organization focuses on neurologic and neurosurgical conditions and techniques, both nursing and technological, which enhance patients' quality of

---

* Modified from *Multiple Sclerosis: The Questions You Have—The Answers You Need* edited by Rosalind C. Kalb. New York: Demos Vermande, 1996.

life and survival. Annual meetings and a professional journal are offered to members and interested nurses

American Association of Spinal Cord Injury Nurses (AASCIN), (75-20 Astoria Blvd), Jackson Heights, NY 11370-1177, tel: 718-803-3782). Although its focus is on spinal cord injury, this organization focuses on research and education with many common concerns with multiple sclerosis

American Nurses Association (600 Maryland Avenue S.W., Suite 100W, Washington, DC 20024-2571, tel: 800-274-4262). The national organization for nurses which offers a wide array of educational, research, and legislative services. In addition, ANCC, a branch of ANA, offers opportunities for certification in nursing specialties

American Society of Neurorehabilitation. (2221 University Avenue S.E., Suite 360, Minneapolis, MN 55414, tel: 612-623-2405). ASNR's membership consists of physicians and non-physicians whose practice is devoted to patients with neurologic disease. ASNR publishes a journal, has an annual meeting, and holds certification courses for specialists.

Association of Rehabilitation Nurses (ARN), (5700 Old Orchard Road, first floor, Skokie, IL 60077-1057, tel: 708-966-3433). The ARN is an international organization of professional rehabilitation nurses. ARN offers a wide range of professional activities that help develop the professional skills of rehabilitation nurses. Included in these are educational conferences, seminars throughout the year, certification examinations, and support of research.

Nurse Practitioner Associates for Continuing Education (NPACE), (5 Militia Drive, Lexington, MA 02173, tel: 617-861-0270). NPACE conducts educational seminars for advanced practice nurses throughout the year.

Respiratory Nursing Society (RNS) (5700 Old Orchard Road, first floor, Skokie, IL 60077-1057, tel: 708-966-3433). RNS is the professional association for nurses who care for clients with pulmonary dysfunction and who are interested in the promotion of pulmonary health.

The Society of Urologic Nurses and Associates, (E. Holly Avenue, Box 56, Pitman, NJ 08071-0056). A specialty group of nurses with a focus on urologic management problems.

Visiting Nurse Associations of America (VNAA), (3801 East Florida Avenue, Suite 900, Denver, CO 80210, tel: 800-426-2547). VNAA is a national non-profit, community-based organization of home health care providers.

Medical Organizations

American Academy of Neurology, (2221 University Avenue S.E., Suite 335, Minneapolic, MN 55414, tel: 612-623-8115). Representing neurologists throughout North America, the AAN has recently established new membership criteria for nurses who specialize in care of the neurologically impaired patient.

American Neurologic Association, (5841 Cedar Lake Road, #108, Minneapolis, MN 55416, tel: 612-545-6284.) The ANA offers membership to neurologists with an academic emphasis.

Information Sources

Accent on Information (P.O. Box 700, Bloomington, IL 61702, tel: 304-378-2961). A computerized retrieval system of information for the disabled about problems relating to activities of daily living and home management. There is a small charge for a basic search and photocopies, but disabled persons unable to pay are never denied services.

Canadian Rehabilitation Council for the Disabled (CRCD) (45 Sheppard Avenue East, Suite 801, Toronto, Ontario M2N 5W9, Canada, tel: 416-250-7490). The Council is a federation of regional and provincial groups serving individuals with disabilities throughout Canada. It operates an information service and publishes a newsletter and a quarterly journal.

Clearinghouse on Disability Information, Office of Special Education and Rehabilitative Services, U.S. Department of Education, Switzer Building, 330 C Street, S.W., Washington, DC 20202, tel: 202-205-8241. Created by the Rehabilitation Act of 1973, the Clearinghouse responds to inquiries about federal laws, services, and programs for individuals of all ages with disabilities. Their quarterly magazine, "OSERS News in Print," is available free of charge.

Disability Rights Center (1616 P Street, N.W., Suite 435, Washington, DC 20036, tel: 202-328-5198). The DIRS provides information about services available to people with disabilities and their families. Through its computerized database, DIRS provides information from both the public and private sectors.

Eastern Paralyzed Veterans Association (EPVA), (75-20 Astoria Boulevard, Jackson Heights, NY 11370, tel: 718-803-3782). EPVA is a private, non-profit organization dedicated to serving the needs of its members and people with disabilities through programs such as benefits services, hospital liaison, sports and recreation, wheelchair repair, information, and referral. EPVA also supports three professional organizations: the American Paraplegia Society, the American Association of Spinal Cord Injury Nurses, and the American Association of Spinal Cord Injury Psychologists and Social Workers. EPVA produces newsletters and journals.

HealthTalk Interactive (800-335-2500). An MS education network is available twenty-four hours a day, providing various kinds of information, including answers to commonly asked questions, a replay of a recent "Living with MS" live broadcast, and presentations on various aspects of symptom management.

Information Center and Library, National Multiple Sclerosis Society (733 Third Avenue, New York, NY 10017, tel: 800-FIGHT MS). The Center will answer questions and send you publications of the Society as well as copies of published articles on any topics related to MS.

Inglis House (2600 Belmont Avenue, Philadelphia, PA 19131, tel: 215-878-5600). A national information exchange network specializing in long-term facilities for mentally alert persons with physical disabilities.

National Health Information Center (P.O. Box 1133, Washington, DC 20013, tel: 800-336-4797). The Center maintains a library and a database of health-related organizations. It also provides referrals related to health issues for consumers and professionals.

President's Committee on Employment of the Handicapped (1111 20th Street N.W. 6th floor, Washington, DC 20036, tel: 202-635-5010). The President's Committee publishes and distributes free pamphlets, publications, and posters covering such topics as education, employment, accessibility, and adapting the worksite. The Committee also publishes "Disabled USA."

Rehabilitation Research Institute (Academic Center T-605, George Washington University, Washington, DC 20502, tel: 202-676-2624). The Institute develops and disseminates materials for rehabilitation professionals and the general public. Publications include annotated bibliographies and cover topics such as attitudinal barriers, employment rights, recreation, and sexual disability.

Electronic Information Sources

One of the most flexible ways to obtain information on multiple sclerosis is by using a computer and a modem. It is possible to dial a number of services that provide access to information about MS. These include the "big three" online services—America OnLine, CompuServe, and Prodigy (see below for customer service numbers). If you are not currently a subscriber and would like information on how to join, call one or more of these numbers. If you are a subscriber, you can access information about MS by entering one of the commands listed below.

Some of these sources of information are available only if you are a subscriber to the service. However, there are also many sources of information available free through the Internet on the World Wide Web. For example, the National Multiple Sclerosis Society has a home page on the World Wide Web at: http://www.nmss.org/. The other sources of MS information on the World Wide Web are too numerous to list. If you are an experienced "net surfer," switch to your favorite search facility and enter the keywords "MS" or "multiple sclerosis." This will generally give you a listing of dozens of web sites that pertain to MS. Keep in mind, however, that the World Wide Web is a free and open medium; while many of the web sites have excellent and useful information, others may contain highly unusual and inaccurate information.

⇨ *America OnLine:* 800-827-6364 (GO TO NMSS).
⇨ *CompuServe:* 800-487-6227 (GO MULTSCLER).
⇨ *Prodigy:* 800-776-3449 (JUMP MS FORUM).

On the Internet: Access USENET NEWSGROUP-ALT.SUPPORT.MULT-SCLEROSIS.

Resource Materials

Assistive Technology Sourcebook. (Written by A. Enders and M. Hall, published by Resna Press, Washington, DC 1990).

The Complete Directory for People with Disabilities. (Edited by L. Mackenzie, published by Grey House Publishing Inc., Lakeville, CT).

Complete Drug Reference. (Compiled by United States Pharmacopoeia, published by Consumer Report Books, A division of Consumers Union, Yonkers, NY). This comprehensive, readable, and easy-to-use drug reference includes almost every prescription and non-prescription medication available in the United States and Canada. A new edition is published yearly.

Directory of National Information Sources on Disabilities. (Published by the National Institute on Disability and Rehabilitation Research, Washington, DC 1994-1995. Vols. I and II).

Exceptional Parent: Parenting Your Child or Young Adult with a Disability. A magazine for families and professionals. (Exceptional Parent, P.O. Box 3000, Dept. EP, Denville, NJ 07834, tel: 800-247-8080. A monthly magazine that celebrated its 25th anniversary by producing the 1996 Resource Guide, which includes 10 directories with more than 1,000 resources in the United States and Canada. This is a very useful directory for adults with disabilities as well.

Living with Low Vision: A Resource Guide for People with Sight Loss. (Resources for Rehabilitation, 33 Bedford Street, Suite 19A, Lexington, MA 02173, tel: 617-862-6455). The only large-print comprehensive guide to services and products designed to assist individuals with vision loss throughout North America.

Resources for People with Disabilities and Chronic Conditions. (Resources for Rehabilitation, 33 Bedford Street, Suite 19A, Lexington, MA 02173, tel: 617-862-6455). A comprehensive resource guide covering a variety of disabling conditions as well as general information on rehabilitation services, assistive technology for independent living, and laws that affect people with disabilities.

Resource Directory for the Disabled. (Written by R.N. Shrout, published by Facts-on-File, 460 Park Avenue South, New York, NY 10016; 1991). A resource directory that includes associations and organizations, government agencies, libraries and research centers, publications, and products of all types for disabled individuals.

Agencies and Organizations

American Self-Help Clearinghouse (St. Clares-Riverside Medical Center, Denville, NJ 07834, tel: 201-625-7101). The Clearinghouse makes referrals to national self-help organizations as well as individual self-help groups for various problems. They also provide referrals to local self-help clearinghouses.

Beach Center on Families and Disabilities (c/o Life Span Institute, University of Kansas, 3111 Haworth Hall, Lawrence, KS 66045, tel: 913-864-7600). The federally funded Center conducts research and training about the functioning of families in which one member is disabled. They have a publications catalog relating to family coping, professional roles, and service delivery. They offer a free newsletter, "Families and Disability."

Consortium of Multiple Sclerosis Centers (CMSC) (c/o Gimbel MS Center at Holy Name Hospital, 718 Teaneck Road, Teaneck, NJ 07666, tel: 201-837-0727). The CMSC is made up of numerous MS centers throughout the United States and Canada. The Consortium's mission is to disseminate information to clinicians, increase resources and opportunities for research, and advance the standard of care for multiple sclerosis. The CMSC is a multidisciplinary organization, bringing together health care professionals from many fields involved in MS patient care.

Department of Veterans Affairs (VA) (810 Vermont Avenue, N.W., Washington, DC 20420, tel: 202-328-5198). The VA provides a wide range of benefits and services to those who have served in the armed forces, their dependents, beneficiaries of deceased veterans, and dependent children of veterans with severe disabilities.

Equal Employment Opportunity Commission (EEOC) (1801 L Street, N.W., 10th floor, Washington, DC 20507, tel: 800-669-3362 (to order publications 800-669-4000; to speak to an investigator 202-663-4900). The EEOC is responsible for monitoring the section of the ADA on employment regulations. Copies of the regulations are available.

Eastern Paralyzed Veterans Association (EPVA) (75-20 Astoria Boulevard, Jackson Heights, NY 11370, tel: 718-803-EPVA). EPVA is a private, non-profit organization dedicated to serving the needs of its members as well as other people with disabilities. While offering a wide range of benefits to member veterans with spinal cord dysfunction (including hospital liaison, sports and recreation, wheelchair repair, adaptive architectural consultations, research and educational services, communications, and library and information services; they will also provide brochures and information on a variety of subjects, free of charge to the general public.

Handicapped Organized Women (HOW) (P.O. Box 35481, Charlotte, NC 28235, tel: 704-376-4735). HOW strives to build self-esteem and confidence among disabled women by encouraging volunteer community involvement. HOW seeks to train disabled women for leadership positions and works in conjunction with the National Organization of Women (NOW).

Multiple Sclerosis Society of Canada (250 Bloor Street East, Suite 820, Toronto, Ontario M4W 3P9, Canada, tel: 416-922-6065; in Canada: 800-268-7582). A national organization that funds research, promotes public education, and produces publications in both English and French. They provide an "ASK MS Information System" database of articles on a wide variety of topics including treatment, research, and social services. Regional divisions and chapters are located throughout Canada.

Health Resource Center for Women with Disabilities (Rehabilitation Institute of Chicago, Chicago, IL 60612, tel: 312-908-7997). The Center is a project run by and for women with disabilities. It publishes a free newsletter, "Resourceful Women," and offers support groups and educational seminars addressing issues from a disabled woman's perspective. Among its many educational resources, the Center has developed a video on mothering with a disability.

National Council on Disability (NCOD) (800 Independence Avenue, S.W., Suite 814, Washington, DC 20591, tel: 202-267-3846). The Council is an independent federal agency whose role is to study and make recommendations about public policy for people with disabilities. Publishes a free newsletter, "Focus."

National Family Caregivers Association (NFCA) (9621 East Bexhill Drive, Kensington, MD 20895, tel: 301-942-6430). NFCA is dedicated to improving the quality of life of America's 18,000,000 caregivers. It publishes a quarterly newsletter, and has a resource guide, an information clearinghouse, and a toll-free hotline: 800-896-3650.

National Multiple Sclerosis Society (NMSS) (733 Third Avenue, New York, NY 10017, tel: 800-FIGHT MS). The NMSS funds both basic and health services research. An office of professional education programs maintains a speakers' bureau and supports professional education programs in the individual chapters. Chapters and branches of the Society provide direct services to people with MS and their families, including information and referral, counseling, equipment loan, and social and recreational support programs. The National Office will put you in touch with your closest chapter. The Information Center and Library is available to answer questions and provide a wide range of educational materials, as well as reprints of articles written about MS.

Office on the Americans with Disabilities Act (Department of Justice, Civil Rights Division, P.O. Box 66118, Washington, DC 20035, tel: 202-514-0301). This office is responsible for enforcing the ADA. To order copies of its regulations, call 202-514-6193.

Paralyzed Veterans of America (PVA) (801 Eighteenth Street N.W., Washington, DC 20006, tel: 800-424-8200). PVA is a national information and advocacy agency working to restore function and quality of life for veterans with spinal cord dysfunction. It supports and funds education and research and has a national advocacy program that focuses on accessibility issues. PVA publishes brochures on many issues related to rehabilitation.

Social Security Administration (6401 Security Boulevard, Baltimore, MD 21235, tel: 800-772-1213). To apply for social security benefits based on disability, call this office or visit your local social security branch office. The Office of Disability within the Social Security Administration publishes a free brochure entitled, "Social Security Regulations: Rules for Determining Disability and Blindness."

Well Spouse Foundation (P.O. Box 801, New York, NY 10023, tel: 212-724-7209). An emotional support network for people married to or living with a chronically ill partner. Advocacy for home health and long-term care and a newsletter are among the services offered.

Assistive Technology

Access to Recreation: Adaptive Recreation Equipment for the Physically Challenged (2509 E. Thousand Oaks Boulevard, Suite 430, Thousand Oaks, CA 91362, tel: 800-634-4351). Products include exercise equipment and assistive devices for sports, environmental access, games, crafts, and hobbies.

adaptABILITY (Department 2082, Norwich Avenue, Colchester, CT 06415, tel: 800-243-9232). A free catalog of assistive devices and self-care equipment designed to enhance independence.

American Automobile Association (1712 G Street N.W., Washington, DC 20015). The AAA will provide a list of automobile hand-control manufacturers.

AT&T Special Needs Center (2001 Route 46, Parsippany, NJ 07054, tel: 800-233-1222). A catalog of special telephone equipment for individuals with physical disabilities.

Enrichments (P.O. Box 5050, Bolingbrook, IL 60440, tel: 800-323-5547). A free catalog of assistive devices and self-care equipment designed to enhance independence.

Medic Alert Foundation International (P.O. Box 1009, Turlock, CA 95380, tel: 800-344-3226; 209-668-3333). A medical identification tag worn to identify a person's medical condition, medications, and any other important information that might be needed in case of an emergency. A file of the person's health data is maintained in a central database to be accessed by a physician or other emergency personnel who need to know the person's pertinent medical information.

National Rehabilitation Information Center (NARIC) (8455 Colesville Road, Silver Spring, MD 20910, tel: 800-346-2742; 301-588-9284; fax: 301-587-1967). NARIC is a library and information center on disability and rehabilitation, funded by the National Institute on Disability and Rehabilitation Research (NIDRR). NARIC operates two databases—ABLEDATA and REHABDATA. NARIC collects and disseminates the results of federally funded research projects and has a collection that includes commercially published books, journal articles, and audiovisual materials. NARIC is committed to serving both professionals and consumers who are interested in disability and rehabilitation. Information specialists can answer simple information requests and provide referrals immediately and at no cost. More complex database searches are available at nominal cost.

ABLEDATA (8455 Colesville Road Suite 935, Silver Spring, MD 20910, tel: 301;588-9284; 800-227-0216; fax: 301-589-3563. ABLEDATA is a national database of information on assistive technology designed to enable persons with disabilities to identify and locate the devices that will assist them in their home, work, and leisure activities. Information specialists are available to answer questions during regular business hours. ABLE INFORM BBS is available twenty-four hours a day to customers with a computer, modem, and telecommunications software.

REHABDATA (8455 Colesville Road, Suite 935, Silver Spring, MD 20910, tel: 301-588-9284; 800-346-2742). REHABDATA is a database containing bibliographic records with abstracts and summaries of the materials contained in the NARIC (National Rehabilitation Information Information Center) library of disability rehabilitation materials. Information specialists are available to conduct a database search on any rehabilitation related topic.

RESNA (1101 Connecticut Avenue N.W., Suite 700, Washington, DC 20036, tel: 202-857-1199). RESNA is an international association for the advancement of rehabilitation technology. Their objectives are to improve the quality of life for the disabled through the application of science and technology and to influence policy relating to the delivery of technology to disabled persons. They will respond by mail to specific questions about modifying existing equipment and designing new devices.

Sears Home Health Care Catalog (P.O. Box 3123, Naperville, IL 60566, tel: 800-326-1750). The catalog includes medical equipment such as hospital beds, commodes, and wheelchairs, as well as adaptive clothing.

Sentry Detection Corporation (exclusive Westinghouse distributor) (tel: 800-695-0110). The company will install a Life Alert system (separately or as part of a total home security system) that allows a disabled person to get immediate assistance in the event of an emergency.

Environmental Adaptations

A Consumer's Guide to Home Adaptation (Adaptive Environments Center, 374 Congress Street, Suite 301, Boston, MA 02210, tel: 617-695-1225). A workbook for planning adaptive. home modifications such as lowering kitchen countertops and widening doorways.

"Adapting the Home for the Physically Challenged" (A/V Health Services, P.O. Box 1622, West Sacramento, CA 95691, tel: 703-389-4339). A 22-minute videotape that describes home modifications for individuals who use walkers or wheelchairs. Ramp construction and room modification specifications are included.

American Institute of Architects (AIA) (1735 New York Avenue, N.W., Washington, DC 20006, tel: 800-365-2724; publications catalog and orders: 202-626-7300). This organization will make referrals to architects who are familiar with the design requirements of people with disabilities.

Barrier-Free Design Centre (2075 Bayview Avenue, Toronto, Ontario M4N 3M5, Canada, tel: 416-480-6000). The Centre provides information and technical consultation in barrier-free design for Canadians with physical disabilities.

Financing Home Accessibility Modifications (Center for Accessible Housing, North Carolina State University, Box 8613, Raleigh, NC 27695, tel: 919-515-3082). This publication identifies state and local sources of financial assistance for homeowners (or tenants) who need to make modifications in their homes.

GE Answer Center (9500 Williamsburg Plaza, Louisville, KY 40222, tel: 800-626-2000). The Center, which is open twenty-four hours a day, seven days a week, offers assistance to individuals with disabilities as well as the general public. They offer two free brochures, "Appliance Help for Those with Special Needs," and "Basic Kitchen Planning for the Physically Handicapped."

National Association of Home Builders (NAHB) (National Research Center, Economics and Policy Analysis Division, 400 Prince George's Boulevard, Upper Marlboro, MD 20772, tel: 301-249-4000). The Research Center produces publications and provides training on housing and special needs. A publication entitled "Homes for a Lifetime" includes an accessibility checklist, financing options, and recommendations for working with builders and remodelers.

National Kitchen and Bath Association (687 Willow Grove Street, Hackettstown, NJ 07840, tel: 908-852-0033). The Association produces a technical manual of barrier-free planning and has directories of certified designers and planners.

Travel

ACCESS: The Foundation for Accessibility by the Disabled (P.O. Box 356, Malverne, NY 11565, tel: 516-887-5798). ACCESS is a clearinghouse for travel services and information on accessibility for the physically disabled. They publish monographs pertaining to travel and accessibility, and will assist in finding resources and services for individuals and corporations.

Directory of Travel Agencies for the Disabled. (Written by Helen Hecker, published by Twin Peaks Press, P.O. Box 129, Vancouver, WA 98666-0129). This directory lists travel agents who specialize in arranging travel plans for people with disabilities.

The Disability Bookshop (P.O. Box 129, Vancouver, WA 98666, tel: 800-637-2256). The Disability Bookshop has an extensive list of books for disabled travelers, dealing with such topics as accessibility, travel agencies, accessible van rentals, medical resources, air travel, and guides to national parks.

Information for Handicapped Travelers (available free of charge from the National Library Service for the Blind and Physically Handicapped, 1291 Taylor Street, N.W., Washington, DC 20542, tel: 800-424-8567; 202-707-5100). A booklet providing information about travel agents, transportation, and information centers for individuals with disabilities.

Society for the Advancement of Travel for the Handicapped (SATH) (347 Fifth Avenue, Suite 610, New York, NY 10016, tel: 212-447-7284). SATH is a non-profit organization that acts as a clearinghouse for accessible tourism information and is in contact with organization in many countries to promote the development of facilities for disabled people. SATH publishes a quarterly magazine, "Access to Travel."

Travel for the Disabled: A Handbook of Travel Resources and 500 Worldwide Access Guides. (Written by Helen Hecker, published by Twin Peaks Press, P.O. Box 129, Vancouver, WA 98666, tel: 800-637-2256). The handbook provides information for disabled travelers about accessibility.

Travel Industry and Disabled Exchange (TIDE) (5435 Donna Avenue, Tarzana, CA 91356, tel: 818-343-6339). The Exchange assists disabled individuals to travel throughout the world. A quarterly newsletter is available to members.

Travel Information Service (Moss Rehabilitation Hospital, 1200 West Tabor Road, Philadelphia, PA 19141, tel: 456-4603). The Service provides information and referrals for people with disabilities.

Travelin' Talk (P.O. Box 3534, Clarksville, TN 37043, tel: 615-552-6670). A network of more than one thousand people and organizations around the world who are willing to provide assistance to travelers with disabilities and share their knowledge about the areas in which they live. Travelin' Talk publishes a newsletter by the same name and has an extensive resource directory.

The Wheelchair Traveler (Accent on Living, P.O. Box 700, Bloomington, IL 61702, tel: 309-378-2961). A directory that provides ratings of hotels and motels in the United States.

Wilderness Inquiry (1313 5th Street, S.E., Box 84, Minneapolis, MN 55414, tel: 800-728-0719; 612-379-3858). Wilderness Inquiry sponsors trips into the wilderness for people with disabilities or chronic conditions.

Visual Impairment

Canadian National Institute for the Blind (CNIB) (1931 Bayview Avenue, Toronto, Ontario M4G 4C8, Canada, tel: 416-480-7580). The Institute provides counseling and rehabilitation services for Canadians with any degree of functional visual impairment. They offer public information literature and operate resource and technology centers. The national office has a list of provincial and local CNIB offices.

The Lighthouse Low Vision Products Consumer Catalog (36-20 Northern Boulevard, Long Island City, NY 11101, tel: 800-829-0500). This large-print catalog offers a wide range of products designed to help people with impaired vision.

The Library of Congress, Division for the Blind and Physically Handicapped (1291 Taylor Street, N.W., Washington, DC 20542, tel: 800-424-8567; 800-424-9100; for application: 202-287-5100). The Library Service provides free talking book equipment on loan as well as a full range of recorded books for individuals with disabilities or visual impairment. It also provides a variety of free library services through one hundred forty cooperating libraries.

Living with Low Vision: A Resource Guide for People with Sight Loss. (Published by Resources for Rehabilitation, 33 Bedford Street, Suite 19A, Lexington, MA 02173, tel: 617-862-6455). A comprehensive directory designed to help individuals with impaired vision to locate the products and services they need in order to remain independent.

Products for People with Vision Impairment Catalog. (American Foundation for the Blind Product Center, P.O. Box 7044, 100 Enterprise Place, Dover, DE 19903, tel: 800-829-0500). The Catalog is available in standard print and audiocassette.

Publishing Companies Specializing in Health and Disability Issues

Demos Vermande (386 Park Avenue South, Suite 201, New York, NY 10016, tel: 800-532-8663).

Resources for Rehabilitation (33 Bedford Street, Suite 19A, Lexington, MA 02173, tel: 617-862-6455).

Twin Peaks Press (P.O. Box 129, Vancouver, WA 98666, tel: 800-637-2256).

Woodbine House (Publishers of the Special-Needs Collection) (6510 Bells Mill Road, Bethesda, MD 20817, tel: 301-897-3570; 800-843-7323).

Medications Commonly Used in Multiple Sclerosis

The information sheets are intended as a patient's guide to drugs commonly used in the treatment and management of multiple sclerosis. They describe the ways in which each medication is most often prescribed in MS, as well as precautions to be noted and the side effects that may occur with their use. Those side effects that could possibly be confused with symptoms of multiple sclerosis are marked with an asterisk.

The information contained in these sheets will help your patients to be more informed about the medications they are taking and therefore more able to discuss their questions and concerns with their physician. This information should never be used as a substitute for professional instructions and recommendations.

The following guidelines will help your patients to manage their medication regime:

- ⊃ Make sure that your physician knows your medical history, including all medical conditions for which you are currently being treated and any allergies you have.
- ⊃ Tell your physician if you are breast-feeding, currently pregnant, or planning to become pregnant in the near future.

*Reprinted with permission of the publisher from *Multiple Sclerosis: The Questions You Have— The Answers You Need* edited by Rosalind C. Kalb. New York: Demos Vermande, 1996.

⊃ Make a list of all of the drugs you are currently taking—including both prescription and over-the-counter medications—and provide your physician with a copy for your medical chart.

⊃ Take your medications only as your physician prescribes them for you. If you have questions about the recommended dosage, ask your physician.

⊃ Unless otherwise instructed, store medications in a cool, dry place; exposure to heat or moisture may cause the medication to break down. Liquid medications that are stored in the refrigerator should not be allowed to freeze.

⊃ Unless otherwise directed by your physician or pharmacist, the general instructions concerning a missed dose of medication are as follows: if you miss a dose, take it as soon as possible. However, if it is almost time for your next dose, skip the one you missed and go back to the regular dosing schedule. Do not double dose.

⊃ Keep all medications out of the reach of children.

Index of Medications

Prescription

Alprostadil
Amantadine
Amitriptyline
Baclofen
Carbamazepine
Ciprofloxacin
Clonazepam
Desmopressin
Diazepam
Fluoxetine
Imipramine
Interferon beta-1a
Interferon beta-1b
Meclizine

Methenamine
Methylprednisolone
Oxybutynin
Papavarine
Paroxetine
Pemoline
Phenazopyridine
Phenytoin
Prednisone
Propantheline bromide
Sertraline
Sulfamethoxazole and
   trimethoprim combination

Non-Prescription
(Over-the-Counter)

Bisacodyl (Dulcolax)—
   tablet or suppository
Docusate (Colace)
Docusate mini enema
   (Therevac Plus)
Glycerin suppository
Magnesium hydroxide
   (Phillips' Milk of Magnesia)

Mineral oil
Psyllium hydrophilic
   mucilloid (Metamucil)
Sodium phosphate
   (Fleet Enema)

Chemical Name: Alprostadil (al-**pross**-ta-dill); also called Prostaglandin E1

Brand Name: Prostin VR (U.S. and Canada)

Generic Available: No

Description: Alprostadil belongs to a group of medicines called vasodilators, which cause blood vessels to expand, thereby increasing blood flow. When alprostadil is injected into the penis, it produces an erection by increasing blood flow to the penis.

Proper Usage

⊃ Alprostadil should never be used as a sexual aid by men who are not impotent. If improperly used, this medication can cause permanent damage to the penis.

⊃ Alprostadil is available by prescription and should be used only as directed by your physician, who will instruct you in the proper way to give yourself an injection so that it is simple and essentially pain-free.

⊃ Alprostadil is sometimes used in combination with a medicine called phentolamine (Regitine—U.S.; Rogitine—Canada).

Precautions

⊃ Do not use more of this medicine or use it more often than it has been prescribed for you. Using too much of this medicine will result in a condition called priapism, in which the erection lasts too long and does not resolve when it should. Permanent damage to the penis can occur if blood flow to the penis is cut off for too long a period of time.

Possible Side Effects

⊃ Side effects that you should report to your physician so he or she can adjust the dosage or change the medication: pain at the injection site; burning or aching during erection.

⊃ Rare side effects that require immediate attention: erection continuing for more than four hours. If you cannot be seen immediately by your physician, you should go to the emergency room for prompt treatment.

Chemical Name: Amantadine (a-**man**-ta-deen)

Brand Name: Symmetrel (U.S. and Canada)

Generic Available: Yes (U.S.)

Description: Amantadine is an antiviral medication used to prevent or treat certain influenza infections; it is also given as an adjunct for the treatment of Parkinson's disease. It has been demonstrated that this medication, through some unknown mechanism, is sometimes effective in relieving fatigue in multiple sclerosis.

Proper Usage

⊃ The usual dosage for the management of fatigue in MS is 100 to 200 mg daily, taken in the earlier part of the day in order to avoid sleep disturbance. Doses in excess of 300 mg daily usually cause livedo reticularis, a blotchy discoloration of the skin of the legs.

Precautions

The precautions listed here pertain to the use of this medication as an antiviral or Parkinson's disease treatment. There are no reports at this time concerning the precautions in the use of the drug to treat fatigue in multiple sclerosis.

⊃ Drinking alcoholic beverages while taking this medication may cause increased side effects such as circulation problems, dizziness, lightheadedness, fainting, or confusion. Do not drink alcohol while taking this medication.

⊃ This medication may cause some people to become dizzy, confused, or lightheaded, or to have blurred vision or trouble concentrating.

⊃ Amantadine may cause dryness of the mouth and throat. If your mouth continues to feel dry for more than two weeks, check with your physician or dentist since continuing dryness may increase the risk of dental disease.

⊃ This medication may cause purplish red, net-like, blotchy spots on the skin. This problem occurs more often in females and usually occurs on the legs and/or feet after amantadine has been taken regularly for a month or more. The blotchy spots usually go away within two to twelve weeks after you stop taking the medication.

⊃ Studies of the effects of amantadine in pregnancy have not been done in humans. Studies in some animals have shown that amantadine is harmful to the fetus and causes birth defects.

⊃ Amantadine passes into breast milk. However, the effect of amantadine in newborn babies and infants is not known.

Possible Side Effects

The side effects listed here pertain to the use of amantadine as an antiviral or Parkinson's disease treatment. There are no reports at the present time of the side effects associated with the use of this drug in the treatment of MS-related fatigue.

- ⊃ Side effects that may go away as your body adjusts to the medication and do not require medical attention unless they continue or are bothersome: difficulty concentrating; dizziness; headache; irritability; loss of appetite; nausea; nervousness; purplish red, net-like, blotchy spots on skin; trouble sleeping or nightmares; constipation*; dryness of the mouth; vomiting.

- ⊃ Rare side effects that should be reported as soon as possible to your physician: blurred vision*; confusion; difficult urination*; fainting; hallucinations; convulsions; unusual difficulty in coordination*; irritation and swelling of the eye; mental depression; skin rash; swelling of feet or lower legs; unexplained shortness of breath.

*Since it may be difficult to distinguish between certain common symptoms of MS and some side effects of amantadine, be sure to consult your health care professional if an abrupt change of this type continues for more than a few days.

Chemical Name: Amitriptyline (a-mee-**trip**-ti-leen)

Brand Name: Elavil (U.S. and Canada)

Generic Available: Yes (U.S. and Canada)

Description: Amitriptyline is a tricyclic antidepressant used to treat mental depression. In multiple sclerosis, it is frequently used to treat painful paresthesias in the arms and legs (e.g., burning sensations, pins and needles, stabbing pains) caused by damage to the pain regulating pathways of the brain and spinal cord.

Note: Other tricyclic antidepressants are also used for the management of neurologic pain symptoms. Clomipramine (Anafranil—U.S. and Canada), desipramine (Norpramin—U.S. and Canada), doxepin (Sinequan—U.S. and Canada), imipramine (Tofranil—U.S. and Canada), nortriptyline (Pamelor—U.S.; Aventyl—Canada), trimipramine (U.S. and Canada). While each of these medications is given in different dosage levels, the precautions and side effects listed for amitriptyline apply to these other tricyclic medications as well.

Precautions

⊃ Amitriptyline adds to the effects of alcohol and other central nervous system depressants (e.g., antihistamines, sedatives, tranquilizers, prescription pain medications, seizure medications, muscle relaxants, sleeping medications), possibly causing drowsiness. Be sure that your physician knows if you are taking these or other medications.

⊃ This medication causes dryness of the mouth. Because continuing dryness of the mouth may increase the risk of dental disease, alert your dentist that you are taking amitriptyline.

⊃ This medication may cause your skin to be more sensitive to sunlight than it is normally. Even brief exposure to sunlight may cause a skin rash, itching, redness or other discoloration of the skin, or severe sunburn.

⊃ This medication may affect blood sugar levels of diabetic individuals. If you notice a change in the results of your blood or urine sugar tests, check with your physician.

⊃ Do not stop taking this medication without consulting your physician. The physician may want you to reduce the amount you are taking gradually in order to reduce the possibility of withdrawal symptoms such as headache, nausea, and/or an overall feeling of discomfort.

⊃ Studies of amitriptyline have not been done in pregnant women. There have been reports of newborns suffering from muscle spasms and heart, breathing, and urinary problems when their mothers had taken tricyclic antidepressants immediately before delivery. Studies in animals have indicated the possibility of unwanted effects in the fetus.

⊃ Tricyclics pass into breast milk. Only doxepin (Sinequan) has been reported to cause drowsiness in the nursing baby.

Possible Side Effects

⊃ Side effects that may go away as your body adjusts to the medication and do not require medical attention unless they continue for more than two weeks or are bothersome: dryness of mouth; constipation*; increased appetite and weight gain; dizziness; drowsiness*; decreased sexual ability*; headache; nausea; unusual tiredness or weakness*; unpleasant taste; diarrhea; heartburn; increased sweating; vomiting.

⊃ Uncommon side effects that should be reported to your physician as soon as possible: blurred vision*; confusion or delirium; difficulty speaking or swallowing*; eye pain*; fainting; hallucinations; loss of balance control*; nervousness or restlessness; problems urinating*; shakiness or trembling; stiffness of arms and legs*.

⊃ Rare side effects that should be reported to your physician as soon as possible: anxiety; breast enlargement in males and females; hair loss; inappropriate secretion of milk in females; increased sensitivity to sunlight; irritability; muscle twitching; red or brownish spots on the skin; buzzing or other unexplained sounds in the ears; skin rash, itching; sore throat and fever; swelling of face and tongue; weakness*; yellow skin.

⊃ Symptoms of acute overdose: confusion; convulsions; severe drowsiness*; enlarged pupils; unusual heartbeat; fever; hallucinations; restlessness and agitation; shortness of breath; unusual tiredness or weakness; vomiting.

*Since it may be difficult to distinguish between certain common symptoms of MS and some side effects of amitriptyline, be sure to consult your health care professional if an abrupt change of this type occurs.

Chemical Name: Baclofen (**bak**-loe-fen)

Brand Name: Lioresal (U.S. and Canada)

Generic Available: Yes (U.S. and Canada)

Description: Baclofen acts on the central nervous system to relieve spasms, cramping, and tightness of muscles caused by spasticity in multiple sclerosis. It is usually administered orally in pill form. Recently, an intrathecal delivery system (via a surgically implanted pump) has been approved for those individuals with significant spasticity who cannot tolerate a sufficiently high dose of the oral form of the medication.

Proper Usage

➲ People with MS are usually started on an initial dose of 5 mg every six to eight hours. If necessary, the amount is increased by 5 mg per dose every five days until symptoms improve. The goal of treatment is to find a dosage level that relieves spasticity without causing excessive weakness or fatigue. The effective dose may vary from 15 mg to 160 mg per day or more.

Precautions

➲ If you are taking more than 30 mg daily, do not stop taking this medication suddenly. Stopping high doses of this medication abruptly can cause convulsions, hallucinations, increases in muscle spasms or cramping, mental changes, or unusual nervousness or restlessness. Consult your physician about how to reduce the dosage gradually before stopping the medication completely.

➲ This drug adds to the effects of alcohol and other CNS depressants (such as antihistamines, sedatives, tranquilizers, prescription pain medications, seizure medications, other muscle relaxants), possibly causing drowsiness. Be sure that your physician knows if you are taking these or other medications.

➲ Studies of birth defects with baclofen have not been done with humans. Studies in animals have shown that baclofen, when given in doses several times higher than the amount given to humans, increases the chance of hernias, incomplete or slow development of bones in the fetus, and lower birth weight.

➲ Baclofen passes into the breast milk of nursing mothers but has not been reported to cause problems in nursing infants.

Possible Side Effects

➲ Side effects that typically go away as your body adjusts to the medication and do not require medical attention unless they continue for several weeks or are bothersome: drowsiness or unusual tiredness*; increased weakness*; dizziness or lightheadedness; confusion; unusual constipation*; new or unusual bladder symptoms*; trouble sleeping; unusual unsteadiness or clumsiness*.

⊃ Unusual side effects that require immediate medical attention: fainting; hallucinations; severe mood changes; skin rash or itching.

⊃ Symptoms of overdose: sudden onset of blurred or double vision*; convulsions; shortness of breath or troubled breathing; vomiting.

*Since it may be difficult to distinguish between certain common symptoms of MS and some side effects of baclofen, be sure to consult your health care professional if an abrupt change of this type occurs.

Chemical Name: Bisacodyl (bis-a-**koe**-dill)

Brand Name: Dulcolax—tablet or suppository (U.S.); Bisacolax—tablet or suppository (Canada)

Generic Available: Yes (U.S. and Canada)

Description: Bisacodyl is an over-the-counter stimulant laxative that can be used in either oral or suppository form. Stimulant laxatives encourage bowel movements by increasing the muscle contractions in the intestinal wall that propel the stool mass. Although stimulant laxatives are popular for self-treatment, they are more likely to cause side effects than other types of laxatives.

Proper Usage

⊃ Laxatives are to be used to provide short-term relief only, unless otherwise directed by the nurse or physician who is helping you to manage your bowel symptoms. A regimen that includes a healthy diet containing roughage (whole grain breads and cereals, bran, fruit, and green, leafy vegetables), six to eight full glasses of liquids each day, and some form of daily exercise is most important in stimulating healthy bowel function.

⊃ If your physician has recommended this laxative for management of constipation, follow his or her recommendations for its use. If you are treating yourself for constipation, follow the directions on the package insert.

⊃ The tablet form of this laxative is usually taken on an empty stomach in order to speed results. The tablets are coated to allow them to work properly without causing stomach irritation or upset. Do not chew or crush the tablets or take them within an hour of drinking milk or taking an antacid.

⊃ A bedtime dose usually produces results the following morning. Be sure to consult your physician if you experience problems or do not get relief within a week.

Precautions

⊃ Do not take any laxative if you have signs of appendicitis or inflamed bowel (e.g., stomach or lower abdominal pain, cramping, bloating, soreness, nausea, or vomiting). Check with your physician as soon as possible.

⊃ Do not take any laxative for more than one week unless you have been told to do so by your physician. Many people tend to overuse laxatives, which often leads to dependence on the laxative action to produce a bowel movement. Discuss the use of laxatives with your health care professional in order to ensure that the laxative is used effectively as part of a comprehensive, healthy bowel management regimen.

⊃ Do not take any laxative within two hours of taking other medication because the desired effectiveness of the other medication may be reduced.

⊃ If you are pregnant, discuss with your physician the most appropriate type of laxative for you to use.

⊃ Some laxatives pass into breast milk. Although it is unlikely to cause problems for a nursing infant, be sure to let your physician know if you are using a laxative and breast-feeding at the same time.

Possible Side Effects

⊃ Side effects that may go away as your body adjusts to the medication and do not require medical attention unless they persist or are bothersome: belching; cramping; diarrhea; nausea.

⊃ Unusual side effects that should be reported to your physician as soon as possible: confusion; irregular heartbeat; muscle cramps; skin rash, unusual tiredness or weakness.

Chemical Name: Carbamazepine (kar-ba-**maz**-e-peen)

Brand Name: Tegretol (U.S. and Canada)

Generic Available: Yes (U.S.)

Description: Carbamazepine is used to relieve shock-like pain, such as the facial pain caused by trigeminal neuralgia (tic douloureux).

Proper Usage

➲ It is very important that you take this medicine exactly as directed by your physician in order to obtain the best results and lessen the chance of serious side effects.

➲ Carbamazepine is not an ordinary pain reliever. It should be used only when your physician prescribes it for certain types of pain. Do not take this medication for other aches or pains.

➲ If you miss a dose of this medication, take it as soon as possible. If it is almost time for your next dose, skip the missed dose and go back to your regular dosing schedule. Do not double dose. If you miss more than one dose in a day, check with your physician.

➲ It is very important that your physician check your progress at regular intervals. Your physician may want to have certain tests done to see if you are receiving the correct amount of medication or to check for certain side effects of which you might be unaware.

Precautions

➲ Carbamazepine adds to the effects of alcohol and other central nervous system depressants that may cause drowsiness (e.g., antihistamines, sedatives, tranquilizers, prescription pain medications, seizure medications, muscle relaxants). Be sure that your physician knows if you are taking these or other medications.

➲ Some people who take carbamazepine may become more sensitive to sunlight than they are normally. Exposure to sunlight, even for brief periods of time, may cause a skin rash, itching, redness or other discoloration of the skin, or severe sunburn.

➲ Oral contraceptives (birth control pills) that contain estrogen may not work properly while you are taking carbamazepine. You should use an additional or alternative form of birth control while taking this drug.

➲ Carbamazepine affects the urine sugar levels of diabetic patients. If you notice a change in the results of your urine sugar tests, check with your physician.

➲ Before having any medical tests or any kind of surgical, dental, or emergency treatment, be sure to let the health care professional know that you are taking this medication.

➲ Carbamazepine has not been studied in pregnant women. There have been reports of babies having low birth weight, small head size, skull and facial defects, underdeveloped fingernails, and delays in growth when their mothers had taken carbamazepine in high doses during pregnancy. Studies in animals have shown that carbamazepine causes birth defects when given in large doses.

➲ Carbamazepine passes into breast milk, and the baby may receive enough of it to cause unwanted effects. In animal studies, carbamazepine has affected the growth and appearance of nursing babies.

Possible Side Effects

➲ Side effects that typically go away as your body adjusts to the medication and do not require medical attention unless they continue for several weeks or are bothersome: clumsiness or unsteadiness*; mild dizziness*; mild drowsiness*; lightheadedness; mild nausea or vomiting; aching joints or muscles; constipation*; diarrhea; dryness of mouth; skin sensitivity to sunlight; irritation of mouth or tongue; loss of appetite; loss of hair; muscle or abdominal cramps; sexual problems in males*.

➲ Check with your physician as soon as possible if any of the following side effects occur: blurred or double vision*; confusion; agitation; severe diarrhea, nausea, or vomiting; skin rash or hives; unusual drowsiness; chest pain; difficulty speaking or slurred speech*; fainting; frequent urination*; unusual heartbeat; mental depression or other mood or emotional changes; unusual numbness, tingling, pain, or weakness in hands or feet*; ringing or buzzing in ears; sudden decrease in urination; swelling of face, hands, feet, or lower legs; trembling; uncontrolled body movements; visual hallucinations.

➲ Check with your physician immediately if any of the following occur: black tarry stools or blood in urine or stools; bone or joint pain; cough or hoarseness; darkening of urine; nosebleeds or other unusual bleeding or bruising; painful or difficult urination; tenderness, swelling, or bluish color in leg or foot; pale stools; pinpoint red spots on skin; shortness of breath or cough; sores, ulcers, or white spots on lips or in the mouth; sore throat, chills, and fever; swollen glands; unusual tiredness or weakness*; wheezing, tightness in chest; yellow eyes or skin.

➲ Symptoms of overdose that require immediate attention: unusual clumsiness or unsteadiness*; severe dizziness or fainting; fast or irregular heartbeat; unusually high or low blood pressure; irregular or shallow breathing; severe nausea or vomiting; trembling, twitching, and abnormal body movements.

*Since it may be difficult to distinguish between certain common symptoms of MS and some side effects of carbamazepine, be sure to consult your health care professional if an abrupt change of this type occurs.

Chemical Name: Ciprofloxacin (sip-roe-**flox**-a-sin) combination

Brand Name: Cipro (U.S. and Canada)

Generic Available: No

Description: Ciprofloxacin is one of a group of antibiotics (fluoro-quinolones) used to kill bacterial infection in many parts of the body. It is used in multiple sclerosis primarily to treat urinary tract infections.

Proper Usage

◌ This medication is best taken with a full glass (eight ounces) of water. Additional water should be taken each day to help prevent some unwanted effects.

◌ Ciprofloxacin may be taken with meals or on an empty stomach.

◌ Finish the full course of treatment prescribed by your physician. Even if your symptoms disappear after a few days, stopping this medication prematurely may result in a return of the symptoms.

◌ This medication works most effectively when it is maintained at a constant level in your blood or urine. To help keep the amount constant, do not miss a dose. It is best to take the doses at evenly spaced times during the day and night.

Precautions

◌ This medication may cause some people to become dizzy, light-headed, drowsy, or less alert.

◌ If you are taking antacids that contain aluminum or magnesium, be sure to take them at least two hours before or after you take ciprofloxacin. These antacids may prevent the ciprofloxacin from working properly.

◌ This medication may cause your skin to become more sensitive to sunlight. Stay out of direct sunlight during the midday hours, wear protective clothing, and apply a sun block product that has a skin protection factor (SPF) of at least 15.

◌ Studies of birth defects have not been done in humans. This medication is not recommended during pregnancy since antibiotics of this type have been reported to cause bone development problems in young animals.

◌ Some of the antibiotics in this group are known to pass into human breast milk. Since they have been reported to cause bone development problems in young animals, breast-feeding is not recommended during treatment with this medication.

Possible Side Effects

- ⊃ Side effects that may go away as your body adjusts to the medication and do not require medical attention unless they continue or are bothersome: abdominal or stomach pain; diarrhea; dizziness; drowsiness*; headache; lightheadedness; nausea or vomiting; nervousness; trouble sleeping.

- ⊃ Rare side effects that should be reported to your physician immediately: agitation; confusion; fever; hallucinations; peeling of the skin; shakiness or tremors*; shortness of breath; skin rash; itching; swelling of face or neck.

*Since it may be difficult to distinguish between certain common symptoms of MS and some side effects of ciprofloxacin, be sure to consult your health care professional if an abrupt change of this type occurs.

Chemical Name: Clonazepam (kloe-**na**-ze-pam)

Brand Name: Klonopin (U.S.); Rivotril; Syn-Clonazepam (Canada)

Generic Available: No

Description: Clonazepam is a benzodiazepine that belongs to the group of medications called central nervous system depressants, which slow down the nervous system. Although clonazepam is used for a variety of medical conditions, it is used in multiple sclerosis primarily for the treatment of tremor, pain, and spasticity.

Proper Usage

⊃ Keep this medication out of the reach of children. An overdose of this medication may be especially dangerous for children.

Precautions

⊃ During the first few months taking clonazepam, your physician should check your progress at regular visits to make sure that this medicine does not cause unwanted effects.

⊃ Take this medication only as directed by your physician; do not increase the dose without a prescription to do so.

⊃ Clonazepam adds to the effects of alcohol and other central nervous system depressants (e.g., antihistamines, sedatives, tranquilizers, prescription pain medications, seizure medications, muscle relaxants, sleeping medications). Consult your physician before taking any of these CNS depressants while you are taking clonazepam. Taking an overdose of this medication or taking it with alcohol or other CNS depressants may lead to unconsciousness and possibly death.

⊃ Stopping this medication suddenly may cause withdrawal side effects. Reduce the amount gradually before stopping completely.

⊃ Clonazepam frequently causes people to become drowsy, dizzy, lightheaded, clumsy, or unsteady. Even if taken at bedtime, it may cause some people to feel drowsy or less alert on awakening.

⊃ Studies in animals have shown that clonazepam can cause birth defects or other problems, including death of the animal fetus.

⊃ Overuse of clonazepam during pregnancy may cause the baby to become dependent on it, leading to withdrawal side effects after birth. The use of clonazepam, especially during the last weeks of pregnancy, may cause breathing problems, muscle weakness, difficulty in feeding, and body temperature problems in the newborn infant.

⊃ Clonazepam may pass into breast milk and cause drowsiness, slow heartbeat, shortness of breath, or troubled breathing in nursing babies.

Possible Side Effects

⊃ Side effects that may go away during treatment as your body adjusts to the medication and do not require medical attention unless they continue for several weeks or are bothersome: drowsiness or tiredness; clumsiness or unsteadiness*; dizziness or lightheadedness; slurred speech*; abdominal cramps or pain; blurred vision or other changes in vision*; changes in sexual drive or performance*; gastrointestinal changes, including constipation* or diarrhea; dryness of mouth; fast or pounding heartbeat; muscle spasm*; trouble with urination*; trembling.

⊃ Unusual side effects that should be discussed as soon as possible with your physician: behavior problems, including difficulty concentrating and outbursts of anger; confusion or mental depression; convulsions; hallucinations; low blood pressure; muscle weakness; skin rash or itching; sore throat, fever, chills; unusual bleeding or bruising; unusual excitement or irritability.

⊃ Symptoms of overdose that require immediate emergency help: continuing confusion; severe drowsiness; shakiness; slowed heartbeat; shortness of breath; slow reflexes; continuing slurred speech*; staggering*; unusual severe weakness*.

*Since it may be difficult to distinguish between certain common symptoms of MS and some side effects of clonazepam, be sure to consult your health care professional if an abrupt change of this type occurs.

Chemical Name: Desmopressin (des-moe-**press**-in)

Brand Name: DDAVP Nasal Spray (U.S. and Canada)

Generic Available: No

Description: Desmopressin is a hormone used as a nasal spray. The hormone works on the kidneys to control frequent urination.

Proper Usage

⊃ Keep this medication in the refrigerator but do not allow it to freeze.

Precautions

⊃ Let your physician know if you have heart disease, blood vessel disease, or high blood pressure. Desmopressin can cause an increase in blood pressure.

⊃ Studies have not been done in pregnant women. It has been used before and during pregnancy to treat diabetes mellitus and has not been shown to cause birth defects.

⊃ Desmopressin passes into breast milk but has not been reported to cause problems in nursing infants.

Possible Side Effects

⊃ Side effects that typically go away as your body adjusts to the medication and do not require medical attention unless they continue for several weeks or are bothersome: runny or stuffy nose; abdominal or stomach cramps; flushing of the skin; headache; nausea; pain in the vulva.

⊃ Unusual side effects that require immediate medical attention: confusion; convulsions; unusual drowsiness*; continuing headache; rapid weight gain; markedly decreased urination.

*Since it may be difficult to distinguish between certain common symptoms of MS and some side effects of desmopressin, be sure to consult your health care professional if an abrupt change of this type occurs.

Chemical Name: Diazepam (dye-**az**-e-pam)

Brand Name: Valium (U.S. and Canada)

Generic Available: Yes (U.S.)

Description: Diazepam is a benzodiazepine that belongs to the group of medicines called central nervous system depressants, which slow down the nervous system. Although diazepam is used for a variety of medical conditions, it is used in multiple sclerosis primarily for the relief of muscle spasms and spasticity.

Proper Usage

⊃ Keep this medication out of the reach of children. An overdose of this medication may be especially dangerous for children.

Precautions

⊃ Your physician should check your progress at regular visits to make sure that this medication does not cause unwanted effects.

⊃ Take diazepam only as directed by your physician; do not increase the dose without a prescription to do so.

⊃ Diazepam adds to the effects of alcohol and other central nervous system depressants (e.g., antihistamines, sedatives, tranquilizers, prescription pain medications, seizure medications, muscle relaxants, sleeping medications). Consult your physician before taking any of these CNS depressants while you are taking diazepam. Taking an overdose of this medication or taking it with alcohol or other CNS depressants may lead to unconsciousness and possibly death.

⊃ Stopping this medication suddenly may cause withdrawal side effects. Reduce the amount gradually before stopping completely.

⊃ Diazepam may cause some people to become drowsy, dizzy, lightheaded, clumsy, or unsteady. Even if taken at bedtime, it may cause some people to feel drowsy or less alert on awakening.

⊃ The use of diazepam during the first three months of pregnancy has been reported to increase the chance of birth defects.

⊃ Overuse of diazepam during pregnancy may cause the baby to become dependent on the medicine, leading to withdrawal side effects after birth. The use of diazepam, especially during the last weeks of pregnancy, may cause breathing problems, muscle weakness, difficulty in feeding, and body temperature problems in the newborn infant. When diazepam is given in high doses (especially by injection) within fifteen hours before delivery, it may cause breathing problems, muscle weakness, difficulty in feeding, and body temperature problems in the newborn infant.⊃ Diazepam may pass into breast milk and cause drowsiness, slow heartbeat, shortness of breath, or troubled breathing in nursing babies.

Possible Side Effects

➲ Side effects that may go away during treatment as your body adjusts to the medication and do not require medical attention unless they continue for several weeks or are bothersome: clumsiness or unsteadiness*; dizziness or lightheadedness; slurred speech*; abdominal cramps or pain; blurred vision or other changes in vision*; changes in sexual drive or performance*; constipation*; diarrhea; dryness of mouth; fast or pounding heartbeat; muscle spasm*; trouble with urination*; trembling*; unusual tiredness or weakness*.

➲ Unusual side effects that should be discussed with your physician as soon as possible: behavior problems, including difficulty concentrating and outbursts of anger; confusion or mental depression; convulsions; hallucinations; low blood pressure; muscle weakness*; skin rash or itching; sore throat, fever, chills; unusual bleeding or bruising; unusual excitement or irritability.

➲ Symptoms of overdose that require immediate emergency help: continuing confusion; unusually severe drowsiness; shakiness; slowed heartbeat; shortness of breath; slow reflexes; continuing slurred speech; staggering; unusually severe weakness*.

*Since it may be difficult to distinguish between certain common symptoms of MS and some side effects of diazepam, be sure to consult your health care professional if an abrupt change of this type occurs.

Chemical Name: Docusate (**doe**-koo-sate)

Brand Name: Colace (U.S. and Canada)

Generic Available: Yes (U.S. and Canada)

Description: Docusate is an over-the-counter stool softener (emollient) that helps liquids to mix into dry, hardened stool, making the stool easier to pass.

Proper Usage

➲ Laxatives are to be used to provide short-term relief only, unless otherwise directed by the nurse or physician who is helping you to manage your bowel symptoms. A regimen that includes a healthy diet containing roughage (whole grain breads and cereals, bran, fruit, and green, leafy vegetables), six to eight full glasses of liquids each day, and some form of daily exercise is most important in stimulating healthy bowel function.

➲ If your physician has recommended this laxative for management of constipation, follow his or her recommendations for its use. If you are treating yourself for constipation, follow the directions on the package insert.

➲ Results usually occur one to two days after the first dose; some individuals may not get results for three to five days. Be sure to consult your physician if you experience problems or do not get relief within a week.

Precautions

➲ Do not take any type of laxative if you have signs of appendicitis or inflamed bowel (e.g., stomach or lower abdominal pain, cramping, bloating, soreness, nausea, or vomiting). Check with your physician as soon as possible.

➲ Do not take any laxative for more than one week unless you have been told to do so by your physician. Many people tend to overuse laxatives, which often leads to dependence on the laxative action to produce a bowel movement. Discuss the use of laxatives with your health care professional in order to ensure that the laxative is used effectively as part of a comprehensive, healthy bowel management regimen.

➲ Do not take mineral oil within two hours of taking docusate. The docusate may increase the amount of mineral oil that is absorbed by the body.

➲ Do not take any laxative within two hours of taking another medication because the desired effectiveness of the other medication may be reduced.

➲ If you are pregnant, discuss with your physician the most appropriate type of laxative for you to use.

➲ Some laxatives pass into breast milk. Although it is unlikely to cause problems for a nursing infant, be sure to let your physician know if you are using a laxative and breast-feeding at the same time.

Possible Side Effects

➲ Side effects that may go away as your body adjusts to the medication and do not require medical attention unless they persist or are bothersome: stomach and/or intestinal cramping.

➲ Unusual side effect that should be reported to your physician as soon as possible: skin rash.

Chemical Name: Fluoxetine (floo-**ox**-uh-teen)

Brand Name: Prozac (U.S. and Canada)

Generic Available: No

Description: Fluoxetine is used to treat mental depression. It is also used occasionally to treat MS fatigue.

Proper Usage

⊃ This medication should be taken in the morning when used to treat depression because it can interfere with sleep. If it upsets your stomach, you may take it with food.

Precautions

⊃ It may take four to six weeks for you to feel the beneficial effects of this medication.

⊃ Your physician should monitor your progress at regularly scheduled visits in order to adjust the dose and help reduce any side effects.

⊃ There have been suggestions that the use of fluoxetine may be related to increased thoughts about suicide in a very small number of individuals. More study is needed to determine if the medicine causes this effect. If you have concerns about this, be sure to discuss them with your physician.

⊃ Fluoxetine adds to the effects of alcohol and other central nervous system depressants (e.g., antihistamines, sedatives, tranquilizers, sleeping medicine, prescription pain medicine, barbiturates, seizure medication, muscle relaxants). Be sure that your physician knows if you are taking these or any other medications.

⊃ This medication affects the blood sugar levels of diabetic individuals. Check with your physician if you notice any changes in your blood or urine sugar tests.

⊃ Dizziness or lightheadedness may occur, especially when you get up from a lying or sitting position. Change positions slowly to help alleviate this problem. If the problem continues or gets worse, consult your physician.

⊃ Fluoxetine may cause dryness of the mouth. If your mouth continues to feel dry for more than two weeks, check with your physician or dentist. Continuing dryness of the mouth may increase the chance of dental disease.

⊃ Studies have not been done in pregnant women. Fluoxetine has not been shown to cause birth defects or other problems in animal studies.

⊃ Fluoxetine passes into breast milk and may cause unwanted effects, such as vomiting, watery stools, crying, and sleep problems in nursing babies. You may want to discuss alternative medications with your physician.

Possible Side Effects

⊃ Side effects that may go away as your body adjusts to the medication and do not require medical attention unless they continue for several weeks or are bothersome: decreased sexual drive or ability*; anxiety and nervousness; diarrhea; drowsiness*; headache; trouble sleeping; abnormal dreams; change in vision*; chest pain; decreased appetite; decrease in concentration; dizziness; dry mouth; fast or irregular heartbeat; frequent urination*; menstrual pain; tiredness or weakness*; tremor*; vomiting.

⊃ Unusual side effects that should be discussed with your physician as soon as possible: chills or fever; joint or muscle pain; skin rash; hives or itching; trouble breathing.

⊃ Symptoms of overdose that require immediate medical attention: agitation and restlessness; convulsions; severe nausea and vomiting; unusual excitement.

*Since it may be difficult to distinguish between certain common symptoms of MS and some side effects of fluoxetine, be sure to consult your health care professional if an abrupt change of this type occurs.

Chemical Name: Glycerin (**gli**-ser-in)

Brand Name: Sani-Supp suppository (U.S.)

Generic Available: Yes (U.S. and Canada)

Description: A glycerin suppository is a hyperosmotic laxative that draws water into the bowel from surrounding body tissues. This water helps to soften the stool mass and promote bowel action.

Proper Usage

⊃ Laxatives are to be used to provide short-term relief only, unless otherwise directed by the nurse or physician who is helping you to manage your bowel symptoms. A regimen that includes a healthy diet containing roughage (whole grain breads and cereals, bran, fruit, and green, leafy vegetables), six to eight full glasses of liquids each day, and some form of daily exercise is most important in stimulating healthy bowel function.

⊃ If your physician has recommended this laxative for management of constipation, follow his or her recommendations for its use. If you are treating yourself for constipation, follow the directions on the package insert.

⊃ If the suppository is too soft to insert, refrigerate it for thirty minutes or hold it under cold water before removing the foil wrapper.

⊃ Glycerin suppositories often produce results within fifteen minutes to one hour. Be sure to consult your physician if you experience problems or do not get relief within a week.

Precautions

⊃ Do not take any type of laxative if you have signs of appendicitis or inflamed bowel (e.g., stomach or lower abdominal pain, cramping, bloating, soreness, nausea, or vomiting). Check with your physician as soon as possible.

⊃ Do not take any laxative for more than one week unless you have been told to do so by your physician. Many people tend to overuse laxatives, which often leads to dependence on the laxative action to produce a bowel movement. Discuss the use of laxatives with your health care professional in order to ensure that the laxative is used effectively as part of a comprehensive, healthy bowel management regimen.

⊃ If you are pregnant, discuss with your physician the most appropriate type of laxative for you to use.

⊃ Use only water to moisten the suppository prior to insertion in the rectum. Do not lubricate the suppository with mineral oil or petroleum jelly, which might affect the way the suppository works.

Possible Side Effects

➲ Side effects that may go away as your body adjusts to the medication and do not require medical attention unless they persist or are bothersome: skin irritation around the rectal area.

➲ Less common side effects that should be reported to your physician as soon as possible: rectal bleeding; blistering, or itching.

Chemical Name: Imipramine (im-**ip**-ra-meen)

Brand Name: Tofranil (U.S. and Canada)

Generic Available: Yes (U.S. and Canada)

Description: Imipramine is a tricyclic antidepressant used to treat mental depression. Its primary use in multiple sclerosis is to treat bladder symptoms, including urinary frequency and incontinence. Imipramine is also prescribed occasionally for the management of neurologic pain in MS.

Proper Usage

➲ To lessen stomach upset, take this medication with food, even for a daily bedtime dose, unless your physician has told you to take it on an empty stomach.

Precautions

➲ Imipramine adds to the effects of alcohol and other central nervous system depressants (e.g., antihistamines, sedatives, tranquilizers, prescription pain medications, seizure medications, muscle relaxants, sleeping medications), possibly causing drowsiness. Be sure that your physician knows if you are taking these or any other medications.

➲ This medication causes dryness of the mouth. Because continuing dryness of the mouth can increase the risk of dental disease, alert your dentist if you are taking imipramine.

➲ Imipramine may cause your skin to be more sensitive to sunlight than it is normally. Even brief exposure to sunlight may cause a skin rash, itching, redness or other discoloration of the skin, or severe sunburn. Stay out of the sun during the midday hours. Wear protective clothing and a sun block that has a skin protection factor (SPF) of at least 15.

➲ This medication may affect blood sugar levels of diabetic individuals. If you notice a change in the results of your blood or urine sugar tests, check with your physician.

➲ Do not stop taking imipramine without consulting your physician. The physician may want you to reduce the amount you are taking gradually in order to reduce the possibility of withdrawal symptoms such as headache, nausea, and/or an overall feeling of discomfort.

➲ Studies of imipramine have not been done in pregnant women. There have been reports of newborns suffering from muscle spasms and heart, breathing, and urinary problems when their mothers had taken tricyclic antidepressants immediately before delivery. Studies in animals have indicated the possibility of unwanted effects in the fetus.

◇ Imipramine passes into breast milk but has not been reported to have any effect on the nursing infant.

Possible Side Effects

⊃ Side effects that may go away as your body adjusts to the medication and do not require medical attention unless they continue for more than two weeks or are bothersome: dizziness; drowsiness*; headache; decreased sexual ability*; increased appetite; nausea; unusual tiredness or weakness*; unpleasant taste; diarrhea; heartburn; increased sweating; vomiting.

⊃ Uncommon side effects that should be reported to your physician as soon as possible: blurred vision*; confusion or delirium; constipation*; difficulty speaking or swallowing; eye pain*; fainting; fast or irregular heartbeat; hallucinations; loss of balance control*; nervousness or restlessness; problems urinating*; shakiness or trembling; stiffness of arms and legs*.

⊃ Rare side effects that should be reported to your physician as soon as possible: anxiety; breast enlargement in males and females; hair loss; inappropriate secretion of milk in females; increased sensitivity to sunlight; irritability; muscle twitching; red or brownish spots on the skin; buzzing or other unexplained sounds in the ears; skin rash; itching; sore throat and fever; swelling of face and tongue; weakness*; yellow skin.

⊃ Symptoms of acute overdose: confusion; convulsions; severe drowsiness*; enlarged pupils; unusual heartbeat; fever; hallucinations; restlessness and agitation; shortness of breath; unusual tiredness or weakness*; vomiting.

*Since it may be difficult to distinguish between certain common symptoms of MS and some side effects of imipramine, be sure to consult your health care professional if an abrupt change of this type occurs.

Chemical Name: Interferon beta-1a

Brand Name: Avonex (U.S.—approval in Canada is pending)

Generic Available: No

Description: Avonex is a medication manufactured by a biotechnological process from one of the naturally occurring interferons (a type of protein). It is made up of exactly the same amino acids (major components of proteins) as the natural interferon beta found in the human body. In a clinical trial of 380 ambulatory patients with relapsing-remitting MS, those taking the currently recommended dose of the medication had a reduced risk of disability progression, experienced fewer exacerbations, and showed a reduction in number and size of active lesions in the brain (as shown on MRI) when compared with the group taking a placebo.

Proper Usage

➲ Avonex is given as a once-a-week intramuscular (IM) injection, usually in the large muscles of the thigh, upper arm, or hip. If your physician decides that you or a care partner can safely administer the injection, you will be taught how to reconstitute the medication (mix the sterile powder with the sterile water that is packaged with it) and instructed in safe and proper IM injection procedures. If you are unable to self-inject, and have no family member or friend available to do the injections, the injections will be given by your physician or nurse. Do not attempt to mix the medication or inject yourself until you are sure that you understand the procedures.

➲ Avonex must be kept cold. Be sure to store it in a refrigerator both before and after the medication is mixed for injection. Do not expose the medication to high temperatures (in a glove compartment or on a window sill, for example) and do not allow it to freeze. Once the medication has been mixed for use, it is recommended that you administer the injection as soon as possible; the reconstituted powder should not be used once it has been stored in the refrigerator longer than six hours.

➲ Do not reuse needles or syringes. Dispose of the syringes as directed by your physician and keep them out of the reach of children.

➲ Since flu-like symptoms are a fairly common side effect during the initial weeks of treatment, it is recommended that the injection be given at bedtime. Taking acetaminophen (Tylenol®) or ibuprofen (Advil®) immediately prior to each injection and during the 24 hours following the injection will also help to relieve the flu-like symptoms.

Precautions

○ Avonex should not be used during pregnancy or by any woman who is trying to become pregnant. Women taking Avonex should use birth control measures at all times. If you want to become pregnant while being treated with Avonex, discuss the matter with your physician. If you become pregnant while using Avonex, stop the treatment and contact your physician.

○ There was no increase in depression reported by people receiving Avonex in the clinical trial. However, since depression and suicidal thoughts are known to occur with some frequency in MS, and depression and suicidal thoughts have been reported with high doses of various interferon products, it is recommended that individuals with a history of severe depressive disorder be closely monitored while taking Avonex.

○ Prior to starting treatment with Avonex, alert your physician if you have any prior history of a seizure disorder.

○ Prior to starting treatment with Avonex, alert your physician if you have any history of cardiac disease, including angina, congestive heart failure, or arrhythmia.

Possible Side Effects

○ Common side effects include flu-like symptoms (fatigue, chills, fever, muscle aches, and sweating). Most of these symptoms will tend to disappear after the initial few weeks of treatment. If they continue, become more severe, or cause you significant discomfort, be sure to talk them over with your physician.

○ Symptoms of depression, including ongoing sadness, anxiety, loss of interest in daily activities, irritability, low self-esteem, guilt, poor concentration, indecisiveness, confusion, and eating and sleep disturbances, should be reported promptly to your doctor.

Avonex Support Line: 800-456-2255

Chemical Name: Interferon beta-1b

Brand Name: Betaseron (U.S. and Canada)

Generic Available: No

Description: Betaseron is a medication manufactured by a biotechnological process from one of the naturally occurring interferons (a type of protein). In a clinical trial of 372 ambulatory patients with relapsing-remitting MS, those taking the currently recommended dose of the medication experienced fewer exacerbations, a longer time between exacerbations, and exacerbations that were generally less severe than those of patients taking a lower dose of the medication or a placebo. Additionally, patients on interferon beta-1b had no increase in total lesion area, as shown on MRI, in contrast to the placebo group, which had a significant increase.

Proper Usage

➲ Betaseron is injected subcutaneously (between the fat layer just under the skin and the muscles beneath) every other day. The physician or nurse will instruct you in the preparation of the medication for injection and the injection procedure itself, using a specially designed set of training materials. Do not attempt to inject yourself until you are sure that you understand the procedures.

➲ Betaseron must be kept cold. Be sure to store it in a refrigerator before and after the medication is mixed for injection.

➲ Do not reuse needles or syringes. Dispose of the syringes as directed by your physician and keep them out of the reach of children.

➲ Since flu-like symptoms are a common side effect associated with at least the initial weeks of taking Betaseron, it is recommended that the medication be taken at bedtime. Taking acetaminophen (Tylenol®) or ibuprofen (Advil®) thirty minutes before each injection will also help to relieve the flu-like symptoms.

➲ Because injection site reactions (swelling, redness, discoloration, or pain) are relatively common, it is recommended that the sites be rotated according to a schedule provided for you by your physician.

Precautions

➲ Betaseron should not be used during pregnancy or by any woman who is trying to become pregnant. Women taking Betaseron should use birth control measures at all times.

➲ During the clinical trial of interferon beta-1b, there were four suicide attempts and one completed suicide among those taking interferon beta-1b. Although there is no evidence that the suicide attempts were related to the medication itself, it is recommended that individuals with a history of severe depressive disorder be closely monitored while taking Betaseron.

Possible Side Effects

➲ Common side effects include flu-like symptoms (fatigue, chills, fever, muscle aches, and sweating) and injection site reactions (swelling, redness, discoloration, and pain). Most of these symptoms tend to disappear over time. If they continue, become more severe, or cause significant discomfort, be sure to talk them over with your physician. Contact your physician if the injection sites become inflamed, hardened, or lumpy, and do not inject into any area that has become hardened or lumpy.

➲ Depression, including suicide attempts, has been reported by patients taking Betaseron. Common symptoms of depression are sadness, anxiety, loss of interest in daily activities, irritability, low self-esteem, guilt, poor concentration, indecisiveness, confusion, and eating and sleep disturbances. If you experience any of these symptoms for longer than a day or two, contact your physician promptly.

Betaseron Customer Service: 800-788-1467

Chemical Name: Magnesium hydroxide (mag-**nee**-zhum hye-**drox**-ide)

Brand Name: Phillips' Milk of Magnesia (available in granule form in Canada, in wafer form in the U.S., and in powder or effervescent powder in the U.S. and Canada) is one of several brands of bulk-forming laxative that are available over-the-counter.

Generic Available: No

Description: Magnesium hydroxide is an over-the-counter hyperosmotic laxative of the saline type that encourages bowel movements by drawing water into the bowel from surrounding body tissue. Saline hyperosmotic laxatives (often called "salts") are used for rapid emptying of the lower intestine and bowel. They are not to be used for the long-term management of constipation.

Proper Usage

⊃ Laxatives are to be used to provide short-term relief only, unless otherwise directed by the nurse or physician who is helping you to manage your bowel symptoms. A regimen that includes a healthy diet containing roughage (whole grain breads and cereals, bran, fruit, and green, leafy vegetables), six to eight full glasses of liquids each day, and some form of daily exercise is most important in stimulating healthy bowel function.

⊃ If your physician has recommended this laxative for management of constipation, follow his or her recommendations for its use. If you are treating yourself for constipation, follow the directions on the package insert. Results are often obtained ninety minutes to three hours after taking a hyperosmotic laxative. Be sure to consult your physician if you experience problems or do not get relief within a week.

⊃ Each dose should be taken with eight ounces or more of cold water or fruit juice. A second glass of water or juice with each dose is often recommended to prevent dehydration. If concerns about loss of bladder control keep you from drinking this amount of water, talk it over with the nurse or physician who is helping you manage your bowel and bladder symptoms.

Precautions

⊃ Do not take any type of laxative if you have signs of appendicitis or inflamed bowel (e.g., stomach or lower abdominal pain, cramping, bloating, soreness, nausea, or vomiting). Check with your physician as soon as possible.

⊃ Do not take any laxative for more than one week unless you have been told to do so by your physician. Many people tend to overuse laxatives, which often leads to dependence on the laxative action to produce a bowel movement. Discuss the use of laxatives with your health care professional in order to ensure that the laxative is used effectively as part of a comprehensive, healthy bowel management regimen.

⊃ Do not take any laxative within two hours of taking another medication because the desired effectiveness of the other medication may be reduced.

⊃ Although laxatives are commonly used during pregnancy, some types are better than others. If you are pregnant, consult your physician about the best laxative for you to use.

⊃ Some laxatives pass into breast milk. Although it is unlikely to cause problems for a nursing infant, be sure to let your physician know if you are using a laxative and breast-feeding at the same time.

Possible Side Effects

⊃ Side effects that may go away as your body adjusts to the medication and do not require medical attention unless they continue or are bothersome: cramping; diarrhea; gas; increased thirst.

⊃ Unusual side effects that should be reported to your physician as soon as possible: confusion; dizziness; irregular heartbeat; muscle cramps, unusual tiredness or weakness*.

---

*Since it may be difficult to distinguish between MS-related fatigue and the tiredness that can result from a hyperosmotic laxative, be sure to consult your health care professional if an abrupt change of this type occurs.

Chemical Name: Meclizine (**mek**-li-zeen)

Brand Name: Antivert (U.S.); Bonamine (Canada)

Generic Available: Yes (U.S.)

Description: Meclizine is used to prevent and treat nausea, vomiting, and dizziness.

Precautions

◗ This drug adds to the effects of alcohol and other central nervous system depressants (e.g., antihistamines, sedatives, tranquilizers, prescriptions pain medications, seizure medications, muscle relaxants, sleeping medications), possibly causing drowsiness. Be sure that your physician knows if you are taking these or any other medications.

◗ Meclizine may cause dryness of the mouth. If dryness continues for more than two weeks, speak to your physician or dentist since continuing dryness of the mouth may increase the risk of dental disease.

◗ This medication has not been shown to cause birth defects or other problems in humans. Studies in animals have shown that meclizine given in doses many times the usual human dose causes birth defects such as cleft palate.

◗ Although meclizine passes into breast milk, it has not been reported to cause problems in nursing babies. However, since this medication tends to decrease bodily secretions, it is possible that the flow of breast milk may be reduced in some women.

Possible Side Effects

◗ Side effects that typically go away as your body adjusts to the medication and do not require medical attention unless they continue for more than two weeks or are bothersome: drowsiness*; blurred vision*; constipation*; difficult or painful urination; dizziness; dryness of mouth, nose, and throat; fast heartbeat; headache; loss of appetite; nervousness or restlessness; trouble sleeping; skin rash; upset stomach.

*Since it may be difficult to distinguish between certain common symptoms of MS and some side effects of meclizine, be sure to consult your health care professional if an abrupt change of this type occurs.

Chemical Name: Methenamine (meth-**en**-a-meen)

Brand Name: Hiprex; Mandelamine (U.S.); Hip-Rex; Mandelamine (Canada)

Generic Available: No

Description: Methenamine is an anti-infective medication that is used to help prevent infections of the urinary tract. It is usually prescribed on a long-term basis for individuals with a history of repeated or chronic urinary tract infections.

Proper Usage

⊃ Before you start taking this medication, check your urine with phenaphthazine paper or another test to see if it is acidic. Your urine must be acidic (pH 5.5 or below) for this medicine to work properly. Consult your health care professional about possible changes in your diet if necessary to increase the acidity of your urine (e.g., avoiding citrus fruits and juices, milk and other dairy products, antacids; eating more protein and foods such as cranberries and cranberry juice with added vitamin C, prunes, or plums).

Precautions

⊃ The effects of methenamine in pregnancy have not been studied in either humans or animals. Individual case reports have not shown that this medication causes birth defects or other problems in humans.

⊃ Methenamine passes into breast milk but has not been reported to cause problems in nursing infants.

Possible Side Effects

⊃ Side effects that typically go away as your body adjusts to the medication and do not require medical attention unless they continue or are bothersome: nausea; vomiting.

⊃ Unusual side effects that should be reported immediately to your physician: skin rash.

*Since it may be difficult to distinguish between certain common symptoms of MS and some side effects of methenamine, be sure to consult your health care professional if an abrupt change of this type occurs.

Chemical Name: Methylprednisolone (meth-ill-pred-**niss**-oh-lone)

Brand Name: Depo-Medrol (U.S. and Canada)

Generic Available: Yes (U.S. and Canada)

Description: Methylprednisolone is one of a group of corticosteroids (cortisone-like medications) that are used to relieve inflammation in different parts of the body. Corticosteroids are used in MS for the management of acute exacerbations because they have the capacity to close the damaged blood-brain barrier and reduce inflammation in the central nervous system. Although methylprednisolone is among the most commonly used corticosteroids in MS, it is only one of several possibilities. Other commonly used corticosteroids include dexamethazone, prednisone, betamethasone, and prednisolone. The following information pertains to all of the various corticosteroids.

Proper Usage

⊃ Most neurologists treating MS believe that high-dose corticosteroids given intravenously are the most effective treatment for an exacerbation, although the exact protocol for the drug's use may differ somewhat from one treating physician to another. Patients generally receive a four-day course of treatment (either in the hospital or as an outpatient), with doses of the medication spread throughout the day. This high-dose, intravenous steroid treatment is then typically followed by a gradually tapering dose of an oral corticosteroid (see Prednisone).

Precautions

⊃ Since corticosteroids can stimulate the appetite and increase water retention, it is advisable to follow a low-salt and/or potassium-rich diet and watch your caloric intake. Your physician will make specific dietary recommendations for you.

⊃ Corticosteroids can lower your resistance to infection and make any infection that you get more difficult to treat. Contact your physician if you notice any sign of infection, such as sore throat, fever, coughing, or sneezing.

⊃ Avoid close contact with anyone who has chicken pox or measles. Tell your physician right away if you think you have been exposed to either of these illnesses. Do not have any immunizations after you stop taking this medication until you have consulted your physician. People living in your home should not have the oral polio vaccine while you are being treated with corticosteroids since they might pass the polio virus on to you.

⊃ Corticosteroids may affect the blood sugar levels of diabetic patients. If you notice a change in your blood or urine sugar tests, be sure to speak to your physician.

⊃ The risk of birth defects for women taking corticosteroids is not known. Overuse of corticosteroids during pregnancy may slow the growth of the infant after birth. Animal studies have demonstrated that corticosteroids cause birth defects.

⊃ Corticosteroids pass into breast milk and may slow the infant's growth. If you are nursing or plan to nurse, be sure to discuss this with your physician. It may be necessary for you to stop nursing while taking this medication.

⊃ Corticosteroids may produce mood changes and/or mood swings of varying intensity. These mood alterations can vary from relatively mild to extremely intense, and can vary in a single individual from one course of treatment to another. Neither the patient nor the physician can predict with any certainty whether the corticosteroids are likely to precipitate these mood alterations. If you have a history of mood disorders (depression or bipolar disorder, for example), be sure to share this information with your physician. If you begin to experience mood changes or swings that feel unmanageable, contact your physician so that a decision can be made about whether or not you need an additional medication to help you until the mood alterations subside.

Possible Side Effects

⊃ Side effects that may go away as your body adjusts to the medication and do not require medical attention unless they continue or are bothersome: increased appetite; indigestion; nervousness or restlessness; trouble sleeping; headache; increased sweating; unusual increase in hair growth on body or face.

⊃ Less common side effects that should be reported as soon as possible to your physician: severe mood changes or mood swings; decreased or blurred vision*; frequent urination*.

⊃ Additional side effects that can result from the prolonged use of corticosteroids and should be reported to your physician: acne or other skin problems; swelling of the face; swelling of the feet or lower legs; rapid weight gain; pain in the hips or other joints (caused by bone cell degeneration); bloody or black, tarry stools; elevated blood pressure; markedly increased thirst (with increased urination indicative of diabetes mellitus); menstrual irregularities; unusual bruising of the skin; thin, shiny skin; hair loss; muscle cramps or pain. Once you stop this medication after taking it for a long period of time, it may take several months for your body to readjust.

*Since it may be difficult to distinguish between certain common symptoms of MS and some side effects of methylprednisolone, be sure to consult your health care professional if an abrupt change of this type occurs.

Chemical Name: Mineral oil

Mineral oil is available in a variety of brands in the U.S. and Canada.

Generic Available: Yes

Description: Mineral oil is a lubricant laxative that is taken by mouth. It encourages bowel movements by coating the bowel and the stool with a waterproof film that helps to retain moisture in the stool.

Proper Usage

⊃ Laxatives are to be used to provide short-term relief only, unless otherwise directed by the nurse or physician who is helping you to manage your bowel symptoms. A regimen that includes a healthy diet containing roughage (whole grain breads and cereals, bran, fruit, and green, leafy vegetables), six to eight full glasses of liquids each day, and some form of daily exercise is most important in stimulating healthy bowel function.

⊃ If your physician has recommended this type of laxative for management of constipation, follow his or her recommendations for its use. If you are treating yourself for constipation, follow the directions on the package insert. Mineral oil is usually taken at bedtime because it takes six to eight hours to produce results. Be sure to consult your physician if you experience problems or do not get relief within a week.

⊃ Mineral oil should not be taken within two hours of mealtime because the mineral oil may interfere with food digestion and the absorption of important nutrients.

⊃ Mineral oil should not be taken within two hours of taking a stool softener (see Docusate) because the stool softener may increase the amount of mineral oil that is absorbed by the body.

Precautions

⊃ Do not take any type of laxative if you have signs of appendicitis or inflamed bowel (e.g., stomach or lower abdominal pain, cramping, bloating, soreness, nausea, or vomiting). Check with your physician as soon as possible.

⊃ Do not take any laxative for more than one week unless you have been told to do so by your physician. Many people tend to overuse laxative products, which often leads to dependence on the laxative action to produce a bowel movement. Discuss the use of laxatives with your health care professional in order to ensure that the laxative is used effectively as part of a comprehensive, healthy bowel management regimen.

⊃ Mineral oil should not be used very often or for long periods of time. Its gradual build-up in body tissues can cause problems, and may interfere with the body's absorption of important nutrients and vitamins A, D, E, and K.

⊃ Do not take any laxative within two hours of taking another medication because the desired effectiveness of the other medication may be reduced.

⊃ Mineral oil should not be used during pregnancy because it may interfere with absorption of nutrients in the mother and, if used for prolonged periods, cause severe bleeding in the newborn infant.

⊃ Be sure to let your physician know if you are using a laxative and breast-feeding at the same time.

Possible Side Effects

⊃ Uncommon side effect that usually does not need medical attention: skin irritation around the rectal area.

Chemical Name: Oxybutynin (ox-i-**byoo**-ti-nin)

Brand Name: Ditropan (U.S. and Canada)

Generic Available: Yes (U.S.)

Description: Oxybutynin is an antispasmodic that helps decrease muscle spasms of the bladder and the frequent urge to urinate caused by these spasms.

Proper Usage

⊃ This medication is usually taken with water on an empty stomach, but your physician may want you to take it with food or milk to lessen stomach upset.

Precautions

⊃ This medication adds to the effects of alcohol and other central nervous system depressants (such as antihistamines, sedatives, tranquilizers, prescription pain medications, seizure medications, muscle relaxants). Be sure that your physician knows if you are taking these or any other medications.

⊃ This medication may cause your eyes to become more sensitive to light.

⊃ Oxybutynin may cause drying of the mouth. Since continuing dryness of the mouth can increase the risk of dental disease, alert your dentist if you are taking oxybutynin.

⊃ Oxybutynin has not been studied in pregnant women. It has not been shown to cause birth defects or other problems in animal studies.

⊃ This medication has not been reported to cause problems in nursing babies. However, since it tends to decrease body secretions, oxybutynin may reduce the flow of breast milk.

Possible Side Effects

⊃ Side effects that typically go away as your body adjusts to the medication and do not require medical attention unless they continue for a few weeks or are bothersome: constipation*; decreased sweating; unusual drowsiness*; dryness of mouth, nose, throat; blurred vision*; decreased flow of breast milk; decreased sexual ability*; difficulty swallowing*; headache; increased light sensitivity; nausea or vomiting; trouble sleeping; unusual tiredness or weakness*.

⊃ Less common side effects that should be reported to your physician immediately: difficulty in urination*.

*Since it may be difficult to distinguish between certain common symptoms of MS and some side effects of oxybutynin, be sure to consult your health care professional if an abrupt change of this type occurs.

Chemical Name: Papaverine (pa-**pav**-er-een)

Brand Name: None

Generic Available: Yes (U.S. and Canada)

Description: Papaverine belongs to a group of medicines called vasodilators, which cause blood vessels to expand, thereby increasing blood flow. Papaverine is used in MS to treat erectile dysfunction. When papaverine is injected into the penis, it produces an erection by increasing blood flow to the penis.

Proper Usage

‚ Papaverine should never be used as a sexual aid by men who are not impotent. If improperly used, this medication can cause permanent damage to the penis.

‚ Papaverine is available by prescription and should be used only as directed by your physician, who will instruct you in the proper way to give yourself an injection so that it is simple and essentially pain-free.

Precautions

‚ Do not use more of this medication or use it more often than it has been prescribed for you. Using too much of this medicine will result in a condition called priapism, in which the erection lasts too long and does not resolve when it should. Permanent damage to the penis can occur if blood flow to the penis is cut off for too long a period of time.

‚ Examine your penis regularly for possible lumps near the injection sites or for curvature of the penis. These may be signs that unwanted tissue is growing (called fibrosis), which should be examined by your physician.

Possible Side Effects

‚ Side effects that you should report to your physician so that he or she can adjust the dosage or change the medication: bruising at the injection site; mild burning along the penis; difficulty ejaculating; swelling at the injection site.

‚ Rare side effects that require immediate treatment: erection continuing for more than four hours. If you cannot be seen immediately by your physician, you should go to the emergency room for prompt treatment.

Chemical Name: Paroxetine (pa-**rox**-uh-teen)

Brand Name: Paxil (U.S. and Canada)

Generic Available: No

Description: Paroxetine is used to treat mental depression.

Proper Usage

⊃ Paroxetine may be taken with or without food, on an empty or full stomach.

Precautions

⊃ It may take up to four weeks or longer for you to feel the beneficial effects of this medication.

⊃ Your physician should monitor your progress at regularly scheduled visits in order to adjust the dose and help reduce any side effects.

⊃ This medication could add to the effects of alcohol and other central nervous system depressants (e.g., antihistamines, sedatives, tranquilizers, sleeping medicine, prescription pain medicine, barbiturates, seizure medication, muscle relaxants). Be sure that your physician knows if you are taking these or any other medications.

⊃ Paroxetine may cause dryness of the mouth. If your mouth continues to feel dry for more than two weeks, check with your physician or dentist. Continuing dryness of the mouth may increase the risk of dental disease.

⊃ This medication may cause you to become drowsy.

⊃ Studies have not been done in pregnant women. Studies in animals have shown that paroxetine may cause miscarriages and decreased survival rates when given in doses that are many times higher than the human dose.

⊃ Paroxetine passes into breast milk but has not been shown to cause any problems in nursing infants.

Possible Side Effects

⊃ Side effects that typically go away as your body adjusts to the medication and do not require medical attention unless they continue for several weeks or are bothersome: decrease in sexual drive or ability*; headache; nausea; problems urinating*; decreased or increased appetite; unusual tiredness or weakness*; tremor*; trouble sleeping; anxiety; agitation; nervousness or restlessness; changes in vision, including blurred vision*; fast or irregular heartbeat; tingling, burning, or prickly sensations*; vomiting.

⊃ Unusual side effects that should be discussed with your physician as soon as possible: agitation; lightheadedness or fainting; muscle pain or weakness; skin rash; mood or behavior changes.

*Since it may be difficult to distinguish between certain common symptoms of MS and some side effects of paroxetine, be sure to consult your health care professional if an abrupt change of this type occurs.

Chemical Name: Pemoline (**pem**-oh-leen)

Brand Name: Cylert (U.S. and Canada)

Generic Available: No

Description: Pemoline is a mild central nervous system stimulant that has been used primarily to treat children with attention deficit hyperactivity disorder and adults with narcolepsy. It is used in multiple sclerosis to relieve certain types of fatigue.

Proper Usage

⊃ The usual starting dose for the treatment of fatigue in MS is 18.75 mg each morning for one week. If necessary, in order to manage the fatigue, the dosage can be gradually increased in increments of 18.75 mg and spread out over the early part of the day. In order to maximize the medication's effectiveness and minimize sleep disturbance, it should all be taken before mid-afternoon. The maximum dose of this medication is not known. Some individuals feel jittery or uncomfortable taking more than the minimum dose; others tolerate higher doses without discomfort. Typically, the drug is not prescribed at levels over 100–140 mgs per day for MS-related fatigue.

Precautions

⊃ Pemoline can increase hypertension. It should not be taken if you have angina and/or known coronary artery disease.

⊃ If you are taking pemoline in large doses for a long time, do not stop taking it without consulting your physician. Your physician may want you to reduce the amount you are taking gradually.

⊃ This drug may interact with the effects of alcohol and other central nervous system depressants (e.g., antihistamines, sedatives, tranquilizers, prescription pain medications, seizure medications, muscle relaxants, sleeping medications). Be sure your physician knows if you are taking these or any other medications.

⊃ Pemoline may cause some people to become dizzy or less alert than they are normally.

⊃ If you have been using this medicine for a long time and think you may have become mentally or physically dependent on it, check with your physician. Some signs of dependence on pemoline are a strong desire or need to continue taking the medicine; a need to increase the dose to receive the effects of the medicine; withdrawal side effects such as mental depression, unusual behavior, unusual tiredness* or weakness* after the medication is stopped.

⊃ Pemoline has not been shown to cause birth defects or other problems in humans. Studies in animals given large doses of pemoline have shown that it causes an increase in stillbirths and decreased survival of the offspring.

⊃ It is not known if pemoline is excreted in breast milk.

Possible Side Effects

Side effects of this medication have not been studied in adults. Side effects that have been reported by some adults in clinical practice include insomnia; elevated heart rate; nervousness; agitation; loss of appetite and weight loss; gastrointestinal upset, including constipation and diarrhea; hallucinations.

*Since it may be difficult to distinguish between certain common symptoms of MS and some side effects of pemoline, be sure to consult your health care professional if an abrupt change of this type occurs.

Chemical Name: Phenazopyridine (fen-az-oh-**peer**-i-deen)

Brand Name: Pyridium (U.S. and Canada)

Generic Available: Yes (U.S.)

Description: Phenazopyridine is used to relieve the pain, burning, and discomfort caused by urinary tract infections. It is not an antibiotic and will not cure the infection itself. This medication is available in the U.S. only with a prescription; it is available in Canada without a prescription. The medication comes in tablet form.

Precautions

⊃ The medication causes the urine to turn reddish orange. This effect is harmless and goes away after you stop taking phenazopyridine.

⊃ It is best not to wear soft contact lenses while taking this medication; phenazopyridine may cause permanent discoloration or staining of soft lenses.

⊃ Check with your physician if symptoms such as bloody urine, difficult or painful urination, frequent urge to urinate, or sudden decrease in the amount of urine appear or become worse while you are taking this medication.

⊃ Phenazopyridine has not been studied in pregnant women. It has not been shown to cause birth defects in animal studies.

⊃ It is not known whether this medication passes into breast milk. It has not been reported to cause problems in nursing babies.

Possible Side Effects

⊃ Uncommon side effects that typically go away as your body adjusts to the medication and do not require medical attention unless they continue or are bothersome: dizziness; headache; indigestion; stomach cramps or pain.

⊃ Unusual side effects that should be reported to your physician: blue or blue-purple color of skin; fever and confusion; shortness of breath; skin rash; sudden decrease in amount of urine; swelling of face, fingers, feet and/or lower legs; unusual weakness or tiredness*; weight gain; yellow eyes or skin.

*Since it may be difficult to distinguish between certain common symptoms of MS and some side effects of phenazopyridine, be sure to consult your health care professional if an abrupt change of this type occurs.

Chemical Name: Phenytoin (**fen**-i-toyn)

Brand Name: Dilantin (U.S. and Canada)

Generic Available: Yes (U.S.)

Description: Phenytoin is one of a group of hydantoin anticonvulsants that are used most commonly in the management of seizures in epilepsy. It is used in MS to manage painful dysesthesias (most commonly trigeminal neuralgia) caused by abnormalities in the sensory pathways in the brain and spinal cord.

Precautions

‫⊃‬ This drug may interact with the effects of alcohol and other central nervous system depressants (e.g., antihistamines, sedatives, tranquilizers, certain prescription pain medications, seizure medications, muscle relaxants, sleeping medications). Be sure your physician knows if you are taking these or any other medications.

⊃ Oral contraceptives (birth control pills) that contain estrogen may not be as effective if taken in conjunction with phenytoin. Consult with your physician about using a different or additional form of birth control to avoid unplanned pregnancies.

⊃ This medication may affect the blood sugar levels of diabetic individuals. Check with your physician if you notice any change in the results of your blood or urine sugar level tests while taking phenytoin.

⊃ Antacids or medicines for diarrhea can reduce the effectiveness of phenytoin. Do not take any of these medications within two to three hours of the phenytoin.

⊃ Before having any type of dental treatment or surgery, be sure to inform your physician or dentist if you are taking phenytoin. Medications commonly used during surgical and dental treatments can increase the side effects of phenytoin.

⊃ There have been reports of increased birth defects when hydantoin anticonvulsants were used for seizure control during pregnancy. It is not definitely known whether these medications were the cause of the problem. Be sure to tell your physician if you are pregnant or considering becoming pregnant.

⊃ Phenytoin passes into breast milk in small amounts.

Possible Side Effects

⊃ Side effects that may go away as your body adjusts to the medication and do not require medical attention unless they continue or are bothersome: constipation*; mild dizziness*; mild drowsiness*.

◌ Side effects that should be reported to your physician: bleeding or enlarged gums; confusion; enlarged glands in the neck or underarms; mood or mental changes*; muscle weakness or pain*; skin rash or itching; slurred speech or stuttering; trembling; unusual nervousness or irritability.

◌ Symptoms of overdose that require immediate attention: sudden blurred or double vision*; sudden severe clumsiness or unsteadiness*; sudden severe dizziness or drowsiness*; staggering walk*; severe confusion or disorientation.

*Since it may be difficult to distinguish between certain common symptoms of MS and some side effects of phenytoin, be sure to consult your health care professional if an abrupt change of this type occurs.

Chemical Name: Prednisone (**pred**-ni-sone)

Brand Name: Deltasone (U.S. and Canada)

Generic Available: Yes (U.S. and Canada)

Description: Prednisone is one of a group of corticosteroids (cortisone-like medicines) that are used to relieve inflammation in different parts of the body. Corticosteroids are used in MS for the management of acute exacerbations because they have the capacity to close the damaged blood-brain barrier and reduce inflammation in the central nervous system. Although prednisone is among the most commonly used corticosteroids in MS, it is only one of several different possibilities. Other commonly used corticosteroids include dexamethasone; prednisone; betamethasone; and prednisolone. The following information pertains to all of the various corticosteroids.

Proper Usage

⊃ Most neurologists treating MS believe that high-dose corticosteroids given intravenously are the most effective treatment for an MS exacerbation, although the exact protocol for the drug's use may differ somewhat from one treating physician to another. Patients generally receive a four-day course of treatment (either in the hospital or as an out-patient), with doses of the medication spread throughout the day (see Methylprednisolone). The high-dose, intravenous dose is typically followed by a gradually tapering dose of an oral corticosteroid (usually ranging in length from ten days to five or six weeks). Prednisone is commonly used for this oral taper. Oral prednisone may also be used instead of the high-dose, intravenous treatment if the intravenous treatment is not desired or is medically contraindicated.

Precautions

⊃ This medication can cause indigestion and stomach discomfort. Always take it with a meal and/or a glass or milk. Your physician may prescribe an antacid for you to take with this medication.

⊃ Take this medication exactly as prescribed by your physician. Do not stop taking it abruptly; your physician will give you a schedule that gradually tapers the dose before you stop it completely.

⊃ Since corticosteroids can stimulate the appetite and increase water retention, it is advisable to follow a low-salt and/or a potassium-rich diet and watch your caloric intake.

⊃ Corticosteroids can lower your resistance to infection and make any infection that you get more difficult to treat. Contact your physician if you notice any sign of infection, such as sore throat, fever, coughing, or sneezing.

◌ Avoid close contact with anyone who has chicken pox or measles. Tell your physician immediately if you think you have been exposed to either of these illnesses. Do not have any immunizations after you stop taking this medication until you have consulted your physician. People living in your home should not have the oral polio vaccine while you are being treated with corticosteroids since they might pass the polio virus on to you.

◌ Corticosteroids may affect the blood sugar levels of diabetic patients. If you notice a change in your blood or urine sugar tests, be sure to discuss it with your physician.

◌ The risk of birth defects in women taking corticosteroids during pregnancy has not been studied. Overuse of corticosteroids during pregnancy may slow the growth of the infant after birth. Animal studies have demonstrated that corticosteroids cause birth defects.

◌ Corticosteroids pass into breast milk and may slow the infant's growth. If you are nursing or plan to nurse, be sure to discuss this with your physician. It may be necessary for you to stop nursing while taking this medication.

◌ Corticosteroids can produce mood changes and/or mood swings of varying intensity. These mood alterations can vary from relatively mild to extremely intense, and can vary in a single individual from one course of treatment to another. Neither the patient nor the physician can predict with any certainty whether the corticosteroids are likely to precipitate these mood alterations. If you have a history of mood disorders (depression or bipolar disorder, for example), be sure to share this information with your physician. If you begin to experience unmanageable mood changes or swings while taking corticosteroids, contact your physician so that a decision can be made whether or not you need an additional medication to help you until the mood alterations subside.

Possible Side Effects

◌ Side effects that may go away as your body adjusts to the medication and do not require medical attention unless they continue or are bothersome: increased appetite; indigestion; nervousness or restlessness; trouble sleeping; headache; increased sweating; unusual increase in hair growth on body or face.

◌ Less common side effects that should be reported as soon as possible to your physician: severe mood changes or mood swings; decreased or blurred vision*; frequent urination*.

⊃ Additional side effects that can result from the prolonged use of corticosteroids and should be reported to your physician: acne or other skin problems; swelling of the face; swelling of the feet or lower legs; rapid weight gain; pain in the hips or other joints (caused by bone cell degeneration); bloody or black, tarry stools; elevated blood pressure; markedly increased thirst (with increased urination indicative of diabetes mellitus); menstrual irregularities; unusual bruising of the skin; thin, shiny skin; hair loss; muscle cramps or pain. Once you stop this medication after taking it for a long period of time, it may take several months for your body to readjust.

*Since it may be difficult to distinguish between certain common symptoms of MS and some side effects of corticosteroids, be sure to consult your health care professional if an abrupt change of this type occurs.

Chemical Name: Propantheline (proe-**pan**-the-leen) bromide

Brand Name: Probanthine (U.S. and Canada)

Generic Available: Yes (U.S.)

Description: Propantheline is one of a group of antispasmodic/anticholinergic medications used to relieve cramps or spasms of the stomach, intestines, and bladder. Propantheline is used in the management of neurogenic bladder symptoms to control urination.

Proper Usage

⊃ Take this medicine thirty minutes to one hour before meals unless otherwise directed by your physician.

Precautions

⊃ Do not stop this medication abruptly. Stop gradually to avoid possible vomiting, sweating, and dizziness.

⊃ Anticholinergic medications such as propantheline can cause blurred vision and light sensitivity. Make sure you know how you react to this medication before driving.

⊃ Anticholinergic medications may cause dryness of the mouth. If your mouth continues to feel dry for more than two weeks, check with your dentist. Continuing dryness of the mouth may increase the chance of dental disease.

⊃ No studies of the effects of this drug in pregnancy have been done in either humans or animals.

⊃ Anticholinergic medications have not been reported to cause problems in nursing babies. The flow of breast milk may be reduced in some women.

⊃ Be sure that your physician knows if you are taking a tricyclic antidepressant or any other anticholinergic medication. Taking propantheline with any of these may increase the anticholinergic effects, resulting in urinary retention.

Possible Side Effects

⊃ Side effects that typically go away as your body adjusts to the medication and do not require medical attention unless they continue for several weeks or are bothersome: constipation*; decreased sweating; dryness of mouth, nose, and throat; bloated feeling; blurred vision*; difficulty swallowing.

⊃ Unusual side effects that require immediate medical attention: inability to urinate; confusion; dizziness*; eye pain*; skin rash or hives.

⊃ Symptoms of overdose that require immediate emergency attention: unusual blurred vision*; unusual clumsiness or unsteadiness*;
unusual dizziness; unusually severe drowsiness*; seizures; hallucinations; confusion; shortness of breath; unusual slurred speech*;
nervousness; unusual warmth, dryness, and flushing of skin.

*Since it may be difficult to distinguish between certain common symp-
toms of MS and some side effects of propantheline, be sure to consult your
health care professional if an abrupt change of this type occurs.

Chemical Name: Psyllium hydrophilic mucilloid (**sill**-i-yum hye-droe-**fill**-ik **myoo**-sill-oid)

Brand Name: Metamucil (available in granule form in Canada, in wafer form in the U.S., and in powder or effervescent powder in the U.S. and Canada) is one of several available brands of bulk-forming laxative.

Generic Available: No

Description: Psyllium hydrophilic mucilloid is a bulk-forming oral laxative. This type of laxative is not digested by the body; it absorbs liquids from the intestines and swells to form a soft, bulky stool. The bowel is then stimulated normally by the presence of the bulky stool.

Proper Usage

⊃ Laxatives are to be used to provide short-term relief only, unless otherwise directed by the nurse or physician who is helping you to manage your bowel symptoms. A regimen that includes a healthy diet containing roughage (whole grain breads and cereals, bran, fruit, and green, leafy vegetables), six to eight full glasses of liquids each day, and some form of daily exercise is most important in stimulating healthy bowel function.

⊃ If your physician has recommended this laxative for management of constipation, follow his or her recommendations for its use. If you are treating yourself for constipation, follow the directions on the package insert. Results are often obtained in twelve hours but may take as long as two or three days. Be sure to consult your physician if you experience problems or do not get relief within a week.

⊃ In order for this type of bulk-forming laxative to work effectively without causing intestinal blockage, it is advisable to drink six to eight glasses (eight ounces) of water each day. Each dose of the laxative should be taken with eight ounces of cold water or fruit juice. If concerns about loss of bladder control keep you from drinking this amount of water, discuss it with the nurse or physician who is helping you manage your bowel and bladder symptoms.

Precautions

⊃ Do not take any type of laxative if you have signs of appendicitis or inflamed bowel (e.g., stomach or lower abdominal pain, cramping, bloating, soreness, nausea, or vomiting). Check with your physician as soon as possible.

⊃ Do not take any laxative for more than one week unless you have been told to do so by your physician. Many people tend to overuse laxatives, which often leads to dependence on the laxative action to produce a bowel movement. Discuss the use of laxatives with your health care professional in order to ensure that the laxative is used effectively as part of a comprehensive, healthy bowel management regimen.

⊃ Do not take any laxative within two hours of taking another medication because the desired effectiveness of the other medication may be reduced.

⊃ Bulk-forming laxatives are commonly used during pregnancy. Some of them contain a large amount of sodium or sugars, which may have possible unwanted effects such as increasing blood pressure or causing fluid retention. Look for those that contain lower sodium and sugar.

⊃ Some laxatives pass into breast milk. Although it is unlikely to cause problems for a nursing infant, be sure to let your physician know if you are using a laxative and breast-feeding at the same time.

Possible Side Effects:

⊃ Check with your physician as soon as possible if you experience any of the following: difficulty breathing; intestinal blockage; skin rash or itching; swallowing difficulty (feelings of lump in the throat).

Chemical Name: Sertraline (**ser**-tra-leen)

Brand Name: Zoloft (U.S. and Canada)

Generic Available: No

Description: Sertraline is used to treat mental depression.

Proper Usage

This medication should always be taken at the same time in relation to meals and snacks to make sure that it is absorbed in the same way. Because sertraline may be given to different individuals at different times of the day, you and your physician should discuss what to do about any missed doses.

Precautions

⊃ It may take four to six weeks for you to feel the beneficial effects of this medication.

⊃ Your physician should monitor your progress at regularly scheduled visits in order to adjust the dose and help reduce any side effects.

⊃ This medication could add to the effects of alcohol and other central nervous system depressants (e.g., antihistamines, sedatives, tranquilizers, sleeping medicine, prescription pain medicine, barbiturates, seizure medication, muscle relaxants). Be sure that your physician knows if you are taking these or any other medications.

⊃ Sertraline may cause dryness of the mouth. If your mouth continues to feel dry for more than two weeks, check with your physician or dentist. Continuing dryness of the mouth may increase the risk of dental disease.

⊃ This medication may cause drowsiness.

⊃ Studies have not been done in pregnant women. Studies in animals have shown that sertraline may cause delayed development and decreased survival rates of offspring when given in doses many times the usual human dose.

⊃ It is not known if sertraline passes into breast milk.

Possible Side Effects

⊃ Side effects that typically go away as your body adjusts to the medication and do not require medical attention unless they continue for several weeks or are bothersome: decreased appetite or weight loss; decrease sexual drive or ability*; drowsiness*; dryness of mouth; headache; nausea; stomach or abdominal cramps; tiredness or weakness*; tremor*; trouble sleeping; anxiety; agitation; nervousness or restlessness; changes in vision including blurred vision*; constipation*; fast or irregular heartbeat; flushing of skin; increased appetite; vomiting.

⊃ Unusual side effects that should be discussed with your physician as soon as possible: fast talking and excited feelings or actions that are out of control; fever; skin rash; hives; itching.

*Since it may be difficult to distinguish between certain common symptoms of MS and some side effects of sertraline, be sure to consult your health care professional if an abrupt change of this type occurs.

Chemical Name: Sodium phosphate

Brand Name: Fleet Enema (U.S. and Canada)

Generic Available: No

Description: Sodium phosphate enemas are available over-the-counter.

Proper Usage

➲ Rectal enemas are to be used to provide short-term relief only, unless otherwise directed by the nurse or physician who is helping you to manage your bowel symptoms. A regimen that includes a healthy diet containing roughage (whole grain breads and cereals, bran, fruit, and green, leafy vegetables), six to eight full glasses of liquids each day, and some form of daily exercise is most important in stimulating healthy bowel function.

➲ If your physician has recommended this rectal laxative for management of constipation, follow his or her recommendations for its use. If you are treating yourself for constipation, follow the directions on the package insert.

➲ Results usually occur within two to five minutes. Be sure to consult your physician if you notice rectal bleeding, blistering, pain, burning, itching, or other signs of irritation that was not present before you began using a sodium phosphate enema.

Precautions

➲ Do not use any type of laxative if you have signs of appendicitis or inflamed bowel (e.g., stomach or lower abdominal pain, cramping, bloating, soreness, nausea, or vomiting). Check with your physician as soon as possible.

➲ Do not use any laxative for more than one week unless you have been told to do so by your physician. Many people tend to overuse laxatives, which often leads to dependence on the laxative action to produce a bowel movement. Discuss the use of laxatives with your health care professional in order to ensure that the laxative is used effectively as part of a comprehensive, healthy bowel management regimen.

➲ If you are pregnant, discuss with your physician the most appropriate type of laxative for you to use.

Possible Side Effects

➲ Side effect that may go away as your body adjusts to the medication and does not require medical attention unless it persists or is bothersome: skin irritation in the rectal area.

➲ Unusual side effects that should be reported to your physician as soon as possible: rectal bleeding, blistering, burning, itching.

Chemical Name: Sulfamethoxazole (sul-fa-meth-**ox**-a-zole) and trimethoprim (try-**meth**-oh-prim) combination

Brand Name: Bactrim; Septra (U.S. and Canada)

Generic Available: Yes (U.S.)

Description: Sulfamethoxazole and trimethoprim combination is used in multiple sclerosis to treat (and sometimes to prevent) urinary tract infections.

Proper Usage

⊃ This medication is best taken with a full glass (eight ounces) of water. Additional water should be taken each day to help prevent unwanted effects.

⊃ Finish the full course of treatment prescribed by your physician. Even if your symptoms disappear after a few days, stopping this medication prematurely may result in a return of the symptoms.

⊃ This medication works most effectively when it is maintained at a constant level in your blood or urine. To help keep the amount constant, do not miss any doses. It is best to take the doses at evenly spaced times during the day and night. For maximum effectiveness, four doses per day would be spaced at six-hour intervals.

Precautions

⊃ This medication may cause dizziness.

⊃ If taken for a long time, sulfamethoxazole and trimethoprim combination may cause blood problems. It is very important that your physician monitor your progress at regular visits.

⊃ This medication can cause changes in the blood, possibly resulting in a greater chance of certain infections, slow healing, and bleeding of the gums. Be careful with the use of your toothbrush, dental floss, and toothpicks. Delay dental work until your blood counts are completely normal. Check with your dentist if you have questions about oral hygiene during treatment.

⊃ This medication may cause your skin to become more sensitive to sunlight. Stay out of direct sunlight during the midday hours, wear protective clothing, and apply a sun block product that has a skin protection factor (SPF) of at least 15.

⊃ Sulfamethoxazole and trimethoprim combination has not been reported to cause birth defects or other problems in humans. Studies in mice, rats, and rabbits have shown that some sulfonamides cause birth defects, including cleft palate and bone problems. Studies in rabbits have also shown that trimethoprim causes birth defects, as well as a decrease in the number of successful pregnancies.

⊃ Sulfamethoxazole and trimethoprim pass into breast milk. This medication is not recommended for use during breast-feeding. It may cause liver problems, anemia, and other problems in nursing babies.

Possible Side Effects

⊃ Side effects that may go away as your body adjusts to the medication and do not require medical attention unless they continue or are bothersome: diarrhea; dizziness; headache; loss of appetite; nausea or vomiting.

⊃ Less common side effects that should be reported to your physician immediately: itching; skin rash; aching of muscles and joints; difficulty in swallowing; pale skin; redness, blistering, peeling, or loosening of skin; sore throat and fever; unusual bleeding or bruising; unusual tiredness or weakness*; yellow eyes or skin.

*Since it may be difficult to distinguish between the tiredness that is common in MS (especially in the presence of an infection) and this side effect of sulfamethoxazole and trimethoprim combination, be sure to consult your physician if an abrupt change of this type occurs.

Index

Abstract reasoning, MS and, 95–96
Acetazolamide, *see* Diamox
Acupuncture, 168
Acute attacks, treatment with
    corticosteroids, 26
Adult education, 151–53, 174–75
Advance directives, 183–84
  durable power of attorney, 184
  trusts, 184
  wills, 183
Advocacy, 181–87
Alprostadil, 219
Alternative therapies, 167–70
  acupuncture, 168
  biofeedback, 169
  bodywork, 168–69
  chiropractic therapy, 169–70
  hypnotherapy, 168
  imagery, 168
  massage, 168–69
  Tai Chi, 169
Amantadine, 220–21
Ambulation, 34–36
  mobility aids, 116, 139
Amitriptyline, 222–23
Ankle edema, 44

Anticholinergic medications, 5, 55, 56,
    57, 60
  sexual functioning and, 111
Antidepressants, orgasmic response
    and, 112
Antivert, 41, 252
Ashworth scale, 75
Atarax, tremor and, 31
Autoimmunity, 13–14
Avonex, 27, 246–47
  results of clinical trials, 160–61
Azathioprine, 27

Back pain, 39
Baclofen, 29, 75, 115, 224–25
  see also Lioresal
Baclofen pump, 30, 76, 77, 115
Bactrim, 279–80
Balance, 33
Benadryl, vertigo and, 41
Benign MS, 5–6
Betaseron, 27, 248–49
  results of clinical trials, 160–61
Biofeedback, 169
Birth, MS and, 121–22
Birth control, 120

Bisacodyl, 226–27
Bisacolax, 226–27
Bladder anatomy and function, 46–47
Bladder diary, 65
Bladder dysfunction, 47–56
 diagnosis of, 50–54
 interventions, 54–56
 measurement of, 74–75
 sexual dysfunction and, 114, 115
 surgical procedures, 56
 symptoms of, 48–50
Bladder management, 46–56
 bladder studies, 51–56
 diagnosis of dysfunction, 50–54
 interventions, 54–56
 normal anatomy and function, 46–47
 problems occurring with MS, 47–50,
  51
 surgical procedures, 56
Bladder studies, 51–54
Bodywork, 168–69
Bonamine, 252
Botox, see Botulinum toxin
Botulinum toxin, 30
Bowel function, 56–57
 sexual dysfunction and, 114
Bowel management, 56–60
 diagnoses of altered elimination,
  57–60
 normal function, 56–57
Braden scale, 78–79
Bulk formers, 58, 59
Buspar, tremor and, 31
Buspirone, see Buspar

Carbamazepine, 116, 228–30
 see also Tegretol
Care models, MS and, 6–8
Case management, 7
Chiropractic therapy, 169–70
Cipro, 231–32
Ciprofloxacin, 231–32
Clinical depression, 89–91, 112
Clinical pathways, 7–8
Clinical trials, 18–22
Clonazepam, 29, 31, 41, 233–34
Cognitive changes, 93–99

attention deficits, 96–97, 116
concentration deficits, 96–97
judgment, 95–96, 116
memory, 94–95, 116
reasoning, 95–96
sexual dysfunction and, 111, 114
spatial organization problems, 97
speed of information processing, 96
word-finding problems, 96, 116
Cognitive dysfunction, course of, 97–98
 interventions, 98–99
 see also Cognitive changes
Cognitive rehabilitation, 98–99, 118
Colace, 58, 238–39
Cold feet, 43
Complications, prevention of in
  disabled, 69–80
 dysphagia, 73–74
 hydration, 73
 nutrition, 69–73
 skin care, 76–80
 spasticity, 74–76
Comprehensive care model, 6–7
Congenital defect, as cause of MS,
  11–12
Constipation, 57–59
 sexual dysfunction and, 115
Contraception, 120
Copaxone, results of clinical trials,
  160–61
Coping styles, 99–100
Copolymer 1, see Copaxone
Corticosteroids, for acute attacks, 26
 side effects, 26
Cyclobenzaprine HCl, see Flexoril
Cyclophosphamide, 27
Cylert, 263–64
 fatigue and, 34, 116
Cystitis, 49
Cytoxan, 27

Dantrium, for spasticity, 29, 75–76
Dantrolene sodium, see Dantrium
DDAVP nasal spray, 235
Decubitus ulcers, 76–80
Deltasone, 268–70
Demyelination, 17–18

as cause of cognitive changes, 93–94
as cause of depression, 90
Depo-Medrol, 254–56
Depression, 88–91
Desmopressin, 235
Dexamethasone, 26
Diamox, tremor and, 31
Diarrhea, 59
Diazepam, 29, 41, 75, 236–37
  see also Valium
Dietary imbalance, as cause of MS,
  12
Dilantin, 266–67
  for trigeminal neuralgia, 37–38, 116
Disability rights, 185
Disabled, prevention of complications
  in, 69–80
Disease course, 4–6
Disease modifying agents, nursing
  implications and, 159–64
Ditropan, 55, 115, 259
Dizziness, 41–42
Docusate, 238–39
Double vision, 41
Dramamine, vertigo and, 41
Dulcolax, 59, 226–27
Durable power of attorney, see Advance
  directives
Dysphagia, 73–74

Elavil, 89, 92, 222–23
Elimination dysfunction, management
  of, 45–65
Emotional challenges, adaptation,
  87–88; 84–92
  denial, 87–88
  depression, 88–92
  grief, 88–92
  mood swings, 91–92
  personality change, 91–92
  stress, 84–86
  uncertainty, 86–87
  unpredictability, 86–87
Emotional release, 92
Enemas, 59, 115
Environmental factors, MS and, 2, 4,
  12, 16–17

Epidemiology, of multiple sclerosis,
  1–3
Erectile dysfunction, treatment of,
  112–14
  inflatable prosthesis, 114
  injections, 113
  surgical implants, 113–14
  vacuum suction devices, 113
Etiology, of multiple sclerosis, 3–4,
  11–13
Exercise
  dizziness and, 42
  immobility and, 36–37
  physical therapist and, 137–38
  spasticity and, 28
  weakness and, 33–34
Experimental allergic
  encephalomyelitis (EAE), 13
  molecular mimicry and, 17

Family issues, MS and, 83–84, 99–105
  communication patterns, 102–104
  coping styles, 99–100
  parenting issues, 104–105, 122–23
  role changes, 100–101
  shared grief, 101–102
Family planning, 119–23
Fatigue, 34
  sexual dysfunction and, 114, 116
Fertility, 120–21
Fleet enema, 59, 277–78
Flexoril, 29, 39
Fluoxetine, 240–41
  fatigue and, 34
  pain and, 116
Food choices, 69–72

Genetic molecular technology, 15–16
Genetics, multiple sclerosis and, 2, 4,
  14–16, 119–20
Glycerin, 242–43
Grief, MS and, 88–91
  sharing of, 101–102

Headache, MS and, 37
Health policy reform, 185
Hip-Rex, 253

Hiprex, 253
Hope, nursing care and, 189–99
Hydration, 73
Hydroxyzine, *see* Vistaril
Hypersexuality, 111, 117
Hypnotherapy, 168

Imagery, 168
Imipramine, 115, 244–45
  see also Tofranil
Immobility, prevention of, 36–37
Immobilization, tremor and, 32
Immunology, multiple sclerosis and,
  13–14
Immunosuppression, 27
Imuran, 27
Incidence, of multiple sclerosis, 1–3
Incontinence, *see* Bladder dysfunction
Inderal, tremor and, 31
Indwelling catheters, 55–56, 115
Infectious agent, as cause of MS, 12
INH, tremor and, 31
Injectable medications, patient
  education and, 159–64
Interferon beta-1a, 246–47
Interferon beta-1b, 248–49
Interferons, 27, 160–61
Intermittent catheterization, 51, 55,
  60–63
  sexual dysfunction and, 115
Intravenous pyelogram (IVP), 51–52
Involuntary bowel, 59–60
Isoniazide, *see* INH

Klonopin, 29, 31, 233–34
  dizziness and, 41
  nystagmus and, 41

Lactation, MS and, 121–22
Laxatives, 59, 115
Learning, MS and, 176–78
Lioresal, 224–25
  spasticity and, 29, 30, 75–76, 115
  trigeminal neuralgia and, 37–38
Low back pain, 39

Magnesium hydroxide, 250–51

Malignant MS, 5–6
Mandelamine, 253
Massage, 168–69
Meclizine, 252
Memory loss, 94–95, 106
Menopause, multiple sclerosis and,
  129–30
Menses, multiple sclerosis and, 129–30
Metamucil, 58, 59, 273–74
Methenamine, 253
Methylphenidate, *see* Ritalin
Methylprednisolone, 26, 254–56
Mineral oil, 257–58
Mobility aids, 139
Molecular mimicry, 16–17
Mood swings, MS and, 91–92
  emotional instability, 91–92
  emotional release, 92
  increased sensitivity, 92
Multiple sclerosis, overview of, 1–8
  course of the disease, 4–6
  epidemiology, incidence, and
    prevalence, 1–3
  nursing implications, 6–8
    care models, 6–8
    wellness model, 6
  pathology and etiology, 3–4
Mysoline, tremor and, 31

Neurogenic bladder, 49–50
Neurologic changes, sexual
  dysfunction and, 110
Norton scale, 76
Numbness, 43
Nurse, role of in rehabilitation, 137,
  146–55
  adult education, 151–53
  case management, 146
  chart review, 153
  cognitive assessment, 148
  communication assessment, 149–50
  community agency input, 153
  community barriers, 155
  data collection, 146–47
  discharge planning, 153–54
  educational needs assessment, 151
  family assessment, 149

patient safety, 154–55
physiologic assessment, 147
psychological assessment, 147–48
recreational assessment, 151
social assessment, 148–49
vocational assessment, 150
Nutrition, 69–73

Occupational therapist, role of, 139–40
Optic neuritis, 40
Oxazepam, *see* Serax
Oxybutynin, 55, 115, 259

Pain, 37–39
sexuality and, 114, 116
Papaverine, 260
Parenting, multiple sclerosis and,
104–105, 122–23
Paroxetine, 261–62
Passive stretching, spasticity and, 28
Pathology, of multiple sclerosis, 3–4
Patient education, 172–74, 175–76
Patients rights, 182–83
Patterning, tremor and, 32
Paxil, 90, 261–62
Pemoline, 263–64
fatigue and, 34, 116
Percutaneous rhizotomy, 38, 76
Personality change, MS and, 91–92
Phenazopyridine, 265
Phenol point block, 30, 76
Phenytoin, 116, 266–67
see also Dilantin
Phillips' Milk of Magnesia, 59, 250–51
Physiatrist, role of, 137
Physical therapist, role of, 137–38
Poser criteria, 4–5
Prednisone, 268–70
Pregnancy, MS and, 121–22
Prevalence, of multiple sclerosis, 1–3
Primary progressive MS, 5–6
Primary sexual dysfunction, 110–12
treatment of, 112–14
Primidone, *see* Mysoline
Probanthine, 55, 115, 271–72
Progressive-relapsing MS, 5–6
Propantheline, 55, 115, 271–72

Propranolol, *see* Inderal
Prostaglandin E1, 219
Prostin VR, 219
Prozac, 90, 240–41
fatigue and, 34
pain and, 116
Pseudobulbar effect, *see* Emotional
release
Psychoeducation, 162–64
Psychologist, role of, 140
Psychosocial issues, 83–106
emotional challenges, 84–93
cognitive changes, 93–99
impact of MS on family life, 83–84,
99–105
nursing role, 84, 105–106
Psyllium hydrophilic mucilloid, 273–74
Pyridium, 265

Quality improvement program,
rehabilitation and, 145
Quality of life goals, 171–72

Range of motion exercises, 28
Recommended dietary allowances,
69–70
Recreational therapist, role of, 141
Rehabilitation, 133–55
definition of, 134
future of, 144–45
goals of, 134–35
interdisciplinary team, 135–42
quality improvement, 145
research studies, 22–23, 143–44
role of nurse in, 146–55
settings. 142–43
Rehabilitation team, 135–42
nurse, 137
occupational therapist, 139–40
physiatrist, 137
physical therapist, 137–38
psychologist, 140
recreational therapist, 141
social worker, 140
speech-language pathologist, 140
vocational rehabilitation counselor,
141–42

Relapsing-remitting MS, 5–6
Relaxation techniques, spasticity and, 28
Research, for new treatments, 18–23
Retrobulbar neuritis, 40
Ritalin, fatigue and, 34
Rivotril, 233–34
Role changes, 100–101
  effect of on sexual relationship, 118

Sani-Supp suppository, 242–43
Secondary progressive MS, 5–6
Secondary sexual dysfunction, 114
  treatment of, 115–17
Seizures, 42
Self-advocacy, 187
Septra, 279–80
Serax, dizziness and, 41–42
Sertraline, 275–76
Sexual dysfunction, 110–19
  evaluation of, 111–12
  incidence and prevalence of, 110
  primary, 110–14
  secondary, 114–17
  tertiary, 117–19
Sexuality, 109–19
Skin care, 76–80
Social worker, role of, 140
Sodium phosphate, 277–78
Spasticity, 27–30, 74–76
  measurement of, 74–75
  sexual dysfunction and, 114
  treatment of, 27–30, 75–76
    exercise, 28
    mechanical aids, 28–29
    medications, 29–30, 75–76
    surgical management, 30, 76
Spasticity scale, 75
Speech difficulties, 40
Speech-language pathologist, role of, 140
SSRI antidepressants, 90
Stool softeners, 58
Stress, MS and, 84–85
Suicide, 89, 90
Sulfamethoxazole and trimethoprim,
  279–80
Symmetrel, 220–21
  fatigue and, 116

Symptom management, 25–44
Syn-Clonazepam, 233–34
Systems advocacy, 184–85

Tai Chi, 169
Tegretol, 228–30
  spasms and, 30
  trigeminal neuralgia and, 37–38, 116
Tertiary sexual dysfunction, 117–18
  treatment for, 118–19
Tizanidine, see Zanaflex
Tofranil, 55, 89, 115, 244–45
Tremor, 30–33
  pharmacologic management of, 31
  physical treatments, 31–33
Tricyclic antidepressants, 55, 89–90, 116
Trigeminal neuralgia, 37–38, 116
Trimethoprim, see Sulfamethoxazole
Trusts, see Advance directives

Urinary symptoms, 48–50, 51–52
Urodynamic testing, 52–54
Uroflowmetry, see Urodynamic testing

Vaginal lubrication, 112
Valium, 236–37
  dizziness and, 41
  spasticity and, 29, 75–76
Vertigo, 41–42
Vestibular stimulation, 33
Virus, as cause of MS, 12, 16
Vision, 40–41
Vistaril, tremor and, 31
Vocational rehabilitation counselor,
  role of, 141–42
Voiding diary, 64

Weakness, 33–34
Weight gain, 42–43, 72
Weighting, tremor and, 32
Wellness model, MS nursing and, 6
Wills, see Advance directives
Women's issues, multiple sclerosis and,
  127–30

Zanaflex, for spasticity, 29, 75–76
Zoloft, 90, 275–76